CONTEMPORARY ANARCHISM

CONTEMPORARY ANARCHISM

Edited by
Terry M. Perlin

Transaction Books
New Brunswick, New Jersey

Copyright © 1979 by Transaction, Inc.
New Brunswick, New Jersey 08903

Library of Congress Catalog Number: 74-20197
ISBN: 0-87855-097-6 (cloth)
Printed in the United States of America

Library of Congress Cataloging in Publication Data
    Main entry under title:

    Contemporary anarchism.

    Includes bibliographical references
    1. Anarchism and anarchists—Addresses, essays,
lectures.   I.   Perlin, Terry M., 1942-
HX828.C637   335'.83   74-20197
ISBN 0-87855-097-6

CONTENTS

Preface

"Let us then have the courage of freedom" wrote Alexander Berkman, the Russo-American anarchist, in 1929. "Let liberty become our faith and our *deed* and we shall grow strong therein." The anarchist challenge to authority and the anarchist promise of freedom and peace did not die with Berkman. It resurfaced, in America and in Europe, during the 1960s and early 1970s.

The present collection of anarchist writings, in which participants in the contemporary movement speak for themselves, is consistent with another anthology of anarchist literature, *The Anarchists,* edited by Irving Louis Horowitz and based on a project begun by the late C. Wright Mills. In that earlier work, nineteenth and twentieth century radicals presented an indictment of the state and offered a series of proposals towards the good society. Clearly the anarchist revolution has not taken place. But, as in the past century, the anarchist assault on the perceived evils of coercion and domination has yielded much important writing. Anti-political agitation has also not been lacking.

The contributors to this volume represent widely divergent points of view. There are perhaps as many anarchisms as there are anarchists. But, I believe, a core of mood and temperament unites most anti-statists: the distrust of authority combined with genuine concern for the travails of daily life among the common people. Yet, perhaps due to the premium put upon individualism by anarchists, the differences among the writers in this collection are significant: communards and hyper-individualists, militants and pacifists, religious heretics and atheists, optimists and pessimists, elderly disciples of Kropotkin and Emma Goldman and youthful activists.

There are several principles of selection I have followed. I wanted to present material not collected elsewhere from journals and sources not normally read by a wide audience. I wished to present a fair sampling of the spectrum of anarchist opinion — from libertarian individualists to anarchist-communists. In addition, I have tried to recapture the electricity and urgency of the resurgence of anarchism during the past decade. This collection, I believe, shows that anarchism is more than critique; it is the affirmation of a new way of life. Many of the contributions show that anarchists, in addition to being conscientious and sometimes strident activists, are also clear and careful thinkers.

An introductory essay by the editor, which sets the revival of anarchism into its historical and social context, is followed by two statements on the nature of the contemporary movement. George Woodcock, the most widely-published historian of anarchism, in "Anarchism Revisited" is at once affectionate toward and critical of the revival. Sam Dolgoff's "The Relevance of Anarchism to Modern Society" adds passionate intelligence in setting the stage for a reconsideration of anarchist thought and practice. Sections on leftist and right-wing anarchism follow. Both kinds of critiques call for the transformation of our political and economic structures, though in markedly different fashions. In the section called "Doing Anarchism," a variety of short pieces from the British anarchist sources *Freedom* and *Anarchy* are included. They demonstrate, I feel, the best of the spontaneous, day-to-day anarchist writing of the recent period. A final section presents three outstanding essays which claim that anarchism's critique is as applicable to our own times as it was to past decades or centuries.

It ought to be clear that I regard this work as more than an interesting collection of materials. These documents speak to a recent recurrence of an old battle: for freedom and happiness and in opposition to the tyrannies of social coercion. The defiant, and sometimes bold, statements made by these contemporary anarchists are a living chapter in an unfinished, perhaps never to be finished, historical drama.

Comradely thanks, rather than mere acknowledgments, are in keeping with the spirit of this book. First, to Irving Louis Horowitz, who suggested and has long supported this work; to Paul Avrich, prime scholar of anarchism, who sees the life in anarchist ideas; to members of the Libertarian Book Club, New York City, whose fidelity to anarchism has inspired me. Miami University's Research Office via Dean Spiro Peterson gave needed financial assistance toward the preparation of this book. I will always be a student of Paul Massing. Finally, thanks to the family.

ACKNOWLEDGMENTS

The author gratefully acknowledges permission to reprint the following material: George Woodcock, "Anarchism Revisited," *Commentary;* Sam Dolgoff, "The Relevance of Anarchism to Modern Society," *Libertarian Analysis;* Staughton Lynd, "The Movement: A New Beginning"; Emile Capouya, "The Red Flag and the Black"; Murray Rothbard, "The Transformation of the American Right," "The Anatomy of the State," "Why Be Libertarian?"; George Lakey, "Manifesto for a Nonviolent Revolution: A Draft for Discussion," "Revolution: A Quaker Prescription for a Sick Society"; Murray Bookchin, "Post-Scarcity Anarchism," Ramparts Press; Howard Zinn, "The Conspiracy of Law," Simon and Schuster.

PART I.
THE RETURN OF ANARCHISM

1.

The Recurrence of Defiance

Terry M. Perlin

Anarchism—literally, a society without government—is less a political philosophy than it is a temperament. Anarchists have been defiant men and women who attempt to organize for the purpose of destroying organization. Anarchism means, for its adherents, a grand struggle against evil, a secular crusade against the debasement of self, a fight against social degradation that the idea and the reality of the state seem to represent. Anarchism is anti-politics, anti-authoritarianism: a mood of perpetual rebellion.

Who are the anarchists? Must we include all social rebels under the anarchist rubric? In the middle of the 19th century Pierre-Joseph Proudhon was the first to proudly proclaim that "I am an anarchist."[1] But self-declaration is insufficient because anarchism is not an orthodox political movement. It has neither party line nor membership criteria. It can be found in unlikely places. The definition of anarchism presented by Emma Goldman, the most notorious American anarchist of the past one hundred years, is quite suggestive: "Anarchism, then, really stands for the liberation of the human mind from the dominion of religion; the liberation of the human body from the dominion of property; liberation from the shackles and restraint of government."[2]

Anarchist rebels have never been satisfied with alteration of the form of the state; they demand its complete aboliton. Often utopian and rarely

3

successful in their plans, anarchists are at once the critics and the consciences of revolutions. If the late Sir Herbert Read, himself a British anarchist, is right in stating that "society exists to transcend itself," then anarchists are those who push hardest and longest for social change of a fundamental kind. They are the perpetually dissatisfied minority who seek virtue through the overturning of the social and political order.

Historically, anarchists have suffered from two contradictory stereotypes. They have been deemed bomb-throwing lunatics *and* muddle-headed utopian dreamers. Neither image has a basis in fact. Though individual anarchists, particularly in the late nineteenth century, have attempted acts of violence and revenge, anarchism has more frequently been a minority social movement infused with ideals. In word and deed, anarchists have condemned war, violence, industrial exploitation, political repression, educational regimentation, religious superstition and economic and political imperialism. They have embodied that critical spirit which Thomas Carlyle more than a century ago claimed characterizes the modern world: that "invincible revolt against false rulers and false teachers."[3]

Anarchism Revived

Across Europe and America during the 1960s and early 1970s anarchism returned. The combative ideas of all the classic nineteenth century anarchist thinkers and practitioners — Proudhon, Bakunin, Stirner, Kropotkin, Tolstoy, Goldman — were published anew. But the rebirth of anarchism was most evident not in the reprinting of works such as *Mutual Aid* or *God and the State,* but rather in concrete anti-statist activity and in the growing mood of distrust of government, the resentment of unchecked technological growth and in the desire for social and individual freedom.

Not all anti-governmental activism was infused with anarchist principles. Few members of the radical movement possessed the historical consciousness of that noisy group of radical feminists called the Emma Goldman brigade, who marched down Fifth Avenue in New York City chanting "Emma said it in 1910, Now we're going to say it again."[4] But within and without the radical culture few doubted that the anarchist heresy has risen again.

When bombs exploded in a corporate headquarters; when dissident intellectuals fled the Soviet Union for the West; when young radicals and innocent bystanders were beaten by police at political conventions in the United States; when bands of squatters occupied buildings in London's East End the typical response of public officials was to label this the work of anarchists. Threats to the public order, in socialist as well as capitalist states, were labeled acts of anarchists and terrorists. Often the terms were made equivalent.

In the United States, the chaos of contemporary events hastened the search for qualified scapegoats and led, as usual, to a search for an enemy within. With traditionally American "historical amnesia," analysts repressed the long saga of labor strife, social and regional conflict, street violence and judicial murder and found only reborn sterotypes.[5] Political scientist Benjamin Barber drew the picture vividly. Anarchism lives, he said: "in the slogans and banners of the French Student Movement, in the New York Townhouse laboratories where amateur chemists forge weapons of terror at the risk of their own lives, in the syncretic vision of the anti-authoritarian young Left and in the street theater and comic braggadocio of the Yippies."[6] The public image of the anarchist changed little since its nineteenth century inception. Mikhail Bakunin was transformed into Abbie Hoffman: both were imagined to be cloaked fanatics, bombs held high in their hands, ready to corrupt innocent believers with cynical impunity.

Historically the official stereotype is fundamentally erroneous. Anarchists have rarely been assassins or bomb-throwers: they have been, most often, propagandists, men and women of ideas and ideals.[7] Yet many anarchists have revelled in notoriety. In the 1960s many radicals reciprocated their condemnation by wearing unearned labels as badges of defiance. As a prominent rock group put it:

> We are the forces of chaos and anarchy
> Everything they say we are we are
> And we are very
> Proud of ourselves.[8]

Rebels and their enemies in this way reified each other. Anarchists prided themselves on their non-legitimacy; state authorities, using the tools of arrest, harassment, public trials and media insinuation, affirmed their commitment to the *status quo*. The skirmishing resultant from such battles over imagery often appeared fantastic — witness the trial of the Chicago Seven. Still, the pride and the prejudice of confrontation was but a small part of the anarchist resurgence. A set of ideals, and a demand for a change in consciousness, infused the radical movement.

Since Proudhon and Bakunin, anarchism has projected models of a new way of life: a pleasant, simple, peaceful, egalitarian and harmonious communal existence based on the abolition of authority and the flowering of individual freedom within the voluntary bonds of social solidarity. How to reach this goal has been the problem. Nineteenth century Russian anarchists, reared in an autocratic milieu, saw revolution, probably a violent one, as the inescapable mode of social change. Unwilling, as the

Marxists demanded, to wait until "conditions were ripe," the anarchists urged revolution now. By propaganda of word and deed, they hoped to mobilize the masses into a revolutionary force. Fiery pamphlets smuggled across borders, agitation among the growing worker class, even acts of assassination, had the same purpose: to show men and women that unfreedom was not a necessity, to demonstrate that liberty could be achieved by those who struggled for it. As Alexander Berkman said: "our social institutions are founded on certain ideas; as long as the latter are generally believed, the institutions built on them are safe. Government remains strong because people think political authority and legal compulsion necessary."[9]

To undermine ideas of governmental necessity has been the major goal of anarchist radicals. The recent New Left, New Right and the advocates of counter-cultural change were also motivated by the presupposition that ideals activated by will can bring about revolutionary transformation. Anarchism thus has had an uncompromising character, a moral absolutism; its emphasis on individual acts also made it an attractive philosophy for the young. As Clemenceau once put it, ironically: "I am sorry for anyone who has not been an anarchist at twenty."[10]

The slogans of the New Left — student power, black power, worker control, community control, freedom for women — were more than responses to recent social and economic changes: they represented the affirmation of the power of ideas. "Participatory democracy," kept alive by the anarchist emphasis (during the nineteenth century) on face-to-face decision-making, was also an effort to enact the principles of Thomas Jefferson. The New Left wanted to raise issues, awaken public opinion and mobilize oppressed minorities. As two former editors of *Studies on the Left* said, radicals wanted to "suggest the basis for a conception of human freedom which demonstrates the need for a new arrangement of social relations."[11]

Like many idealistic nineteenth century anarchists, New Leftists found it difficult to gain the sympathetic attention of the working class. They more often recruited their membership from the ranks of disenchanted intellectuals, from students suddenly made aware of bourgeois hypocrisy, from the artistic avant-garde and, sometimes, from members of awakened minorities. Like their predecessors, the New Left was defamed, hunted and abused, driven underground and, on occasion, imprisoned.

The term New Left is actually a covering phrase, historically and ideologically. It describes activists ranging from civil rights protestors in the early 1960s through the underground radical factions of the 1970s. It encompasses a wide spectrum: from advocates of Black separatism and worker control to University reformers and free school organizers. What united the New Left, for all its diversity, was spontaneity. What distinguished it from the Old Left was the absence of an enforceable ideological orthodoxy. There was no revealed path to revolution.

To be sure, there were among the New Left a number of puritanically fanatic and rigorously dogmatic Marxists, from Progressive Laborites to certain members of the Black Panthers. But to the extent that ideological conformity and internecine rituals of purification were present, the New Left was Old. What was surprising and refreshing about the New Left was the absence of certainty and a plan. Instead one found an experimental attitude toward social change, a willingness to see things as they were (to "tell it like it is") without the blinders of a dogma. As the Diggers, a San Fransisco group of communal agitators, warned: "Beware of leaders, heroes, organizers. Watch that stuff. Beware of Structure-freaks. They do not understand. We know the system doesn't work because we're living in the ruins."[12] One of the best New Left scholar-activists, Howard Zinn, showed the restraint of the movement when he described his purpose as an effort "to participate *a bit* in the social combat of our time."[13] This ambition—to dip in and try revolutionary activity — was no frivolous task. In its commitment to variable tactics and in its eschewing of ideological conformity, it retained the special flavor of anarchist spontaneity.

Anarchist solutions to social questions have ranged from a total communism to an equally zealous indiviualism. In between are found sundry recipes, from anarcho-syndicalism to anarcho-capitalism. A recent indication of the breadth of the anarchist spectrum can be seen in the phenomenon of the New Right. Emerging from the American conservative youth movement, notably the Young Americans for Freedom (YAF), these self-declared anarchists, who took the name "radical libertarians," presented an anti-political program that demanded an end to public education, to the draft, to the "robbery" of taxation and to the repression of individual freedom that is the main task of the corporate state. But New Rightists would not yield to their New Left counterparts on the issue of private property.

Odd counter-stances developed. One former conservative, who became a follower of libertarians Murray Rothbard and Karl Hess, a believer in totally free enterprise, regarded himself as an anarchist and stated: "The military draft must be regarded as the most brutal and unjust government institution in existence today. . .Libertarians should align themselves with draft resisters throughout the country."[14] Personally, I met a right-wing attorney who devoted himself to libertarian causes: organizing tax payer revolts and working on civil liberties cases. He also wrote revisionist essays which blamed the United States for originating the Cold War. Affecting the life-style of the counter-culture, this lawyer travelled to colleges and universities to propagandize, edited a monthly anarchist journal and expressed considerable sympathy toward anarcho-communism. When I asked him how this work was consistent with his being a lawyer, he answered, "We will use the law to destroy the law."

The anarchist impetus can be seen in what has been called the counter-culture. Anarchists have always been bohemian in style of dress, family life, sexual mores and public presence. Contemporary "freaks" looked much more like the systematically slovenly Bakunin than the neatly bourgeoisified Marx. But more than appearance united the new culture with anarchism.

In their defiance of the main trends of modern industrial society— urbanization, conformity, technological efficiency, planned, rational social change — many young people rejected the ideals of their families. More than a mere generational rebellion, this fight was closer to the wholesale rejection of values found in Ivan Turgenev's nineteenth-century novel *Fathers and Sons*. The emphasis upon sensual experience, upon face-to-face encounters, upon communal living had its counterparts in the pursuits of earlier generations of anarchist comrades.

Like other heretical movements, the counter-culture was by definition ephemeral. It was easily bought out or converted by established forces. Yet its impact was undeniable, especially in the realm of values. Each young man who refused the draft, each family that rejected the atomism of isolated suburban existence in search of communal harmony, each young rebel who rejected the authority of political party politics, preferring the authenticity of the autonomous political act, behaved in the anarchist idiom.

The young rebels were constantly frustrated. The trends were against them. Government grew more powerful and its authority over the citizen tightened. West German agitators, *Kabouters* in the Netherlands, followers of Daniel Cohn-Bendit in France learned, at their peril, that the chance for revolution was slim. But, like the nineteenth century generation of Russian anarchists, they constantly asked: what is to be done?

And where was it to be done? What is the proper scene of action? Do we remain in the city or do we try to create a microcosm of the new society in the wilderness? Such debates were not new. Harry Kelly, an early twentieth century disciple of Emma Goldman, once admonished those anarchists who wanted to desert the urban battleground. A few years later he founded the most successful and long-lived anarchist colony in America, in the meadows of then rural New Jersey. He had discovered that constant police harassment, coupled with no real prospect of converting the working class, led anarchism to one direction: the creation of a small-scale, cooperative community based on a libertarian school.[15]

Anarchists, old and new, have been accused by their Marxist critics of being reactionaries: of seeking to postpone progress and growth by hiding in the past. And it is true that if progress means unlimited urbanization, automation, alienation and the coordination of human life through economic and political centralization, the anarchists have sought—and will continue to desire — an arrest of the trends of modernity. Yet Robert Nisbet, the conservative social theorist, finds in anarchism the early recognition, and continuous pursuit, of one of the most significant social problems of the last two hundred years: the quest for community. Kropotkin and his heirs, says Nisbet, have worked consistently for a "genuine and lasting community." They have wanted to build such unstructured structures, "on the most natural of interdependences among men, such as the village, autonomous association, and region, and, finally, on the natural division of man's intellectual and manual abilities."[16]

During the 1960s, and continuing into the present, in a new wave of "returning to the land," young people, and some older ones as well, abandoned the city for reasons beyond a simple distaste for the terrors of urban life. Many sought simplicity and the implicit virtue that comes from a life close to the land. Others erected a set of economic arrangements that were radically egalitarian. Disgusted with competitive capitalism, and equally disenchanted by the maintenance of hierarchy in the orthodox socialist systems, the new communards sought a "natural" economic order. Even now, many continue to live the life described by Kropotkin in *Mutual Aid* and *Fields, Factories and Workshops.* No person owns property. Eating is a common experience. The group works for the group, not for individual gain. The aim is self-sufficiency, though there is usually some commercial interaction with the outside world. Most communes have failed, economically.

Yet at the root of the communal movement has been an effort at redefining labor. Often unconsciously, young "pioneers" put Marx's early repudiation of alienated labor into action. Affecting the clothing and even the language of an imaginary peasantry, many followed Marx's description of what the simple communist life could look like: "to hunt in the morning, fish in the afternoon, rear cattle in the evening, criticize after dinner just as I have a mind, without ever becoming hunter, fisherman, shepherd or critic." Anarchists in recent years have been attracted to the youthful writings of Marx. His disgust at alienation, his sympathetic treatment of the human side of industrial development, they claim, differs from his later dogmatism and concern for party rigidity. Many anarchists have moved towards syndicalism — just as their predecessors did in late nineteenth century France, Spain and Italy — and have urged the control of the economy by the workers themselves.

No group, left or right, has made so fundamental or passionate an attack on capitalist *and* socialist state systems. Murray Bookchin, the contemporary critic, agrees with Bakunin and Kropotkin and speaks in the same idiom as Emma Goldman and Alexander Berkman who were the first radicals to report to the world the excesses of Soviet power after the 1917 Bolshevik Revolution. The anarchists today — virtually non-partisan in their condemnation of eastern and western state systems — who point out that state industrial planning is not any better than unregulated competition: both waste resources; both depend on the abridgement of personal freedoms; both result in inequality and special privilege. Nation-states, say the anarchists, preserve and distribute power. Anarchists demand its liquidation.

The core of the anarchist attitude is a moral vision, not a "Lawlike" notion of the economic system. Thus a wide variety of opinions characterizes the movement. There are free-market anarchists, often called anarcho-capitalists, who preach a total laissez-faire. For them only the pursuit of individual gain will guarantee personal freedom. Allowing the state any role in economic life abrogates man's natural right to the fruits of his labor. Anarchist-communists, on the other hand, advocate complete abolition of private property. For them the monopolization of wealth is a presupposition of authoritarianism and, hence, evil. They envision a communal existence and imagine the birth of new social forms which will guarantee the means of life to all. In between these two visions a variety of schemes have been suggested: syndicalism, mutualism, collectivism and many admixtures.

The ambiguity and inconsistency one sees in anarchist economic schemes reproduces the confusion many anarchists face in their attitude towards social change. For example, they regard the French and Russian revolutions as liberating events and recognize that the growth of industrialism has unleashed the power of the working class. Many admire machines as potential liberators of the alienated working class. But so-called progress has not been uncorrupted. The Russian revolution has turned into a sour autocracy; the machine now symbolizes servitude, not possible freedom. Growth has issued an ecological nightmare.

Anarchists, thus, continue to be torn between a simultaneous admiration for, and disgust with, modernity. They feel that factories are here to stay, yet they are nostalgic for the village commune. The frightening present and the idealized past compete in their desire for a realistic viewpoint. So, while anarchism can be a penetrating social critique, it has rarely been a sensible, concrete guide to economic action.

Though the anarchist vision has varied, the anarchist attact on social problems has remained remarkably consistent. Anarchists — who refuse to vote, or to align themselves with political parties or reformist movements — have attacked injustice directly, without calling for more laws, committees or governmental action. Emma Goldman, who died in 1940, was a founder of the women's liberation movement, the birth control movement, the free school movement and the struggle to end bourgeois marriage.[18] Her criticism had nothing to do with urging legislative or judicial reforms: she went to the root of social questions and many contemporary radicals are her disciples.

The question of women's liberation illustrates my point. Genuinely radical women do not want more laws or more female representation in corporations, political or educational institutions. These matters are peripheral. What truly radical feminists seek is a transvaluation of the male/female relationship. They want an end to the imbalance of power that *is* marriage; an end to the requirements of role-playing. They want the liberation of men as well. As two radical women declare:

> Sex and love have been so contaminated for women by economic dependence that the package deal of love and marriage looks like a con and a shill. We will not be able to sort out what we do want from men and we want to give them until we know that our own physical and pyschological survival — at home and at work —does not depend on men. Like all oppressed people, first of all, we need *self-determination.*[19]

The right to possess one's own body, and to live according to one's own desires, is a premise of anarchism. The state, through abortion laws, intervenes into the private realm. By licensing human relationships, the state violates fundamental rights. Advocates of free love — of the abolition of marriage and, consequently, of divorce — are not eccentrics or perverts: they are advocates of freedom per se.

Because some anarchists have recognized that revolution is not imminent, they have tried other means of bringing about basic social change. One central premise has been: if you want to change minds, start with the children. The assumption is that a new generation kids, reared happily with anarchist principles, can be the first step in the value-change that is indispensable to the new life. Anarchists for a century — from Bakunin to Paul Goodman — have urged freedom in education. Schools, publicly run and administered, are tools of statist indoctrination. Even if they are not blatantly "patriotic," they teach such established values as competitiveness, respectability, sexual inhibition and the business ethic. At the most long-lived American free school, the Modern School (*Escuela Moderna*) in Stelton, New Jersey, which lasted from 1915 until the 1950s, a generation of children startlingly free from the competitiveness and aggressiveness which characterizes most public school graduates was produced. Many of the hundreds of free schools in operation today work under similar premises: to change the world you must begin at the beginning; the natural vehicle is the child.[20]

Such enterprises which attempt the transvaluation of values, the enemies of anarchism claim, amount to nothing less than nihilism. In their zeal to destroy power, the critics say, anarchists wish to destroy the traditional bonds among men which give security and solidarity to communities. Yet there are many anarchists who are religious, in some broad sense of the term, and who perform rituals gladly and consciously. Many of them have been followers of Tolstoy, who was among the first to combine a rigorous anti-statism with belief in divinity. One such religious anarchist calls for the enactment of the original Biblical ethic:

> to live and let live, treating others as we would like them to treat us, loving one another, forgiving one another, not judging, not seeking restitution of damages, but centering always upon the greater needs of others rather than on our own desire.[21]

Religious idealism of this sort has sometimes led to pacifism. The non-violent activism of many anarchists has given the lie to the stereotype that anarchism is violence per se. From Thoreau to Tolstoy to Gandhi, anarchists and decentralists have shown that non-resistance techniques, combatting violence with non-violence, can react upon the conscience of the wider community. Of course, such non-violent activity has not eventuated in an anarchist revolution: from Gandhi's struggle issued the Indian state.[22] But a tradition of protest rooted in ideals does exist.

Since the early 1960s, beginning with the American civil rights movement, but continuing through the Vietnam War until the present, anarchist groups, particularly the Catholic workers movement, have used pacifist methods. Resisters of the draft in the past decade, morally repugned by an unjust war, went to jail or into exile and affirmed the pacifist tenet of refusal to cooperate. All those protestors who went limp rather than strike back at the strong arms of the state might not have been anarchists. But their actions reinforced one of the goals of anarchists and pacifists: to embarrass the state and to present it to the public as an immoral force. When Mayor Daley's police beat the demonstrators at the Democratic National Convention in Chicago in 1968, the spontaneous cry that arose was compelling: "The whole world is watching... The whole world is watching."

Anarchist moralism has led to stands both utopian and dogmatic. For example, the anarchist attitude toward politics is unambiguous: politics involves the distribution of power and authority. Since anarchists despise the delegation of power and authority they can have no political platform, no plan for using the state in any way. Anarchists ignore the francise.

Unlike the Marxists who coveted the extension of the ballot as a means to capturing the state, the anarchists have derogated any scheme which would legitimize state authority and symbolize any grant of individual freedom from a political body.

Such dogmatism has had considerable value: it has yielded both a critique of politics *and* a series of specific plans for the dissolution of centralized power. In the late 1960s and early 1970s anarchism caught the mood of anti-politics. Consider the phrases associated with government during the decade: liars, credibility gap, imperialists, Tweedledee and Tweedledum, Watergate, tape gap, impeachment. Real-life events have matched the slogans: the Vietnam war, the massive increase of bureaucracy on all levels, the publication of the Pentagon Papers, the trials of protestors, the attempt at packing the Supreme Court with "strict constructionists," the omnipresent FBI and CIA snooping, the continuous revelation of business bribery of public officials and, of course, the demonstration of presidential culpability in high crimes and misdemeanors. These resulted in massive discontent with government as usual; clearly many non-anarchists hate Washington, but the general pessimism about the uses of state power reinforced the anarchist position.

Historically, anarchists have been forced into skepticism about government. Liberal and conservative regimes — from the frontier America which framed the Haymarket "rioters" to Czarist Russia which liquidated opponents summarily — have treated anarchism in a single way. As a result, anarchists have no reason to want to try the approved political methods: they decry the ballot; they will not enter coalition governments (though there are a few notable exceptions); they prefer "direct action" to Machiavellian tactics. No doubt, probably as a result of their isolation, anarchist platitudes are often hyperbolic. A recent example: "anarchists [must] recognize the validity of the ongoing Third World revolution, for they are in the belly of the Monster."[23]

Yet practice can be more revealing than rhetoric. As the late Paul Goodman noted: "[Anarchists] believe in local power, community development, rural reconstruction, decentralist organization."[24] Goodman stands out as *the* pragmatically-oriented anarchist, the man who made plans for the beautification of New York City, the humanization of the educational system, the decentralization of social life. His writings inspired many to think and act concretely. Some have chosen to leave the urban scene; others have sought, through community organization, to challenge the bureaucracy. Most share a contempt for "due process," for administrators and professionals, for remote agencies appointed to solve local problems. "All this adds up to the community Anarchism of Kropotkin, the resistance anarchism of Malatesta, the agitational anarchism of Bakunin," said Goodman.[25]

Anarchism's extremism, its fervent idealism, seems to link it with the utopian tradition. From this perspective anarchists are a cross-breed of hopeful dreamers: their realm is neither in, nor of, this world. Such a critique has a foundation — among the anarchists are many wide-eyed preachers of both apocalyptic and harmonious visions. Yet the social conflict of the late sixties and early seventies seemed to validate the anarchist analysis and to open the door a crack to the anarchist viewpoint. "The kids" were dropping out of school; a new class of *Lumpenproletariat* filled the streets; technology failed to provided the advertised panacea. The lessons of the decade had an anarchist flavor: the credibility of states, socialist and capitalist, were nearly destroyed; decentralization of power became a popular notion; free love, birth control, abortion became more than slogans; a new ruralism attracted the young to the land; communes burgeoned.

All these phenomena — some ephemeral, other more fundamental — had been seen before. What was unique about the period of anarchist revival was that such events combined within a single decade. A revolution was not made, but rebellion filled the air.

A Tradition of Novelty

Anarchism is enchanted by chaos and is, almost by definition, a non-systematic social philosophy. Caught up in the present, anarchists are perplexed by the past and the future. Emma Goldman refused to look very far ahead "because I believe that Anarchism can not consistently impose an iron-clad program or method on the future. The things every new generation has to fight, and which it can least overcome, are the burdens of the past, which holds us all as in a net."[26] This contempt for the past suggests the problem of an anarchist attitude toward history. History is something which (unfortunately) must be studied and comprehended, but it is an uncongenial thing. The past wears many masks — religious tradition, hereditary power, economic inheritance, conventional mores — and they all obscure and weigh down human freedom. Unlike the followers of Karl Marx who sought to achieve freedom by mastering an understanding of history, the anarchists have tried to transcend historical bonds. They affirmed spontaneity, adventurism, a break with the old, not discipline or conformity to the "laws" of history.

Contemporary anarchism also expresses a disdain for the old, for the traditional and the dated. Modern communalists attempt to break with the trends of industrialization, bureaucratization and homogenization which they identify with twentieth-century living. Catholic radicals want to set aside what they consider the meaningless obscurantism of their Church, to discover new forms of religious expression. The culture of the youth movement repudiated parental values, the overtly materialistic life-styles and institutions of bourgeois accumulation. Anarchism, as always, affirms the new and condemns the old.

This perhaps unconscious avant-gardism is not precisely anti-historical: rather it is ahistorical. The older anarchists, the generation of Goldman and Berkman, for example, were rarely scholars, but the most prominent of them were intellectuals, men and women devoted to ideas, to the forms of their expression. They were writers, journalists, novelists, public speakers, cafe debaters, manifesto writers and, of course, activists. The state was their enemy, but so was its history. Today, and in the late sixties and early seventies, contempt for the past is replaced by ignorance of it. The best work of contemporary anarchists has been ahistorical. Murray Bookchin's *Post-Scarcity Anarchism* portrays a fruitful present for anarchist agitation and schematically outlines a technological cornucopia in an anarchist future, but cares little about the past. There is scarcely an allusion to Kropotkin or Bakunin, many of whose ideas predate and parallel those offered by Bookchin.[27] An ahistorical consciousness can safely ignore predecessors. "Seize the time" and "Freedom, Now" require no antecedents.

Philosophical idealism and absolutistic ethic lend support to the ahistorical consciousness. The good society, the free life, the cooperative integration of individual and group — these are the conditions of happiness which ought to be found everywhere, forever. Unlike the historicist Marxists, anarchists have an unyielding, nondynamic vision of the true community. As George Woodcock has described it: the anarchists portray "the vision of a society in which every relation would have moral rather than political characteristics." The zealousness and willfulness of anarchists replicate this consciousness. Why wait? Why remain attached to outmoded institutions? Ignore the past!

But this break — from an immersion in anarchist tradition into an ahistorical presentism — has its roots in the core of anarchist thought. Anarchism is a search for freedom, for an end to the tyrannies of personal and social life which inhibit all men and women. Even Emma Goldman recognized this: situations change; all is flux; anarchists do not fear this. A new affirmation of the new is no betray of the essential message of anarchism.

We are not suprised, then, to find that the revival of anarchist activity in the 1960s and 1970s triggered no special nostalgia. Very faint were the memories of earlier defiances: the labor militancy of the 1880s; the non-conscription campaigns before World War I; the Sacco and Vanzetti protests. If the past was clearly over, how did anarchists see this revival.

Before World War II, the last generation of American anarchists, and many of the European comrades, had either grown old or died; their children had prospered. The surviving remnant of anarchist activists had either retired or, during the Depression, joined the Trotskyite opposition to Stalin. This new era of anarchist agitation had few tangible links to the anarchist tradition. Many young radical youth knew only the names of Bakunin or Kropotkin and cared little for the European militants of an earlier epoch. They saw anarchism as "new, again," a response to changed conditions in the social fabric of American and European life, a reflex to the structural, cultural and psychological tensions that made the past decade turbulent and rebellious.

Contemporary anarchism was a piece of the torn fabric of a conflict-ridden society. Especially after the assassination of John Kennedy in 1963, the consensual base of American society seemed to be cracking. The normally quiet institutions, such as the universities, the ghettoes, even the churches, seemed incapable of holding together. One president, Lyndon Johnson, was virtually forced to abdicate after a single term. Another was hounded out of office. A useless foreign war smoldered to an inconclusive finish. Racial conflict, generational feuding, the strains of rapid urbanization, environmental destruction, artistic nihilism, sexual normlessness — all these frightening things symbolized culture in danger.

For some of the older generation of anarchists, long-waiting during the forties and fifties, the new discontents seemed to validate long-held suspicions. In the spring of 1970, for example, a group of elderly disciples of Goldman and Berkman spoke to me of their joy in witnessing current student revolts, anti-war agitations and the wide-ranging contempt for state-imposed solutions to social problems. The new emphasis upon direct learning experience, the experimentalism of the rural communes, the growth of free sexuality and libertarian schools seemed to these seventy and eighty-year old anarchists proof that, once the rotteness in the social structure becomes evident, young people with an advanced consciousness would act along anarchist lines.

The repudiaton of the bourgeois ethic, it seemed to them, was the beginning of a new dream, a practical one. The very success of American industrial culture would cause a reaction in the direction of decentralization. The end of the Cold War (engineered, it was admitted, by the state systems) might issue in a real era of peace. The very limits of state power had been reached; a helpless giant could easily be dismantled.

Many less sanguine citizens were also convinced, in no small part by the daily bombardment of newspaper, radio and television warnings, that civil conflict was inevitable. The Paris uprising in the summer of 1968, a youthful rebellion, shocked many, including President Charles DeGaulle. Despite the insurrection, the French Republic remained. By the time of the departure of Richard Nixon, it apeared that the radicalism of the sixties and early seventies was again ephemeral. Campuses quieted down, the Vietnam War ended with a whimper, minorities and the poor withdrew their pickets. The liberation of women, due to its middle-class base, moved toward reformist solutions.

But the story is not quite so simple. A bit of retrospect should not lead to the conclusion that the activism of the rebellious decade was either unreal or insignificant. Certainly, great states did not fall, power was not redistributed, values did not change with lightning speed. Utopia was not achieved. But it never is! The anxiety of the period was genuine and the contributions of anarchists were vital. A kind of shift in socio-cultural possibilities was made. The strains of the noisy decade provided an opening: it let previously unspoken factions be heard. Blacks, Chicanos, Puerto Rican-Americans, the poor, women, homosexuals, pacifists, defrocked priests and nuns, students, draft-dodgers—not only did they get headlines, they achieved a sort of counter-legitimacy rarely seen in earlier epochs. Anarchist anti-politics was at the core of this move from marginality to centrality among a host of previously ignored social characters.

Broadly defined, it was the *Lumpenproletariat,* that non-class of outsiders, the group Marx pejoratively mocked as the flotsam and jetsam of industrial society who became politcally significant and morally interesting. The anarchists addressed themselves to this agglomeration. Murray Bookchin, wrote expressly for them. He belived, perhaps naively, that the dispossessed would follow the black flag of anarchy, where more comfortable working men had failed to go. These groups, which had no use for the normal legitimacy of political forms or economic enterprise, achieved a new kind of power. The resurfacing of anarchism thrust the light on some oft-hidden alternatives. Though a revolution may not be made, a revolutionary life-style became possible. Though the civil-rights movement or the anti-war campaigns have faded, the flowering of the marginality they engendered has not. As Marx might recognize, a part of the superstructure has taken on a life of its own.

And principal among the spokesmen for these growing interests — whether birth control or free love or free schools or an earthly religion — have been anarchists or their sympathizers. That is why we can regard the period as an age of anarchist revival. Once again the least likely group gained the attention of the many; once again, the strange became normal. Old solutions were penetrated and exposed. This may not be revolution, but it is a special kind of rebellion. The revival of anarchism exemplifies George Woodcock's picture of the anarchist ideal as "water percolating through porous ground." Anarchism is, he says, "a strong underground current, there gathering into a swirling pool, trickling through crevices, disappearing from sight, and then re-emerging where the cracks in the social structure may offer it a course to run. As a doctrine it changes constantly; as a movement it grows and disintegrates, in constant fluctuation, but it never vanishes."[28]

In a postscript to *The Anarchists,* the collection of early anarchist writings, Irving Louis Horowitz related the radical, anti-statist critique to a general cultural phenomenon. Each age, he said, confronts its own crises and all ages are critical. "The modern world, however, has a particularly unique consciousness of crisis. Part of that consciousness originates with the critique offered by anarchist and various radical thinkers. . . ." At the heart of that novel consciousness, Horowitze argued, is "the contradiction between power and principles." The anarchists have presented the bifurcation vividly, defiantly.

Anarchism, the recurrent condemnation of abuse, the recurrent dream of justice, will continue to revive until power vanishes and principles are harmonized.

NOTES

1. Proudhon, quoted by George Woodcock in *Anarchism: A History of Libertarian Ideas and Movements* (Cleveland: Meridian, 1962), p.12.
2. Emma Goldman, "Anarchism," *Anarchism and Other Essays* (New York: Mother Earth, 1911), p. 68.
3. Carlyle, cited by Karl Lowith, *From Hegel to Nietzsche: The Revolution in Nineteenth-Century Thought* (Garden City: Anchor, 1967), p.181. James Joll agrees that anarchism is fundamentally a mood: "if there is a living anarchist tradition, it should be sought in psychological and temperamental attitudes to society as much as in a sociological analysis of the societies in which anarchism has flourished." "Anarchism—A Living Tradition," David Apter and James Joll, eds., *Anarchism Today* (Garden City: Anchor, 1972), p.260.
4. Introduction to Alix Kates Shulman, ed., *Red Emma Speaks: Selected Writings and Speeches of Emma Goldman* (New York: Vintage, 1972), p.5.
5. See Ted Robert Gurr, Introduction to *The History of Violence in America* (New York: Bantam Books, 1969), p.xiv.
6. Benjamin Barber, *Superman and Common Men: Freedom, Anarchy and the Revolution* (New York: Praeger, 1971), p.15.
7. I have argued that anarchists are primarily ideologists in some detail in "The Sublime Cause: Anarchists and Idealists," *Berkshire Review* (Winter 1972): 21-31.
8. Jefferson Airplane, cited in Arthur Lothstein, *All We are Saying. . . : The Philosophy of the New Left* (New York: Capricorn, 1971), p.11.

9. Alexander Berkman, *What Is Communist Anarchism?* (New York: Vanguard Press, 1929), p.v.

10. See James Joll, *The Anarchists* (New York: Universal Library, 1966), p.279.

11. Ronald Aronson and John C. Crowley, "The New Left in the United States," in Arthur Lothstein, *All We Are Saying,* p.43.

12. "Free City," in Peter Stansill and David Z. Mairowitz, eds., *BAMN (By Any Means Necessary): Outlaw Manifestos and Ephemera 1965-70* (Harmondsworth: Penguin Books, 1971), p.49.

13. Howard Zinn, *The Politics of History* (Boston: Beacon Press, 1970), p.3. Italics mine.

14. Jerome Tucille, *Radical Libertarianism: A New Political Alternative* (New York: Harper and Row, 1970), pp.100-1.

15. Harry Kelly, *The Ferrer Modern School* (Stelton, New Jersey: Modern School, 1920).

16. Robert Nisbet, *The Social Philosophers: Community and Conflict in Western Thought* (New York: Crowell, 1973), p.382.

17. Karl Marx and Friedrich Engels, "The German Ideology," in Lewis Feuer, ed., *Marx and Engels: Basic Writings on Politics and Philosophy* (New York: Anchor, 1959), p.254.

18. This is not a subject for this anthology, for it extends far beyond the range of anarchist theory and practice. Yet it is useful to recall that most of the recent work on the subject is heavily dependent upon the writings of the anarchist Emma Goldman.

19. Connie Brown and Jane Seitz, " 'You've Come a Long Way Baby': Historical Perspectives," in Robin Morgan, ed., *Sisterhood is Powerful* (New York: Vintage, 1970), p.28.

20. See Terry M. Perlin, "Anarchism in New Jersey: The Ferrer Colony at Stelton," *New Jersey History* (Fall 1971).

21. Neville Fowler, "A Religious View of Anarchism," *Freedom,* vol. 32, no. 17, May 29, 1971.

22. See Irving Louis Horowitz, Introduction to *The Anarchists* (New York: Dell, 1964), p. 55.

23. Steve Halbrook "Northamerican Anarchism: problems and tasks," *Anarchy,* no. 8 (second series, 1972), p.6.

24. Paul Goodman, quoted in April Carter, *The Political Theory of Anarchism* (New York: Harper and Row, 1971), p.9-10.

25. Ibid. None of the great anarchist thinkers of the nineteenth century even drew a sketch of the new society.

26. Richard Drinnon quoting Emma Goldman, new introduction to *Anarchism and Other Essays* (New York: Dover, 1969), p.xiii.

27. Murray Bookchin, *Post-Scarcity Anarchism* (Berkeley: Ramparts Press, 1971). This book has become perhaps the most influential piece of new anarchist writing.

28. George Woodcock, *Anarchism: A History of Libertarian Ideas and Movements* (Cleveland: Meridian Books, 1961), pp.17-18.

PART II.

The Revival

"No matter: Man always hopes; Life always hopes," wrote Voltairine de Cleyre, the anarchist poet and agitator, early in this century. Anarchism is a special kind of idealism; inextricably linked to the defiant mood of anarchist criticism is a vision of a cooperative, peaceful, happy future. Those anarchists who are aware of their movement's history could become easily disillusioned. But most have not. The seventy and eighty year old anarchists I talked with in the late 1960s were filled with fire and enthusiasm; their hope had not wearied.

The reason for the persistence of anarchism as an anti-political force — and as a movement is has been active for more than a century and a half — is that anarchism's "power" is fundamentally moral. The outrage of individual radicals, their very deeply felt sense of injustice, comes not from a finely honed political or economic theory. It surfaces from a ferment of anger and resentment against statist injustice. In nearly all epochs one can find sensitive enemies of the status quo.

Still, anarchism has always been the movement of a tiny minority. Often speaking in the name of entire socieities, or at least of their working classes, the anarchists have met with resistance, contempt and sometimes mere ignorance. But still they persist and, as in the last decade, when the times provided an opening, their words are heard, disseminated and, even, acted upon.

George Woodcock has been active in the anarchist movement since the era of World War II, in Britain, America and Canada. He has written many works, biographies of the anarchists "masters" such as Proudon and

Kropotkin. He is the author of the best-known general work, *Anarchism* (1961). In 1968, he reflected on the revival of anarchism in a sensitive, yet somewhat skeptical essay, "Anarchism Revisited." Woodcock seeks to teach the younger generation some of the lessons learned from earlier anarchist experimentation and confrontation with authority.

Sam Dolgoff, in "The Relevance of Anarchism to Modern Society," composed in 1971, writes polemically and with passion. For years the member, often with two or three comrades, of tiny American anarchist groups, Dolgoff presents anarchism as a program for social reconstruction. The moral imperative is very prominent in his writing, yet there is also a demand for concreteness and an emphasis upon the utility of anarchist decentralization in a world growing increasingly complex and unmanageable. Dolgoff's flexibility and willingness to try out new ideas and techniques issues from a typical anarchist attitude toward experimentalism.

2.
Anarchism Revisited

George Woodcock

There are still thousands of anarchists scattered thinly over many countries of the world. There are still anarchist groups and anarchist periodicals, anarchist schools and anarchist communities. But they form only the ghost of the historical anarchist movement, a ghost which inspires neither fear among governments nor hope among people nor even interest among newspapermen. Clearly, as a movement anarchism has failed. In almost a century of effort it has never even approached the fulfillment of its great aim to destroy the state and build Jerusalem in its ruins. During the past forty years the influence it once established has dwindled, by defeat after defeat and by the slow draining of hope, almost to nothing. Nor is there any reasonable likelihood of a renaissance of anarchism as we have known it since the foundation of the First International in 1864; history suggests that movements which fail to take the chances it offers them are never born again.

So I wrote seven years ago in a book called *Anarchism* which was largely a reckoning with my own youth. For more than a decade, from the early 1940s to the early 1950s, I had served my radical time working with anarchist groups in Britain, France, the United States. I was for a time an editor of the British anarchist papers, *War Commentary* and *Freedom*. My magazine *Now* was the main organ of the literary anarchists who gathered around

Herbert Read and Alex Comfort during the 1940s. I contributed regularly to Dwight Macdonald's *Politics* when Dwight too considered himself an anarchist. I compiled a jejune manual of anarchist tenets *(Anarchy or Chaos)*, as narrowly sectarian as a Trotskyite tract, which Kenneth Rexroth used as a text in his pre-beat gatherings of San Francisco poets during the late 1940s. I was considered unpleasant enough by the State Department to be refused an immigration visa in 1955, a good four years after I had abandoned any kind of connection with organized anarchism. Whether in the changed circumstances of the 1960s that ban still holds I cannot say. My pride has not let me test it again, and in any case I feel it is primarily the business of Americans if their regulations mean that, alone among the frontiers of the world, a libertarian finds those of the United States and China closed against him.

During that decade of activity in the dwindling rump of the historic anarchist movement, I received a sustained exposure to the ideas of a series of libertarian thinkers from the seventeenth century, Winstanley through Godwin and Proudhon down to Sorel and Kropotkin, which I have found a lasting gain. I received also an education in the history of the labor movement somewhat different from that of the average Old Leftist, since it was sharply critical of Marx, and this I have found invaluable in assessing reactionary developments in socialist and Communist countries, which seem to surprise other far more than they do me. I met some intelligent people, of whom a few were charming and one was beautiful, and some of them are still my friends.

But I also lived at that time in the atmosphere of dense and parochial fanaticism which is characteristic of the remnants of dying movements. I watched bitter factional feuds over minor points of anarchosyndicalist doctrine which history had in any case made irrelevant; I even took part in them. I witnessed, with a horrified excitement, one group of English anarchists turning bandits and carrying out an armed raid to raise funds; the victims were not wicked capitalist, but other anarchists with whom the raiders had quarreled over the ownership of a printing press, and whose code of honor they knew would not allow them to report the raid to the police. And I found myself agreeing more and more (against my will) with George Orwell, whom I met at this point, and who—despite his own libertarian tendencies—pointed out the danger that anarchist intolerance might create a moral dictatorship which would imperil the very freedom for which anarchists claimed to fight. I knew already that within anarchist groups pressures to orthodoxy of belief existed; the more dedicated a militant, the more priggish and intolerant he was likely to be. I felt the infection touching me, knew it would probably ruin me as a writer, and stepped aside to become a free-wheeling radical of my own kind. I have never been forgiven, particularly by those who fawned most upon me when I was a young and promising writer who also appeared to be a true believer. But that is nothing exceptional; it is the experience of all intellecturals who became involved, in whatever direction, with the sects of the Old Left.

The distinction I have emphasized—between what I gained positively from studying the writers and the history of the generative period of anarchism, and what I wasted in time and energy (though perhaps not finally in experience) by becoming too deeply involved with the conservators of a movement which had lost its relevance because it lost its constituency among the peasant and artisan masses of the Latin and Slav countries—is closely related to a point I made in *Anarchism,* where, after tolling a knell for old-line forms of anarchist organization, I went on to say: "Here of course we must distinguish between the historical anarchist movement that sprang from the efforts of Bakunin and his followers, and the anarchist idea which established it. The idea, in various forms and under various names, was alive more than two centuries before the historical movement began, and since ideas are more durable than organizations and causes, it is possible that the theoretical core of anarchism may still have the power to give life to a new form under changed historical circumstances." And later, as I moved into the last page of my book, I found "a purpose and a function" which anarchism may possess in the modern world.

> If human values are to survive, a counter-ideal must be posed to the totalitarian goal of a uniform world, and that counter-ideal exists precisely in the vision of pure liberty that has inspired the anarchist and near-anarchist writers from Winstanley in the seventeenth century. Obviously, it is not immediately realizable, and since it is an ideal, it will probably never be realized. But the very presence of such a concept of pure liberty can help us to judge our condition and see our aims; it can help us to safeguard what liberties we still retain against the further encroachments of the centralizing state; it can help us to conserve and even enlarge those areas in which personal values still operate; it can help in the urgent task of mere survival, of living out the critical decades ahead until the movement of world centralization loses its impetus like all historical movements, and the moral forces that depend on individual choice and judgment can reassert themselves in the midst of its corruption.

Anarchism, published in 1962, has enjoyed a modest continuing popularity, with editions appearing in Italy, Sweden, now Japan, which I suspect has had as much to do with the fortunes of the doctrine it discusses as with the book's own merits. For anarchism, as a doctrine rather than as a movement, has had a revival during the last few years of the kind I thought possible. The old revolutionary sect has not been resurrected, but in its place has appeared a moral-political movement typical of the age. The development began about a year after my book appeared, but that particular link is accidental.

Let me begin with facts. One reached me only recently. A political science teacher in a Canadian university wrote me of the curious results of a quiz on political preferences which he had given to the 160 students in his class on Contemporary Ideologies. Ninety of them chose anarchism in preference to democratic socialism (which came next with twenty-three votes), liberalism, Communism, and conservatism. Most of the voters seemed as square as students run in the late 1960s; only a small minority were ever hippies or New Leftists.

That was a fact for December, 1967. Part of its background was of course the unparalled academic interest in anarchism during the past decade. Since 1960 more serious and dispassionate studies of anarchism have appeared than during the preceding sixty years of the century. Apart from my own book, these have included James Joll's excellent *The Anarchists,* and some very good paperback anthologies of key libertarian texts, of which the best is probably that edited by Irving Horowitz, which is also called *The Anarchists.* (The French have been somewhat ahead of us in this; Jean Maitron's definitive *Histoire du mouvement anarchiste en France* appeared in 1955, and the first excellent volume of the never completed *Histoire de l'anarchie,* by Alain Sergent and Claude Harmel, in 1949.)

The interest of historians is sometimes the equivalent of a death certificate. All is safely past and ended and can be entombed in books without the fear of a knock in the coffin. The interest of the press, on the other hand, is usually a sign of life in the subject, and furing the past few years anarchism has been popping in and out of newspapers on both sides of the Atlantic because of the new role it has been playing as an element in contemporary youth movements.

I first became aware of this trend in 1963, when newspaper accounts began to reach me describing the Easter demonstrations in London, following on the annual Aldermaston march against nuclear armament. I read that behind the banner of the London Anarchists five hundred young men and women marched twenty abreast. "The London Anarchists came ringleted and bearded and pre-Raphaelite," enthused one reporter. "It was a frieze of non-conformists enviable in their youth and gaiety and personal freedom." In the 1940s the anarchists in London had not taken part in street demonstrations for fear of revealing the smallness of their number. We would have thought ourselves lucky to assemble fifty behind the tattered red-and-black which had been preserved from Spanish Civil War days, and half of these would have been veterans, now dead, who bored one with reminiscences of Kropotkin and Edward Carpenter. And nobody would have talked of us as enviable in our gaiety. The Old Left was solemn through and through. At parties we might take down our unringleted hair, but in public we were as earnest as any of the steeltoothed Trotskyites with whom we competed to sell a few dozen papers every Sunday at Marble Arch. Perhaps, I began to think as I read of those hundreds of gay comrades, perhaps I had been rash in so officiously burying the historic anarchist movement. But this was in fact no knock in the coffin. The anarchists of the 1960s were not the historic anarchist movement resurrected. They were something quite different, a new manifestation of the idea.

The anarchists of the 1940s were bellicose barricaders, dreaming inoffensively of the violent overthrow of the state, and identifying themselves with the great assassins like Ravachol and Emile Henry as a hearth cat might imagine himself a lion. Only a minority of us followed the pacifist revolutionary line and, provided we were allowed an occasional say in *Freedom,* we did not obtrude our point of view. The tradition of Bakunin and the syndicalist cult of romantic death still hung too heavily over the movement. Our yesterday was Spain.

In 1963, it was evident, things had changed. The new anarchists who marched ringleted and pre-Raphaelite, had forgotten Spain and had no use for the old romanticism of the *dynamitero* and the *petroleuse.* They were militant pacifists. They represented a trend which had appeared from outside Old Anarchism. It had come into being through radical protest drives against nuclear warfare like the Campaign for Nuclear Disarmament and the Committee of 100. Among the leaders of the Committee of 100, in particular, were older libertarians, unorthodox anarchists like Herbert Read, Alex Comfort, and the pacifist activist, Laurie Hislam. Within the Committee and its groups of supporters grew up a philosophy of direct action and defiance of the state which created anarchists without traditions, and in the English provinces especially scores of small groups sprang up and maintained largely autonomous existences. Their anarchism was pacifist in nature, and concerned itself little with the dogmatic disputes of the past. Glancing through the announcement columns of *Freedom* in 1967, one realizes these groups are still numerous and widely scattered, representing many times the number of individual supporters the anarchists could muster twenty years ago.

One of the great sustaining influences on this youthful neo-anarchist movement in Britain has been the intellectual quarterly, *Anarchy,* edited for the past seven years by Colin Ward. *Anarchy* has kept a level higher than that of any anarchist magazine I know of since the French 1890s, escaping from old ideological disputes to discuss pratical radical approaches to a great range of current problems. Its contributors have included men as various and vital as Colin MacInnes, Alan Sillitoe, Alex Comfort, Paul

Goodman, Maurice Cranston. It has been influential in the universities, where mushroom anarchist magazines have also been founded in many places by the students, usually going out of existence after a few issues, but giving expression in the meantime to the local form of the general ferment.

All this (hundreds of new anarchists marching through London, one good durable magazine, a lot of ephemeral ones) might seem to mean very little if Britain's reborn anarchism had not lost the holy isolationism of the past, and become allied with all the radical youth trends in present-day Britain, which it influences by its libertarian approach. Thirty years ago in Britain the leaders of the community were shocked when sons and daughters joined the Communists (the present poet laureate among them, singing "Why do we all, seeing a Communist, feel small?"). Today one is more likely to hear a sigh of resignation when young David or Sybil comes home to announce that he or she has become an anarchist. Mark the change. Becoming rather than joining. A change of heart rather than a party ticket. That is how the young tend to see their revolutionism, with a stress on feeling and faith that would have aroused derision among past ideologists.

Britain is not the only country where, in a loose way, the new anarchists maintain a link with the remnants of the old Anarchist Left. In Holland the Provos, rebels against the welfare state who have stirred smug Amsterdam to the depths of its canals with their demonstrations, happenings, and occasional riots, are frankly anarchist in orientation, paying tribute to the Dutch pacifist anarchists of the past (Domela Nieuwenhuis and Bart de Ligt), and giving revolutionary doctrines a new twist so that the despair at ever attaining the libertarian paradise becomes in its own way a weapon, to be used in goading governments into showing their most brutal faces. The weak provoke; the strong unwillingly expend themselves.

> Through provocation (says one Provo manifesto) we force authority to tear off its mask. Uniforms, boots, helmets, sabers, truncheons, firehoses, police dogs, tear gas, and all the other means of suppression they have lined up for us, must be produced. The authorities must be forced to rage, threatening us right and left, commanding, forbidding, condemning, convicting. They will become more and more unpopular and the popular spirit will ripen for revolution. A revolutionary feeling will once again be in the air: crisis.
>
> A crisis of provoked authority.
>
> Such is the gigantic provocation we call for from the International Provotariat.

In North America, in all the kaleidoscope of New Radical organizations, with names compounded of initials impossible to remember, there is no such obvious revival of anarchism as one finds in Britain and Holland. But only if one seeks explicit statements or anarchistic loyalties. In practice many observers regard anarchism as an important and central element in the pluralistic specturm of New Radical thought. Probably the best study of the movement from the inside is Jack Newfield's *A Prophetic Minority,* and Newfield has no hesitation in placing anarchism, with pacifism and socialism, as one of the three basic influences on the New Left. Sometimes the influence becomes a long but concentrated beam stretching across centuries: that of seventeenth-century Winstanley, for example, on the modern Diggers. In general, however, it is hard to find North American New Radicals who have read an anarchist classic as recent as Kropotkin's *Mutual Aid* or *Memoirs of a Revolutionist,* though many have read that surviving but untypical Old Anarchist, Paul Goodman. In general, the basic ideas of anarchism, like those of traditional socialism and pacifism, have come down to the New Radicals (that generation of voluntary semi-literates) not through direct reading, but in a kind of mental nutrient broth of remnants of the old ideologists which pervades the air of certain settings in New York, the Bay Area, Los Angeles, Vancouver, and Montreal. But the key tenets that have been on anarchist lips for generations are there: the rejection of the state, the abandonment of the comfortable in favor of the good life, direct action, decentralization, the primacy of the functional group, participation.

Where neo-anarchists, avowed or unavowed, flourish, one notices at least two important differences from the Old Anarchists in their heyday. The historic movement that died in Barcelona sprang from the poorest classes, the illiterate and wretched peasants of Andalucia and the Ukraine, the hard-run French and Lombard factory workers of the turn-of-the-century, the marble cutters of Carrara, dock-workers of Ancona, watchmakers of the Jura; a few aristocrats (Bakunin and Kropotkin), unfrocked parsons (Godwin and Nieuwenhuis), and working-class intellectuals (Proudhon and Weitling) were among their leaders; neo-Romantic painters and poets (Courbet and Pissarro and Signac, Octave Mirbeau and Oscar Wilde) skirmished on their flanks. Now the conscience-stricken noblemen and priests have been replaced by the conscience-stricken middle class, and these, with the vastly increased bohemian contingent, have almost completely displaced the old anarchist constituency of the peasants and the poor.

Six years ago the British anarchist magazine *Freedom* conducted a survey of the backgrounds of its readers. Out of 457 who answered the questionnaire, forty were engaged industry, but of these six were managers. Twenty-three worked on the land, but eight ran their own farms and holdings and one was an estate manager. Nineteen worked in communications and transport. And that, fifteen percent when one had counted out the managers and owners, was about the total of those who belonged to the traditional groupings of workers and peasants. On the other hand, there were fifty-two teachers, thirty students, twenty architects, sixteen journalists and writers, twenty-three in the arts and entertainments, twelve in the book trade, twenty-five in scientific research and twenty-five in health and welfare, forty, finally, in various administrative and clerical posts. The preponderance of white-collar workers was striking. So was the predominance of youth. Anarchists in the 1940s included a high proportion of the elderly, but of this batch in 1962, sixty five percent were under forty, and if the count were taken again now it would show an even higher proportion. Even more significant was the stronger class shift among the young. Forty-five percent of those over sixty were working-class, as against twenty-three percent of those in their thirties and ten percent of those in their twenties. The new anarchists in Britain, and this applies as much to the Provos in Holland and the New Radicals in the United States, are a movement of dissident middle class youth.

The historic anarchist movement was strongest in countries which, apart from France, were technologically and socially backward and where authority took on a reactionary and half-feudal form. The new anarchism, on the other hand, is strongest in countries where the state has assumed a bland welfare face, and where its pervading influence on daily life rather than its brutality affronts the young.

Perhaps, in this situation, the failures of anarchism, splendid and comic as they have variously been, speak in its favor. Anarchism can claim, almost alone among modern ideologies, the equivocal merit of never having really been tried out. Not having come to power, it was never discredited in power, and in this sense it presents an untarnished image, the image of an idea which, in practical terms, has had nothing but a future. Success has not sullied it, and with the young in their present mood this is a unique and powerful advantage. "Flowers for the rebels who failed," the Old Anarchists used to sing. The flowers are descending on their successors.

Though its ideas were originally framed in situations totally different from those in which the young of today find themselves, anarchism, with its cult of the spontaneous, has always shown a strikingly Protean fluidity in adapting its approach and methods to special historical circumstances. Winstanley in Civil-War England concentrates on direct action to cultivate the wastelands. Godwin at the height of the Enlightenment interests himself in the spread of discussion groups. Proudhon works through the pioneer credit unions (his People's Banks). Bakunin's romantic insurrectionism is balanced by Kropotkin's scientific-sociological approach, from which arose some seminal insights on the relations between town and country, industry and agriculture. The tragically flamboyant gestures of the Terrorists in the 1890s gave place to the syndicalists' myth of the regenerative general strike. The Andalucian peasants in the early months of the Spanish Civil War set up communes of idyllic and altruistic simplicity. The means were always fluid, adapting to changing social norms, but always keeping close to the ground, to the ideal of a society deep at the roots, and always keeping away from ordinary politics, away from power.

None of these specific phases of the anarchist past seems to matter greatly to the New Anarchists. Unlike their predecessors, they do not have the historic urge which loved to relive past battles and to dwell on what birds might lodge on the libertarian family tree between Zeno and Sir Herbert Read. What mainly concerns them in ideas is applicability to their own situation, and here anarchism certainly seems to have a great deal to give them.

Consider that situation. They are in full revolt against a society dominated by material goals, by established power. They are facing, perhaps more realistically than their elders, the great revolution which automation will wreak within a few years on our concepts of the dignity and necessity of toil. They see at the same time that the world which provides material security and leisure for tens of millions, leaves, even in North America, other millions in poverty and alienation, to which there appear at present no certified cures. They see the most condemned war in their country's history being fought in their name and, for many of them, with their blood. But they cannot even applaud unreservedly the other side, since only the most naively gullible among them believe that the Vietcong is really better than its enemies. They see the traditional great American and Canadian parties concerned with despicable goals of power and material reward. They revolt against the hierarchic institutionalization of revolutionism by the Old Left, which is why, despite the fantasies that crowd the mind of J. Edgar Hoover, the Communists have never made any appreciable headway among them. They see the unions concerned almost wholly with money. Labor radicalism is dead, and its one great manifestation in the American past revives for a grotesque and ghostly Sabbath each year when the few surviving veterans of the IWW gather to shout old slogans at the annual convention in Chicago and to sing old songs of defiance to an unlistening world.

What the anarchist tradition has to give the radical young is perhaps, first of all, the vision of a society in which every relation would have moral rather than political characteristics. The anarchist believes in a moral urge in man powerful enough to survive the destruction of authority and still to hold society together in the free and natural bonds of fraternity. Recent events, the civil-rights campaigns, the revolts in the Negro ghettos, the behavior of have-not countries toward their prosperous benefactors, have shown that even in a materialist culture, non-materialist values will make an irrational but convincing clamor. The relations among men are moral in nature, and politics can never entirely embrace them. This the anarchists have always insisted.

Within such a non-materialist attitude they have posed, against the TUC and AFL-CIO drives to bring the workers into line materially with the rich, the ideal of a dignified poverty. Paul Goodman has written a great deal on this, but we should not forget those magnificently poetic passages of *La guerre et la paix* in which Proudhon draws the distinction between pauperism and poverty. Pauperism, he contends, is destitution. Poverty is the state in which a man gains from his work just enough for his needs, and this condition Proudhon praises in lyrical terms as the ideal human state, in which we are most free, in which, masters of our senses and our appetites, we are best able to spiritualize our needs. In material terms anarchists have never asked for more than the sufficiency that will allow men to be free. One has only to read the moving accounts of Gerald Brenan and Franz Borkenau to realize how deeply the peasant anarchists of southern Spain felt their freedom. They were willing to give up not merely alcohol and tobacco, but even tea and coffee, so that their newly communized villages could escape more completely from the golden chains of the money system.

The great anarchists, and here I am not considering the embittered last-ditch defenders who represented the historic movement in the 1940s, laid a constant stress on the natural, the spontaneous, the unsystematic. For them individual judgment held primacy; dogmas impeded one's understanding of the quality of life. That life, they believed, should be as simple and as near to nature as possible. This urge toward the simple, natural way of life made men like Kropotkin urgently concerned over the alienation of men in modern cities and the destruction of the countryside, themes that are dear to New Radicals. The anarchists were ever conscious of the danger of rule by experts. Bakunin was frankly hostile to professional scientists. Even Kropotkin, scientist by training, stressed the great role of the amateur in scientific development, and when it came to the organization of a trade or a village or a city quarter to fulfill its material needs, he believed that responsibility should lie with those nearest to the problem. People must learn to make their own decisions. This strong sense of the appropriateness of those directly concerned deciding on all matters affecting them alone became the basis of Proudhon's federalism. He saw society organized in functional groups, industrial and social in character, in which people would decide what should be done at their place of work or their place of living. Above these primary levels, and dependent always upon them, would be constructed, in the most loosely federal manner possible, the few national and international institutions that might be necessary. At every level the people would participate as widely as possible, but at the lowest level, in workshops and living areas, participation would be complete.

It is easy to see how such views may appeal to New Radicals today and, indeed, how far New Radical views derive half-consciously from those of the anarchist past. But perhaps the way in which the anarchists have most interestingly anticipated the preoccupations of the young today is in their concern over what they firmly believed would be the death of the relation between man and his work as we have known it. As long ago as 1793, writing his *Enquiry Concerning Political Justice* (the first major anarchist text), Godwin foresaw with great accuracy the age of automation and forced leisure which today seems almost upon us.

At present, to pull down a tree, to cut a canal, to navigate a vessel requires the labor of many. Will it always require the labor of many? When we look at the complicated machines of human contrivance, various sorts of mills, of weaving engines, of steam engines, are we not astonished at the compendium of labor they produce? Who shall say where this species of improvement must stop? The conclusion of the progress which has here been sketched is something like a final close to the necessity of human labor.

With a daring that seemed more astonishing 175 years ago than it does today, Godwin ventured the prophecy that one day man might have to work no more than an average of half an hour a day. The rest he could devote to the cultivation of his nature. Kropotkin, writing almost a quarter of a century later in *The Conquest of Bread,* was more cautious than his predecessor, merely making a suggestion whose fulfillment is now almost upon us in the Western world. The physical comfort of society might be assured, he ventured, if all men worked "five hours a day from the age of twenty or twenty-five to forty-five or fifty." But Kropotkin also realized what is becoming steadily more clear to us today, that the small amount of work necessary in the near future will be of far less concern than the long hours away from the factory and the office. We are faced with the problem of what happens, to borrow phraseology from that other old libertarian, William Morris, when Useless Toil is eliminated and we have to find Useful Work. Kropotkin believed optimistically that when the problems of excessive toil had been solved, men would adjust themselve, creatively. "Man is not a being whose exclusive purpose in life is eating, drinking, and providing a shelter for himself. As soon as his material wants are satisfied, other needs, which generally speaking may be described as of an artistic nature, will thrust themselves forward. These needs are of the greatest variety; they vary in each and every individual, and the more society is civilized, the more will individuality be developed, and the more desires be varied." So Kropotkin wrote in 1892. I think New Radicals today would see the problem in exactly the same way, though I doubt if many would be as optimistic.

To a great extent I still share many of the libertarian attitudes I have been describing, though I answer to no whip and accept no label. I am not seeking converts to them. My propagandist days are ended. But I am, as a historian, extremely interested in the phenomenon of a group of ideas, which only a decade ago seemed tied to the dying animal of a nineteenth-century working-class movement, but which today have taken on new company among the young and the middle class, and which seem to be giving the young at least some of the answers they want to the questions of the 1960s.

I am also interested in the absence of some of the elements which were part of classic anarchism. There is no longer much talk of barricades and revolutionary heroism, and while "direct action" is a phrase continually on the lips of New Radicals, it means something very near to Gandhian civil disobedience, which Old Anarchists would despise ostentatiously. I believe all these changes are to the good, since they represent the liberation of useful libertarian ideas from many of those elements of the historic anarchist movement which its critics, with a degree of justification, condemned. The anarchists of the past were too much inclined, despite their fervent anti-Marxism, to accept the stereotypes of nineteenth-century left-wing thinking; the idea of the class struggle as a dominant and constructive force in society, the romantic cult of insurrectionism and terror, and even, though this they rarely admitted, a vision of proletarian dictatorship, particularly among the anarcho-syndicalists who envisaged a society run by monolithic workers' unions. Those who openly or unwittingly advocate anarchistic ideas today have mostly shed these outdated concepts, together with much else of the ideological baggage of the Old Left. The revolutionary tactics of Bakunin are as dead as if they were buried with him among the solid burghers of Berne. It is unlikely that we shall see the revival of a movement dedicated to pursuing them, however far libertarian ideas and impulses may spread among the young and influence their social and moral concepts.

As to the kind of society their efforts might lead to, the anarchists were never great utopians. They liked to keep the future flexible and felt that elaborate plans laid burdens on generations which had not made them. I am sure most New Radicals would agree. But there was nevertheless an unbending rigidity about one aspect of the Old Anarchist view of the future. It was a hard, no-compromise view; either the completely non-governmental society, or nothing at all. The Old Anarchists never came within light years of attaining such a goal; hence the glorious record of unsuccess which is now so much to anarchism's advantage.

Today I doubt if anyone in the West seriously believes in the possibility of creating a uniform society of any kind, and I suspect the Russians too are fast abandoning such a hope. We no longer think terminally, thanks paradoxically to the threat of nuclear destruction. The future is open-ended, open-sided, and as far as we can see ahead we are likely to be involved in pluralistic permutations that will embrace many philosophies, many nuances of approach.

The anarchists, in other words, will never create their own world. The free society of which they have dreamed is as pleasant and as remote a myth as the idyllic libertarian society William Morris portrayed in *News from Nowhere*. The material and social complexity of the modern world obviously precludes such simplistic solutions. But this does not mean that the ideas which have emerged within the libertarian tradition are, outside the context of an anarchist utopia, irrelevant in the real world. Taken individually, as I have suggested, they often have a striking relevance to current problems. At the same time, it seems to me, they can only become useful if those who respect the positive aspects of anarchist thought are willing to make a number of radical admissions.

Classic anarchists, for instance, believed that the destruction of an authoritarian society must precede the creation of its libertarian successor. But history in the past fifty years has shown that the revolutionary destruction of an authoritarian society tends to create a more efficiently coercive society in its place. The liberalization of a society is, in fact, an evolutionary and not an apocalyptic process, and can only be attained by concentrating on piecemeal changes. These changes are to be attained not by rejecting all laws, since some restraints are manifestly necessary in any foreseeable future society, but by searching out those areas in which authoritarian and bureaucratic methods have manifestly failed or over-extended themselves, and by endeavoring to give practical application to libertarian concepts of decentralization, voluntarism, and direct participation in decision-making. Such an admission implies that it is time for those who still find some virtue in basic libertarian teachings to recognize that, despite the moralistic pretensions of past anarchists, anarchism has never been genuinely non-political. It has always represented politics carried out by other means. A recognition of this kind would free those who hold libertarian convictions to seek the social changes they think necessary within an existing political framework which, needless to say, is also changeable.

Finally, one must accept a more existential view of human nature than the historic anarchists upheld. They believed that, even if man was not naturally good, he was naturally social. Such an assumption presupposed impossibly ideal circumstances; given freedom and sufficiency and time to heal their psychic wounds, men would perhaps begin behaving with perfect sociability. But this, again is a utopian vision, unlikely to be realized. We live in the present, where most men are probably better fitted for responsibility than the pessimists assume, and where a few are more chronically anti-social than the optimists wish to admit. This, impossible to define as it may be, is the only human nature we know from experience. We must therefore accept its existence, and limit anti-sociality where it impinges on the lives of others.

Our aim should be to preserve as much freedom as possible for men as they are, rather than dream of a hypothetical total freedom for men as they at present are not.

What I have left, I can hear my old comrades complaining, is no longer anarchism. Perhaps not. But it is an attempt to bring the constructive insights of anarchist thinkers, too often neglected in the past because of the tactics they were wedded to, into a context where they may at last wield some positive and beneficial influence in the shaping of society. The fact that we are now thinking in political and social matters more openly and more pluralistically than in the past makes it possible for the ideas that emerged within the libertarian tradition to play a vital part in shaping, not an anarchist utopia, but a world that will really exist as the product of the vast technological changes of our age. But this can only happen if, as Paul Goodman does so admirably, libertarians are willing to make their social criticisms and their proposals for reform relevant to our concrete and rapidly changing present and not to some idealized future.

The Relevance of Anarchism
to Modern Society

Sam Dolgoff

Bourgeois Neo-Anarchism

Meaningful discussion about the relevance of anarchist ideas to modern industrialized societies must first, for the sake of clarity, outline the difference between today's "neo-anarchism" and the classical anarchism of Proudhon, Bakunin, Kropotkin, Malatesta and their successors. With rare exceptions one is struck by the mediocre and superficial character of the ideas advanced by modern writers on anarchism. Instead of presenting fresh insights, there is the repetition of utopistic ideas which the anarchist movement had long since outgrown and rejected as totally irrelevant to the problems of our increasingly complex society.

Many of the ideas which the noted anarchist writer Luigi Fabbri a half century ago labeled "Bourgeois Influences in Anarchism" are again in circulation.[1] For example, there is Kingsley Widmer's article, "Anarchism Revived Right—Left and All Around." Like similar bourgeois movements in the past, Widmer correctly points out that: "Anarchism's contemporary revival . . . mostly comes from the dissident middle class-intellectuals, students and other marginal groups who [base themselves] on individualist, utopian and other non-working class aspects of anarchism...."[2] Like the old bourgeois anarchists, Widmer too, practically denies the link between anarchism and free socialism and chides Noam Chomsky for seeing "anarchism as purely integral to socialism."

Other typical bourgeois anarchist characteristics are: *Escapism*—the hope that the establishment will be gradually undermined if enough people "cop out" of the system and "live like anarchists in communes ... and other life-style institutions" (Widmer). *Nechayevism*—romantic glorification of conspiracy, ruthlessness, violence in the amoral tradition of Nechayev. *Bohemianism*—total irresponsibility; exclusive preoccupation with one's picturesque "life-style"; exhibitionism; rejection of any form of organization or self-discipline. *Anti-Social Individualism*—the urge to "idealize the most anti-social forms of individual rebellion" (Fabbri).

"Intolerance of oppression [writes Malatesta], the desire to be free and to develop one's personality to its full limits, is not enough to make one an anarchist. That aspiration toward unlimited freedom, if not tempered by a love for mankind and by the desire that all should enjoy equal freedom, may well create rebels who ... soon become exploiters and tyrants."[3] Still other neo-anarchists are obsessed with "action for the sake of action." One of the foremost historians of Italian anarchism, Pier Carlo Masini, notes that for them "spontaneity" is the panacea that will automatically solve all problems. No theoretical or practical preparation is needed. In the "revolution" which is "just around the corner" the fundamental differences between libertarians and our mortal enemies, authoritarian groups like the "Marxist-Leninists" will miraculously vanish. Masini observes, "Paradoxically enough, the really modern anarchists are those with white hair, those who guided by the teachings of Bakunin and Malatesta, who in Italy and in Spain (as well as in Russia) had learned from bitter personal participation how serious a matter revolution can be."[4]

It is not our intention to belittle the many fine things the scholars do say, nor to downgrade the magnificent struggles of our young rebels against war, racism and the false values of that vast crime "The Establishment" — struggles which sparked the revival of the long dormant radical movement. But they stress the negative aspects and ignore or misinterpret the constructive principles of anarchism. Bakunin and the classical anarchists always emphasized the necessity for constructive thinking and action: "It [1848 revolutionary movement] was rich in instincts and negative theoretical ideas which gave it full justification for its fight against privilege, but it lacked completely any positive and practical ideas which would have been needed to enable it to erect a new system upon the ruins of the old bourgeois setup."[5]

Distorting Anarchist Ideas

Recent works on anarchism, like George Woodcock's *Anarchism* and the two books by Horowitz and Joll, both titled *The Anarchists*, perpetuate the myth that the anarchists are living antiques, visionaries yearning to return to an idyllic past. According to Woodcock, "The historical anarchist movement that sprang from Bakunin and his followers is dead." The cardinal principles of classical anarchism: economic and political decentralization of power, individual and local autonomy, self-management of industry ("workers' "control") and federalism are "obsolete forms of organization [running counter] to the world wide trend toward political and economic centralization. . . . The real social revolution of the modern age has in fact been this process of centralization toward which every development of scientific and technological progress has contributed. [the trend is in the opposite direction] . . . the anarchist movement failed to present an alternative to the state or the capitalist economy."[6]

It is hard to understand how scholars even slightly acquainted with the vast libertarian literature on social reconstruction could possibly come to such absurd conclusion!! A notable exception is the French sociologist-historian Daniel Guerin whose excellent little book *L'anarchisme* has just been translated into English with an introduction by Noam Chomsky (Monthly Review Press, N. Y.) Guerin concentrates on the constructive aspects of anarchism. While not without its faults (he underestimates the importance of Kropotkin's ideas and exaggerates Stirner's) it is still the best short introduction to the subject. Guerin effectively refutes the arguments of recent historians, particularly Jean Maitron, Woodcock, and Joll, concluding that their "image of anarchism is not true. Constructive anarchism which found its most accomplished expression in the writings of Bakunin, relies on organization, on self-discipline, on integration, on a centralization which is not coercive, but federalist. It relates to large scale industry, to modern technology, to the modern proletariat, to genuine internationalism . . . In the modern world the material, intellectual and moral interests have created between all parts of a nation and even different nations, a real and solid unity, and this unity will survive all states."[7] To assess the extent to which classical anarchism is applicable to modern societies it is first necessary to summarize briefly its leading constructive tenets.

Complex Societies Necessitate Anarchism

It is a fallacy to assume that anarchists ignore the complexity of social life. On the contrary, the classical anarchists have always rejected the kind of "simplicity" which camouflages regimentation in favor of the natural complexity which reflects the many faceted richness and diversity of social and individual life. The Cybernetic mathematician John B. McEwan, writing on the relevance of anarchism to cybernetics explains that: "Libertarian socialists, [synonym for non-individualist anarchism] especially Kropotkin and Landauer, showed an early grasp of the complex structure of society as a complex network of changing relationships, involving many structures of correlated activity and mutual aid, independent of authoritarian coercion. It was against this background that they developed their theories of social organization."[8]

Like his predecessors, Proudhon and Bakunin, Kropotkin elaborated the idea that the very complexity of social life demanded the decentralization and self-management of industry by the workers. From his studies of economic life in England and Scotland he concluded that: "production and exchange represented an undertaking so complicated that no government [without establishing a cumbersome, inefficient bureaucratic dictatorship] would be able to organize production if the workers themselves, through their unions, did not do it in each branch of industry; for, in all production there arises daily thousands of difficulties that . . . no government can hope to foresee . . . Only the efforts of thousands of intelligences working on problems can cooperate in the development of the new social system and find solutions for the thousands of local needs."[9]

Decentralization and autonomy does not mean the breakup of society into small, isolated, economically self-sufficient groups, which is neither possible nor desireable. The Spanish anarchist, Diego Abad De Santillan, Minister of the Economy in Catalonia in the early period of the Spanish Civil War, (December 1936) reminded some of his comrades: "Once and for all we must realize that we are no longer . . . in a little utopian world . . . we cannot realize our economic revolution in a local sense; for economy on a localist basis can only cause collective privation . . . economy is today a vast organism and all isolation must prove detrimental . . . We must work with a social criterion, considering the interests of the whole country and if possible the whole world."[10]

A balance must be achieved between the suffocating tyranny of unbridled authority and the kind of "autonomy" that leads to petty local patriotism, separatism of little grouplets and the fragmentation of society. Libertarian organization must reflect the complexity of social relationships and promote solidarity on the widest possible scale. It can be defined as federalism: coordination through free agreement, locally, regionally, nationally and internationally. A vast coordinated network of voluntary alliances embracing the totality of social life, in which all the groups and associations reap the benefits of unity while still exercising autonomy within their own spheres and expanding the range of their freedom. Anarchist organizational principles are not separate entities. Autonomy is impossible without decentralization, and decentralization is impossible without federalism.

The increasing complexity of society is making anarchism *more* and *not less* relevant to modern life. It is precisely this complexity and diversity, above all their overriding concern for freedom and human values that led the anarchist thinkers to base their ideas on the principles of diffusion of power, self-management and federalism. The greatest attribute of the free society is that it is self-regulating and "bears within itself the seeds of its own regenration" (Buber). The self-governing associations will be flexible enough to adjust their differences, correct and learn from their mistakes, experiment with new, creative forms of social living and thereby achieve genuine harmony on a higher, humanistic plane. Errors and conflicts confined to the limited jurisdiction of special purpose groups, may do limited damage. But miscalculations and criminal decisions made by the state and other autocratically centralized organizations affecting whole nations, and even the whole world, can have the most disasterous consequences.

Modern Industry Better Organized Anarchistically

Bourgeois economists, sociologists, and administrators like Peter Drucker, Gunnar Myrdal, John Kenneth Galbraith, and Daniel Bell, now favor a large measure of decentralization not because they have suddenly become anarchists, but primarily because technology has rendered anarchistic forms of organization "operational necessities." The bourgeois reformers have yet to learn that as long as these organizational forms are tied to the state or to capitalism, which connotes the monopoly of political economic power, decentralization and fedealism will remain a fraud—a more efficient device to enlist the cooperation of the masses in their own enslavement. To illustrate wherein their ideas inadvertently demonstrate the practicality of anarchist organization and how they contradict themselves, we cite the "free enterpriser" Drucker and the "welfare statist" Myrdal. In the chapter titled, "The Sickness of Government" Drucker writes:

> Disenchantment with government cuts across national boundaries and ideological lines. . . . Government itself has become one of the vested interests. . . . The moment government undertakes anything it becomes entrenched and permanent. . . . The unproductive becomes built into the political process itself. . . . Social theory to be meaningful at all, must start with the reality of pluralism of institutions, a galaxy of

suns rather than one big center surrounded by moons that shine only by reflected light . . . a society of institutional diversity and diffusion of power. . . . In a pluralist society of organizations [each unit would be] limited to the specific service it renders to the members of society which it meant to perform—yet, since every institution has power in its own sphere, it would be as such, affected with the public interest. . . . Such a view of organizations as being autonomous and limited are necessary both to make the organization perform and to safeguard the individual's freedom.[11]

After demonstrating the "monstrosity of government, its lack of performance and its impotence" Drucker flatly contradicts himself and comes to the surprising conclusion that "never has strong, effective government been needed more than in this pluralist society of organizations . . ."

Myrdal convincingly demonstrates that both the Soviet and the "free world states" need decentralization for administrative efficiency in order that (political and economic life) shall not succumb to the rigidity of the central apparatus. But then he expects the paternalistic welfare state to loosen "its controls over everyday life" and gradually transfer most of its powers to "all sorts of organizations and communities controlled by the people themselves . . . " No anarchist could refute Myrdal's argument better than he does himself: "to give up autocratic patterns, to give up administrative controls and . . . to withdraw willingly from intervening when it is no longer necessary, are steps which do not correspond to the inner workings of a functioning bureaucracy."[12] If these advocates of decentralization and autonomy were consistent, they would realize that the diffusion of power leads to anarchism.

The anarchists have always opposed the Jacobins, Blanquists, Bolsheviks and other would-be dictators, who would in Proudhon's words: "reconstruct society upon an imaginary plan, much like the astronomers who for respect for their calculations would make over the system of the universe."[13]

The anarchist theoreticians limited themselves to suggest the utilization of all the useful organisms in the old society in order to reconstruct the new. They envisioned the generalization of practices and tendencies which are already in effect. The very fact that autonomy, decentralization and federalism are more practical alternatives to centralism and statism already presupposes that these vast organizational networks now performing the functions of society are prepared to replace the old bankrupt hyper-centralized administrations. That the "elements of the new society are already developing in the collapsing bourgeois society" (Marx) is a fundamental principle shared by all tendencies in the socialist movement.

Kropotkin was very explicit on this subject: "The anarchists . . . build their previsions of the future upon those data which are supplied by the observations of life at the present time . . .[14] The idea of independent communes for the territorial organizations and of federations of trade unions for the organization of men in accordance with their different functions, gives a concrete conception of a society generated by a social revolution. There remained only to add to these two modes of organization, a third, which we saw rapidly developing during the last fifty years. . . . The thousands upon thousands of free combines and societies growing up everywhere for the satisfaction of all possible and imaginable needs, economic, sanitary, and educational; from mutual protection, for the propaganda of ideas, for art, for amusement, and so on. All of them covering each other, and all of them ready to meet new needs by new organizations and adjustments."[15]

One need not, in view of modern developments, agree with all of Kropotkin's specific suggestions to see that, in general, the concepts sketched out by him constitute a realistic basis for the reconstruction of society. Society is a vast interlocking network of cooperative labor: and all the deeply rooted institutions listed by Kropotkin, now functioning, will in some form continue to function for the simple reason that the very existence of mankind depends upon this inner cohesion. This has never been questioned by anyone. What is needed is emancipation from authoritarian institutions over society and authoritarianism with the organizations themselves: above all, they must be infused with revolutionary spirit and confidence in the creative capacities of the people. Kropotkin in working out the sociology of anarchism, has opened an avenue of fruitful research which has been largely neglected by social scientists busily engaged in mapping out new areas for state control.

The anarchist's insistence on worker's control—the idea of self-management of industry by workers' associations "in accordance with their different functions" rests on very solid foundations. this tendency traces back to Robert Owen, the first International Workingmens' Association, the Guild Socialist movement in England and the pre-World War I syndicalist movements. With the Russian Revolution, the trend towards workers' control in the form of free soviets (councils) which arose spontaneously, was finally snuffed out with the Kronstadt massacre of 1921. The same tragic fate awaited the workers' councils in the Hungarian, Polish and East German risings around 1956. Among the many other attempts that were made, there is of course, the classic example of the Spanish Revolution of 1936, with the monumental constructive achievements in the libertarian rural collectives and workers' control of urban industry. The prediction of the *New Bulletin* of the reformist International Union of Food and Allied

Workers Associations[16] (July 1964) that: "The demand for workers' control may well become the common ground for advanced sectors in the labor movement both 'east' and 'west' " is now a fact.

Although the purged Bolshevik "left oppositionist," Victor Serge, refers to the economic crisis that gripped Russia during the early years of the revolution, his remarks are, in general still pertinent and incidentally illustrate Kropotkin's theme: "certain industries could have been revived (and) an enormous degree of recovery achieved by appealing to the initiative of groups of producers and consumers, freeing the state strangled cooperatives and inviting the various associations to take over management of different branches of economic activity . . I was arguing for a Communism of Associations—in contrast to Communism of the State—the total plan not dictated on high by the State, but resulting from the harmonizing by congresses and special assemblies from below."[17]

"After the Revolution"

The anarchist thinkers were not so naive as to expect the installation of the perfect society composed of perfect individuals who would miraculously shed all their ingrained prejudices and old habits on the day after the revolution. They were primarily concerned with the immediate problems of social reconstruction that will have to be faced in any country—industrialized or not.

They are issues which no serious revolutionary has the right to ignore. It was for this reason that the anarchists tried to work out measures to meet the pressing problems most likely to emerge during what Malatesta called: ". . . the period of reorganization and transition."[18] We summarize Malatesta's discussion of some of the more important questions.[19]

Crucial problems cannot be avoided by postponing them to the distant future—perhaps a century or more—when anarchism will have been fully realized and the masses will have finally become convinced and dedicated anarchist-communists. We anarchists must have our own solutions if we are not to be relegated to the role of useless and impotent grumblers, while the more realistic and unscrupulous authoritarians seize power. Anarchy or no anarchy, the people must eat and be provided with the necessities of life. The cities must be provisioned and vital services cannot be disrupted. Even if poorly served, the people in their own interests would not allow us or anyone else to disrupt these services unless and until they are reorganized in a better way; and this cannot be achieved in a day.

The urbanization of the anarchist-communist society on a large scale can only be achieved gradually as material conditions permit, and as the masses convince themselves of the benefits to be gained and as they gradually become psychologically accustomed to radical alterations in their way of life. Since free and voluntary communism (Malatesta's synonym for anarchism) cannot be imposed, Malatesta stressed the necessity for the coexistence of various economic forms, collectivist, mutualist, individualist; on the condition that there will be no exploitation of others. Malatesta was confident that the convincing example of successful libertarian collectives will "attract others into the orbit of the collectivity... for my part I do not believe that there is 'one' solution to the social problem, but a thousand different and changing solutions, in the same way as social existence is different in time and space."[20]

"Pure" Anarchism is a Fiction

Aside from the "individualists" (a very ambiguous term) none of the anarchist thinkers were "pure" anarchists. The typical "pure" anarchist grouping, explains George Woodcock "... is the loose and flexible affinity group," which needs no formal organization and carries on anarchist propaganda through an "invisible network of personal contacts and intellectual influences." Woodcock argues that "pure" anarchism is incompatable with mass movements like Anarcho-Syndicalism because they need "stable organizations precisely because it moves in a world that is only partly governed by anarchist ideals . . . and make compromises with day-to-day situations. . . .[It] has to maintain the allegiance of masses of working men who are only remotely conscious of the final aim of anarchism."[21]

If these statements are true, then "pure" anarchism is a pipe dream. First, because there will never be a time when everybody will be a "pure" anarchist, and humanity will forever have to make "compromises with the day-to-day situation." Second, because the intricate economic and social operations of an interdependent world cannot be carried on without these "stable organizations." Even if every inhabitant were a convinced anarchist, "pure" anarchism would still be impossible for technical and functional reasons alone. This is not to say that anarchism excludes affinity groups. Anarchism envisions a flexible, pluralist society where all the needs of mankind would be supplied by a infinite variety of voluntary associations. The world is honeycombed with affinity groups from chess clubs to anarchist propaganda groups. They are formed, dissolved and reconstituted according to the fluctuating whims and fancies of the individual adherents. It is precisely because they *reflect individual preferences* that such groups are the lifeblood of the free society.

But the anarchists have also insisted that since the necessities of life and vital services must be supplied without fail and cannot be left to the whims of individuals, they are social obligations which every able bodied individual is honor-bound to fulfill, if he expects to enjoy the benefits of collective labor. The large scale organizations, federations, and confederations supplying these necessities must therefore underpin the free society. Such stable associations, anarchistically organized, are not a deviation. They are the very essence of anarchism as a viable social order.

There is no "pure" anarchism. There is only the application of anarchist principles to the realities of social living. The aim of anarchism is to stimulate forces that propel society in a libertarian direction. It is only from this standpoint that the relevance of anarchism to modern life can be properly assessed.

Automation Could Expedite Anarchism

We consider that the constructive ideas of anarchism are rendered even more timely by the cybernetic revolution still in its early stages, and will become increasingly more relevant as this revolution unfolds. There are, even now, no insurmountable *technical-scientific barriers* to the introduction of anarchism. The greatest material drawback to the realization of the ideal (which the anarchists hold in common with all socialist tendencies: "To each according to his needs from each according to his ability,") has been the scarcity of goods and services. ". . . Cybernation, a system of almost unlimited productive capacity which requires progressively less human labor . . . would make possible the abolition of poverty at home and abroad . . . "[22] In a consumer economy where purchasing power is not tied to production, the wage system becomes obsolete and the preconditions for the realization of the socialist ideal immeasurably enhanced.

When Kropotkin in 1899 wrote his *Fields, Factories and Workshops* to demonstrate the feasability of decentralizing industry to achieve a greater balance between rural and urban living, his ideas were dismissed a premature. It is now no longer disputed that the problem of scaling down industry to manageable human proportions, rendered even more acute by the pollution threatening the very existence of life on this planet, can now be largely solved by modern technology. There is an enormous amount of literature on this topic. (Murray Bookchin has done an enormous amount of research on this subject—see his *Post-Scarcity Anarchism,* Ramparts Press, 1971)

One of the major obstacles to the establishment of the free society is the cumbersome, all pervasive, corporate-statist manned by an entrenched bureaucratic elite class of administrators, managers and officials who at all levels exercise de facto control over the operations of society. This has up till now been regarded as an unavoidable evil, but thanks to the development of computerized technology, this byzantine apparatus can now be dismantled.

Alan Toffler (*Future Shock,* Random House, 1970, p.141) summing up the evidence, concludes that: "Far from fastening the grip of bureaucracy on civilization more than before, *automation leads to its overthrow . . ."* (emphasis ours). Another source, quoting *Business Week,* emphasizes that "automation not only makes economic planning necessary—it also makes it possible. The calculations required for planning on nationwide scale are complicated and difficult, but they can be performed by the new electronic computers in an amazingly short time."[23]

The libertarian principle of workers' control will not be invalidated by changes in the composition of the work force or in the nature of work itself. With automation, the economic structure of the new society must be based on self-administration by the people directly involved in economic functions. Under automation millions of highly trained technicians, engineers, scientists, educators, etc. who are already organized into local, region, national, and international federations will freely circulate information, constantly improving both the quality and availability of goods and services and developing new products for new needs.

By closely intermeshing and greatly expanding the already existing networks of consumer cooperative associations with the producers associations at every level, the consumers will make their wants known and be supplied by the producers. The innumberable variety of supermarkets chain stores and service centers of every description now blanketing the country, though owned by corporations or privately, are so structured that they could be easily socialized and converted into cooperative networks. In general, the same holds true for production, exchange, and other branches of the economy. The integration of these economic organisms will undoubtedly be greatly facilitated because the same people are both producers and consumer.

The progress of the new society will depend greatly upon the extend to which its self-governing units will be able to ·speed up direct communication—to understand each other's problems and better coordinate activities. Thanks to modern communications technology, all the essential facilities are now available: tape libraries, "computer laundromats," closed television and telephone circuits, communication satellites and a plethora of other devices are making instant, direct communication of a world scale accessible to all (visual and audio contact between earth and moon within seconds!) "Face to face democracy," a cornerstone of a free society, is already foreshadowed by the increasing mobility of peoples.

There is an exaggerated fear that a minority of scientific and technical workers would, in a free society, set up a dictatorship over the rest of society.

They certainly do not now wield the power generally attributed to them. In spite of their "higher" status, they are no less immune to the fluctuations of the economic system than are the "ordinary" workers. (nearly 100,000 are jobless) Like lower paid workers, they too must on pain of dismissal obey the orders of their employers.

Tens of thousands of frustrated first-rate technical and scientific employees, not permitted to exercise their knowledge creatively find themselves trapped in monotonous, useless and anti-social tasks. And nothing is more maddening than to stand helplessly by, while ignoramuses who do not even understand the language of science, dictate the direction of research and development. Nor are these workers free to exercise these rights in Russia or anywhere else.

In addition to these general considerations there are two other preventative checks to dictatorship of the techno-scientific elite. The first is that the wider diffusion of scientific and technical training, providing millions of new specialists, would break up any possible monopoly by a minority and eliminate the threat of dictatorship. ". . . The number of scientists and technologists in this country has doubled in little more than ten years and now forms twenty percent of the labor force—this growth is much faster than that of the population . . ." (*New York Times,* December 29, 1970)

The second check to dictatorship is not to invest specialists or any other group with political power to rule over others. While we must ceaselessly guard against the abuse of power, we must never forget that in the joint effort to build a better world, we must also learn to trust each other. If we do not, then this better world will forever remain a utopia.

The True Relevance of Anarchism

I have tried to show that anarchism is not a panacea that will miraculously cure all the ills of the body social, but rather, a twentieth century guide to action based on a realistic conception of social reconstruction. The well-nigh insurperable. material obstacles to the introduction of anarchism— scarcity of goods and services and excessive industrial-managerial centralization—have or can be removed by the cybernetic-technical revolution. Yet, the movement for emancipation is threatened by the far more formidable political, social and brainwashing techniques of "The Establishment."

In their polemics with the Marxists, the anarchists insisted that the political state subjects the economy to its own ends. A highly sophisticated economic system, once viewed as the prerequisite for the realization of socialism, now serves to reinforce the domination of the ruling classes with the technology of physical and mental repression and the ensuing obliteration of human values. The very abundance which can liberate man from want and drudgery, now enables the state to establish what is, in effect, a nationalized poorhouse, where the millions of technologically unemployed—forgotten, faceless outcasts—on public "welfare" will be given only enough to keep them quiet. The very technology that has opened new roads to freedom, has also armed states with unimaginably frightful weapons for the annihilation of humanity.

While the anarchists never underestimated the great importance of the economic factor in social change, they have nevertheless rejected fanatical economic fatalism. One of the most cogent contributions of anarchism to social theory is the proper emphasis on how political institutions, in turn, mold economic life. Equally significant is the importance attached to the will of man, his aspirations, the moral factor, and above all, the spirit of revolt in the shaping of human history. In this area too, anarchism is particularly relevant to the renewal of society. To indicate the importance attached to this factor, we quote a passage from a letter that Bakunin wrote to his friend Elisee Reclus: "the hour of revolution is passed, not because of the frightful disaster [the Franco-Prussian War and the slaughter of the Paris Commune, May 1871] but because, to my great despair, I have found it a fact, and I am finding it every day anew, that revolutionary hope, passion, are absolutely lacking in the masses; and when these are absent, it is vain to make desperate efforts."

The availability of more and more consumer goods plus the sophisticated techniques of mass indoctrination has corrupted the public mind. Bourgeoisification has sapped the revolutionary vitality of the masses. It is precisely this divorce from the inspiring values of socialism, which, to a large extent, accounts for the venality and corruption in modern labor and socialist movements.

To forge a revolutionary movement, which, inspired by anarchist ideas, would be capable of reversing this reactionary trend, is a task of staggering proportions. But therein lies the true relevance of anarchism.

NOTES

1. Luigi Fabbri, *Influences Bourgueses en el Anarquismo* (Paris: Solidaridad Obrera, 1959).
2. Kingsley Widmer, "Anarchism Revived Right," *The Nation,* November 16, 1970.
3. *Errico Malatesta—Life and Ideas* (London: Freedom Press, 1965), p.24.
4. Quoted in letter from a friend—no date.
5. *Federalism—Socialism—Anti-Theologism.*
6. George Woodcock, *Anarchism* (Cleveland: World Publishing, 1962), pp.469, 473.

7. Daniel Guerin, *L'anarchisme* (Paris: Gallimard, 1965), pp.180-81.
8. John B. McEwan, *Anarchy,* no. 25, March 1963, London.
9. Peter Kropotkin, *Revolutionary Pamphlets* (New York: Vanguard Press, 1927), pp. 76-77. Proudhon's position was similar, "through the progress of ideas and the complexity of interests, society is forced to abjure the state."
10. Diego Abad De Santillan, *After the Revolution* (New York: Greenberg, 1937), pp. 85, 100.
11. Peter Drucker, *The Age of Discontinuity* (New York: Harper and Row, 1968), pp. 212, 217, 222, 225, 226, 251-52.
12. Gunnar Myrdal, *Beyond the Welfare State* (New Haven: Yale University, 1960), pp. 97, 102, 108.
13. Pierre Proudhon, *General Idea in the Revolution in the 19th Century* (London: Freedom Press, 1923), p.90.
14. Peter Kropotkin, *Revolutionary Pamphlets,* p.168.
15. Ibid., pp. 166-67.
16. A confederation of national unions affiliated to the International Labor Organization, a branch of the United Nations.
17. Kropotkin, *Memoirs of a Revolutionary* (London: Oxford University Press, 1963), pp. 147-48.
18. *Malatesta,* p.100
19. Ibid., pp.36, 103, 159.
20. Ibid., pp. 99, 151.
21. Woodcock, *Anarchism,* pp.273-74.
22. *Manifesto . . . Committee for the Triple Revolution,* quoted in *Liberation,* April 1964.
23. *Robot Revolution,* Socialist Party, U.S.A., 1965, pp.43, 44.

PART III

ANARCHISM ON THE LEFT

In the middle of the nineteenth century, Marxists, communists, anarchists and their nameless comrades could be lumped together under the rubric "socialist." But after the schism between Karl Marx and Mikhail Bakunin in the 1870s — a struggle precipitated as much by temperament as ideological hostility — Marxists and anarchists demonstrated quite clearly their differences. The Marxist infatuation with historical development, rapid industrialization, seizure of a centralized state appartus and, especially, creation of an organized, orthodox ideology was anathema to the anarchists. They preferred spontaneity to planning, decentralized communes to workers' states; many anarchists were militantly individualistic.

Since 1917 anarchists, starting with Emma Goldman and Peter Kropotkin, have shown themselves enemies not only of capitalist states but of Soviet centralization as well. The anarchist challenge, one taken up by many New Leftists, was to define an ideology that was rigorously radical, yet untainted by the errors of Marx's statist heirs. The sense of spontaneity, of movement, of utopian yearning for social justice was expressed very early in the 1960s by C. Wright Mills, as unorthodox a radical as imaginable. Mills' "Letter to the New Left," widely read, discussed, and criticized, was anarchist in spirit. Full of contempt for officialdom, it made hope and desire as legitimate forces as ideological orthodoxy had once been.

Antipathy towards dogmatism, affirmation of the idea of revolution from "below" is expressed concretely in Staughton Lynd's "The Movement: A New Beginning." An historical overview by a gifted historian and engaged

51

activist, the essay centers on resistance to the draft during the Vietnam war. It gives an insider's account of the day-to-day activities, and problems, of radical resisters. But in emphasizing the personal dimension of non-cooperation, it displays the New Left's ethical perspective. Lynd's friends were engaged in both opposition and construction and his words have the spirit of anarchism in them.

Murray Bookchin, whose writings on anarchism, especially *Post-Scarcity Anarchism,* are clearly in the tradition of the anarchist classics, has been engaged in radical activity for more than thirty years. During the 1960s and 1970s his voice was the clearest and most systematic among those who proclaimed themselves anarchists. In an interview ("The Anarchist Revolution"), Bookchin shows the anarchist commitment to, and concern with, the here and now — he was among the first radicals to deal with the environmental catastrophe — and also gives a plea for a stateless society of decentralized communities which is clearly non-Marxist.

Both the nay-saying protest and the positive goals of anarchism are reviewed by Emile Capouya in "The Red Flag and the Black." At once critical of anarchist extremism and sympathetic towards anarchist faith in human possibility, Capouya, an editor and writer, applauds the ideals of the left anarchists: "every man must do his own work, living in his own person the life of an emancipated social being."

4.
Letter to the New Left

C. Wright Mills

When I settle down to write to you, I feel somehow "freer" than usual. The reason, I suppose, is that most of the time I am writing for people whose ambiguities and values I imagine to be rather different from mine; but with you, I feel enough in common to allow us "to get on with it" in more positive ways. Reading your book, *Out of Apathy,* prompts me to write to you about several problems I think we now face. On none of these can I hope to be definitive; I only want to raise a few questions.

It is no exaggeration to say that since the end of World War II in Britain and the United States smug conservatives, tired liberals and disillusioned radicals have carried on a weary discourse in which issues are blurred and potential debate muted; the sickness of complacency has prevailed, the bi-partisan banality flourished. There is no need — after your book — to explain again why all this has come about among "people in general" in the NATO countries; but it may be worth while to examine one style of cultural work that is in effect an intellectual celebration of apathy.

Many intellectual fashions, of course, do just that; they stand in the way of a release of the imagination — about the cold war, the Soviet bloc, the politics of peace, about any new beginnings at home and abroad. But the fashion I have in mind is the weariness of many NATO intellectuals with what they call "ideology," and their proclamation of "the end of ideology." So far as I know, this began in the mid-fifties, mainly in intellectual circles more or less associated with the Congress for Cultural Freedom and the magazine *Encounter*. Reports on the Milan Conference of 1955 heralded it; since then, many cultural gossips have taken it up as a posture and an unexamined slogan. Does it amount to anything?

Its common denominator is not liberalism as a political philosophy, but the liberal rhetoric, become formal and sophisticated and used as an uncriticized weapon with which to attack Marxism. In the approved style, various of the elements of this rhetoric appear simply as snobbish assumptions. Its sophistication is one of tone rather than of ideas: in it, the *New Yorker* style of reportage has become politically triumphant. The disclosure of fact, set forth in a bright-faced or in a deadpan manner, is the rule. The facts are duly weighed, carefully balanced, always hedged. Their power to outrage, their power truly to enlighten in a political way, their power to aid decision, even their power to clarify some situation — all that is blunted or destroyed.

So reasoning collapses into reasonableness. By the more naive and snobbish celebrants of complacency, arguments and facts of a displeasing kind are simply ignored; by the more knowing, they are duly recognized, but they are neither connected with one another nor related to any general view. Acknowledged in a scattered way, they are never put together: to do so is to risk being called, curiously enough, "one-sided."

This refusal to relate isolated facts and fragmentary comment with the changing institutions of society makes it impossible to understand the structural realities which these facts might reveal; the longer-run trends of which they might be tokens. In brief, fact and idea are isolated, so the real questions are not even raised, analysis of the meanings of fact not even begun.

Practitioners of the no-more-ideology school do of course smuggle in general ideas under the guise of reportage, by intellectual gossip, and by their selection of the notions they handle. Ultimately, the end-of-ideology is based upon a disillusionment with any real commitment to socialism in any recognizable form. *That* is the only "ideology" that has really ended for these writers. But with its ending, *all* ideology, they think, has ended. *That* ideology they talk about: their own ideological assumptions, they do not.

Underneath this style of observation and comment there is the assumption that in the West there are not more real issues or even problems of great seriousness. The mixed economy plus the welfare state plus prosperity — that is the formula. U.S. capitalism will continue to be workable, the welfare state will continue along the road to ever greater justice. In the meantime, things everywhere are very complex, let us not be careless, there are great risks. . . .

This posture, one of "false consciousness" if there ever was one, stands in the way, I think, of considering with any chances of success what may be happening in the world.

First and above all, it does rest upon a simple provincialism. If the phrase "the end of ideology" has any meaning at all, it pertains to self-selected circles of intellectuals in the richer countries. It is in fact merely their own self-image. The total population of these countries is a fraction of mankind; the period during which such a posture has been assumed is very short indeed. To speak in such terms of much of Latin America, Africa, Asia, the Soviet bloc is merely ludicrous. Anyone who stands in front of audiences, intellectual or mass, in any of these places and talks in such terms will merely be shrugged off (if the audience is polite) or laughed at out loud (if the audience is more candid and knowledgeable). The end-of-ideology is a slogan of complacency, circulating among the prematurely middle-aged, centered in the present, and in the rich Western societies. In the final analysis, it also rests upon a disbelief in the shaping by men of their own futures — as history and as biography. It is a consensus of a few provincials about their own immediate and provincial position.

Second, the end-of-ideology is of course itself an ideology — a fragmentary one, to be sure, and perhaps more a mood. The end-of-ideology is in reality the ideology of an ending: the ending of political reflection itself as a public fact. It is a weary know-it-all justification, by tone of voice rather than by explicit argument, of the cultural and political default of the NATO intellectuals.

All this is just the sort of thing that I at least have always objected to, and do object to, in the "socialist realism" of the Soviet Union.

There too, criticism of milieux are of course permitted — but they are not to be connected with criticism of the structure itself: one may not question "the system." There are no "antagonistic contradictions."

There too, in novels and plays, criticisms of characters, even of party members, are permitted — but they must be displayed as "shocking exceptions": they must be seen as survivals from the old order, not as systematic products of the new.

There too, pessimism is permitted — but only episodically and only within the context of the big optimism: the tendency is to confuse any systematic or structural criticism with pessimism itself. So they admit criticisms, first of this and then of that: but engulf them all by the long-run historical optimism about the system as a whole and the goals proclaimed by its leaders.

I neither want nor need to overstress the parallel, yet in a recent series of interviews in the Soviet Union concerning socialist realism I was very much struck by it. In Uzbekistan and Georgia as well as in Russia, I kept writing notes to myself, at the end of recorded interviews: "This man talks in a style just like Arthur Schlesinger Jr." "Surely this fellow's the counterpart of Daniel Bell, except not so — what shall I say? — so gossipy; and certainly neither so petty nor so vulgar as the more envious status-climbers. Perhaps this is because here they are not thrown into such a competitive status-panic about the ancient and obfuscating British models of prestige." The would-be enders of ideology, I kept thinking, "are they not the self-coordinated, or better the fashion-coordinated, socialist realists of the NATO world?" And: "Check this carefully with the files of *Encounter* and *The Reporter*."

Certainly there are many differences — above all, the fact that socialist realism is part of an official line; the end-of-ideology is self-managed. But the differences one knows. It is more useful to stress the parallels — and the generic fact that both of these postures stand opposed to radical criticisms of their respective societies.

In the Soviet Union, only political authorities at the top, or securely on their way up there, can seriously tamper with structural questions and ideological lines. These authorities, of course, are much more likely to be intellectuals (in one or another sense of the word — says a man who actually writes his own speeches) then are American politicians (about the British, you would know better than I). Moreover, such Soviet authorities, since the death of Stalin, *have* begun to tamper quite seriously with structural questions and basic ideology — although for reasons peculiar to the tight and official joining of culture and politics in their set-up, they must try to disguise this fact.

The end-of-ideology is very largely a mechanical reaction, not a creative response, to the ideology of Stalinism. As such it takes from its opponent something of its inner quality. What does it all mean? That these people have become aware of the uselessness of Vulgar Marxism, but not yet aware of the uselessness of the liberal rhetoric.

But the most immediately important thing about the "end of ideology" is that it is merely a fashion, and fashions change. Already this one is on its way out. Even a few Diehard Anti-Stalinists are showing signs of a reappraisal of their own past views; some are even beginning to recognize publicly that Stalin himself no longer runs the Soviet party and state. They begin to see the poverty of their comfortable ideas as they come to confront Khrushchev's Russia.

We who have been consistently radical in the moral terms of our work throughout the post war period are often amused nowadays that various writers, sensing another shift in fashion, begin to call upon intellectuals to work once more in ways that are politically explicit. But we shouldn't be merely amused — we ought to try to make their shift more than a fashion change.

The end-of-ideology is on the way out because it stands for the refusal to work out an explicit political philosophy. And alert men everywhere today do feel the need of such a philosophy. What we should do is to continue directly to confront this need. In doing so, it may be useful to keep in mind that to have a working political philosophy means to have a philosophy that enables you to work. And for that, at least four kinds of work are needed, each of them at once intellectual and political.

In these terms, think for a moment longer of the end-of-ideology:

1. It is kindergarten fact that any political reflection that is of possible public significance is *ideological:* in its terms, policies, institutions, men of power are criticized or approved. In this respect, the end-of-ideology stands, negatively, for the attempt to withdraw oneself and one's work from political relevance; positively, it is an ideology of political complacency which seems the only way now open for many writers to acquiesce in or to justify the *status quo.*

2. So far as orienting *theories* of societies and of history are concerned, the end-of- ideology stands for, and presumably stands upon, a fetishism of empiricism: more academically, upon a pretentious methodology used to state the trivialities about unimportant social areas; more essayistically, upon a naive journalistic empiricism, which I have already characterized above, and upon a cultural gossip in which "answers" to the vital and pivotal issues are merely assumed. Thus political bias masquerades as epistemological excellence, and there are no orienting theories.

3. So far as the *historic agency of change* is concerned, the end-of-ideology stands upon the identification of such agencies with going institutions; perhaps upon the piecemeal reform, but never upon the search for agencies that might be used or that might themselves make for a structural change of society. The problem of agency is never posed as a problem to solve, as our problem. Instead there is talk of the need to be pragmatic, flexible, open. Surely all this has already been adequately dealt with: such a view makes sense politically only if the blind drift of human affairs is in general beneficent.

4. So far as political and human *ideals* are concerned, the end-of-ideology stands for a denial of their relevance — except as abstract ikons. Merely to hold such ideals seriously is in this view "utopian."

But enough. Where do *we* stand on each of these four aspects of political philosophy? Various of us are of course at work on each of them, and all of us are generally aware of our needs in regard to each. As for the articulation of ideals: there I think your magazines have done their best work so far. That is *your* meaning, is it not?, of the emphasis upon cultural affairs. As for ideological analysis, and the rhetoric with which to carry it out: I don't think any of us are nearly good enough, but that will come with further advance on the two fronts where we are weakest: theories of society, history, human nature; and the major problem — ideas about the historical agencies of structural change.

We have frequently been told by an assorted variety of dead-end people that the meanings of Left and Right are now liquidated, by history and by reason. I think we should answer them in some such way as this:

The Right, among other things, means — what you are doing, celebrating society as it is, a going concern. Left means, or ought to mean, just the opposite. It means: structural criticism and reportage and theories of society, which at some point or another are focused politically as demands and programs. These criticisms, demands, theories, programs are guided morally by the humanist and secular idea of Western civilization — above all, reason and freedom and justice. "To be Left" means to connect up cultural with political criticism, and both with demands and programs. And it means all this inside *every* country of the world.

Only one more point of definition: absence of public issues there may well be, but this is not due to any absence of problems or of contradictions, antagonistic and otherwise. Impersonal and structural changes have not eliminated problems or issues. Their absence from many discussions — that *is* an ideological condition, regulated in the first place by whether or not intellectuals detect and state problems as potential *issues* for probable publics, and as *troubles* for a variety of individuals. One indispensible means of such work on these central tasks is what can only be described as ideological analysis. To be actively Left, among other things, is to carry on just such analysis.

To take seriously the problem of the need for a political orientation is not of course to seek for A Fanatical and Apocalyptic Vision, for An Infallible and Monolithic Lever of Change, for Dogmatic Ideology, for A Startling New Rhetoric, for Treacherous Abstractions — and all the other bogeymen of the dead-enders. These are of course "the extremes," the straw men, the red herrings, used by our political enemies as the polar opposite of where they think they stand.

They tell us, for example, that ordinary men can't always be political "heroes." Who said they could? But keep looking around you; and why not search out the conditions of such heroism as men do and might display? They tell us we are too "impatient," that our "pretentious" theories are not well enough grounded. That is true, but neither are they trivial; why don't they get to work, refuting or grounding them? They tell us we "don't really understand" Russia, and China, today. That is true; we don't; neither do they; we are studying it. They tell us we are "ominous" in our formulations. That is true: we do have enough imagination to be frightened — and we don't have to hide it: we are not afraid we'll panic. They tell us "we are grinding axes." Of course we are: we do have, among other points of view, morally grounded ones; and we are aware of them. They tell us, in their wisdom, we don't understand that The Struggle is Without End. True: we want to change its form, its focus, its object.

We are frequently accused of being "utopian" — in our criticisms and in our proposals; and along with this, of basing our hopes for a New Left *politics* "merely on reason," or more concretely, upon the intelligentsia in its broadest sense.

There is truth in these charges. But must we not ask: what now is really meant by utopian? And: is not our utopianism a major source of our strength? "Utopian" nowadays I think refers to any criticism or proposal that transcends the up-close milieux of a scatter of individuals: the milieux which men and women can understand directly and which they can reasonably hope directly to change. In this exact sense, our theoretical work is indeed utopian — in my own case, at least, deliberately so. What needs to be understood, and what needs to be changed, is not merely first this and then that detail of some institution or policy. If there is to be a politics of a New Left, what needs to be analysed is the *structure* of institutions, the *foundation* of policies. In this sense, both in its criticisms and in its proposals, our work is necessarily structural, and so, *for us,* just now, utopian.

Which brings us face to face with the most important issue of political reflection, and of political action, in our time: the problem of the historical agency of change, of the social and institutional means of structural change. There are several points about this problem I would like to put to you.

First, the historic agencies of change for liberals of the capitalist societies have been an array of voluntary associations, coming to a political climax in a parliamentary or congressional system. For socialists of almost all varieties, the historic agency has been the working class — and later the peasantry; also parties and unions variously composed of members of the working class or (to blur, for now, a great problem) of political parties acting in its name — "representing its interests."

I cannot avoid the view that in both cases, the historic agency (in the advanced capitalist countries) has either collapsed or become most ambiguous: so far as structural change is concerned, these don't seem to be at once available and effective as our agency any more. I know this is a debatable point among us, and among many others as well; I am by no means certain about it. But surely the fact of it, if it be that, ought not to be taken as an excuse for moaning and withdrawal (as it is by some of those who have become involved with the end-of-ideology); it ought not to be bypassed (as it is by many Soviet scholars and publicists, who in their reflections upon the course of advanced capitalist societies simply refuse to admit the political condition and attitudes of the working class).

Is anything more certain than that in 1970, indeed this time next year, our situation will be quite different, and, the chances are high, decisively so? But of course, that isn't saying much. The seeming collapse of our historic agencies of change ought to be taken as a problem, an issue, a trouble — in fact, as *the* political problem which *we* must turn into issue and trouble.

Second, is it not obvious that when we talk about the collapse of agencies of change, we cannot seriously mean that such agencies do not exist. On the contrary, the means of history-making, of decision and of the enforcement of decision, have never in world history been so enlarged and so available to such small circles of men on both sides of The Curtains as they now are. My own conception of the shape of power, the theory of the power elite, I feel no need to argue here. This theory has been fortunate in its critics, from the most diverse points of political view, and I have learned from several of these critics. But I have not seen, as of this date, any analysis of the idea that causes me to modify any of its essential features.

The point that is immediately relevant does seem obvious: what is utopian for us is not at all utopian for the presidium of the Central Committee in Moscow, or the higher circles of the Presidency in Washington, or, recent events make evident, for the men of SAC and CIA. The historic agencies of change that have collapsed are those which were at least thought to be open to *the left* inside the advanced Western nations: those who have wished for structural changes of these societies. Many things follow from this obvious fact; of many of them, I am sure, we are not yet adequately aware.

Third, what I do not quite understand about some New Left writers is why they cling so mightily to "the working class" of the advanced capitalist societies as *the* historic agency, or even as the most important agency, in the face of the really impressive historical evidence that now stands against this expectation.

Such a labor metaphysic, I think, is a legacy from Victorian Marxism that is now quite unrealistic.

It is an historically specific idea that has been turned into an a-historical and unspecific hope.

The social and historical conditions under which industrial workers tend to become a-class-for-themselves, and a decisive political force, must be fully and precisely elaborated. There have been, there are, there will be such conditions; of course these conditions vary according to national social structure and the exact phase of their economic and political development. Of course we can't "write off the working class." But we must *study* all that, and freshly. Where labor exists as an agency, of course we must work with it, but we must not treat it as The Necessary Lever — as nice old Labor Gentlemen in your country and elsewhere tend to do.

Although I have not yet completed my own comparative studies of working classes, generally it would seem that only at certain (earlier) stages of industrialization, and in a political context of autocracy, etc., do wage-earners tend to become a-class-for-themselves, etc. The "etcs." mean that I can here merely raise the question.

It is with this problem of agency in mind that I have been studying, for several years now, the cultural apparatus, the intellectuals — as a possible, immediate, radical agency of change. For a long time, I was not much happier with this idea than were many of you; but it turns out now, in the spring of 1960, that it may be a very relevant idea indeed.

In the first place, is it not clear that if we try to be realistic in our utopianism, and that is no fruitless contradiction, a writer in our countries on the Left today *must* begin there? For that is what we are, that is where we stand.

In the second place, the problem of the intelligentsia is an extremely complicated set of problems on which rather little factual work has been done. In doing this work, we must, above all, not confuse the problems of the intellectuals of West Europe and North America with those of the Soviet bloc or with those of the underdeveloped worlds. In each of the three major components of the world's social structure today, the character and the role of the intelligentsia is distinct and historically specific. Only by detailed comparative studies of them in all their human variety can we hope to understand any one of them.

In the third place, who is it that is getting fed up? Who is it that is getting disgusted with what Marx called "all the old crap"? Who is it that is thinking and acting in radical ways? All over the world, in the bloc, outside the bloc and in between, the answer's the same: it is the young intelligentsia.

I cannot resist copying out for you, with a few changes, some materials I've just prepared for a 1960 paperback edition of a book of mine on war:

"In the spring and early summer of 1960 — more of the returns from the American decision and default are coming in. In Turkey, after student riots, a military junta takes over the state, of late run by Communist Container Menderes. In South Korea too, students and others knock over the corrupt American-puppet regime of Syngman Rhee. In Cuba, a genuinely left-wing revolution begins full scale economic reorganization — without the domination of US corporation. Average age of its leaders: about 30 — and certainly a revolution without any Labor As Agency. On Taiwan, the eight million Taiwanese under the American — imposed idctatorship of Chaing Kai-Shek, with his two million Chinese, grow increasingly restive. On Okinawa, a US military base, the people get their first chance since World War II ended to demonstrate against US seizure of their island: and some students take that chance, snake dancing and chanting angrily to the visiting President: "Go home, go home — take away your missiles." (Don't worry, 12,000 US troops easily handled the generally grateful crowds; also the President was "spirited out the rear end of the United States compound" — and so by helicopter to the airport.) In Great Britain, from Aldermaston to London, young — but you were there. In Japan, weeks of student rioting succeed in rejecting the President's visit, jeopardise a new treaty with the U.S.A., displace the big-business, pro-American prime minister, Kishi. And even in our own pleasant Southland, Negro and white students are — but let us keep that quiet: it really *is* disgraceful.

"That is by no means a complete list; that was yesterday; see today's newspaper. Tomorrow, in varying degree, the returns will be more evident. Will they be evident enough? They will have to be very obvious to attract real American attention: sweet complaints and the voice of reason — these are not enough. In the slum countries of the world today, what are they saying? The rich Americans, they pay attention only to violence — and to money. You don't care what they say, American? Good for you. Still, they may insist; things are no longer under the old control; you're not getting it straight, American: your country, it would seem, may well become the target of a world hatred the like of which the easy-going Americans have never dreamed. Neutralists and Pacifists and Unilateralists and that confusing variety of Leftists around the world — all those tens of millions of people, of course they are misguided, absolutely controlled by small conspiratorial groups of trouble-makers, under direct orders straight from Moscow and Peking. Diabolically omnipotent, it is *they* who create all this messy unrest. It is *they* who have given the tens of millions the absurd idea that they shouldn't want to remain, or to become, the seat of American nuclear bases — those gay little outposts of American civilization. So now they don't want U-2's on their territory; so now they want to contract out of the American military machine; they want to be neutral among the crazy big antagonists. And they don't want their own society to be militarized.

"But take heart, American: you won't have time to get really bored with your friends abroad: they won't be your friends much longer. You don't need them: it will all go away; don't let them confuse you."

Add to that: in the Soviet bloc, who is it that has been breaking out of apathy? It has been students and young professors and writers; it has been the young intelligentsia of Poland and Hungary, and of Russia too. Never mind that they've not won; never mind that there are other social and moral types among them. First of all, it has been these types. But the point is clear — isn't it?

Thats why we've got to study these new generations of intellectuals around the world as real live agencies of historic change. Forget Victorian Marxism, except whenever you need it; and read Lenin again (be careful) — Rosa Luxemburg, too.

"But it's just some kind of moral upsurge, isn't it?" Correct. But under it: no apathy. Much of it is direct non-violent action, and it seems to be working, here and there. Now we must learn from their practice and work out with them new forms of action.

"But it's all so ambiguous. Turkey for instance. Cuba, for instance." Of course it is; history-making is always ambiguous; wait a bit; in the meantime, *help* them to focus their moral upsurge in less ambiguous political ways; work out with them the ideologies, the strategies, the theories that will help them consolidate their efforts: new theories of structural changes of and by human societies in our epoch.

"But it's utopian, after all, isn't it?" No — not in the sense you mean. Whatever else it may be, it's not that: tell it to the students of Japan.

Isn't all this, isn't it something of what we are trying to mean by the phrase, "The New Left"? Let the old men ask sourly, "Out of Apathy — into what?" The Age of Complacency is ending. Let the old women complain wisely about "the end of ideology." We are beginning to move again.

Yours truly,

C. WRIGHT MILLS

5.

The Movement: A New Beginning

Staughton Lynd

I'm going to talk in a way that may seem to some of you abstract or theoretical. Usually I, too, feel impatient of theory and concerned that people relate what they say today to what they, personally, are going to do tomorrow. But at this conference I feel differently. If our discussion is limited to problems which arise in daily resistance work, then we tacitly take for granted our present definition of that work. This procedure will not serve if we want to take a fresh look at how that work has been defined. My own conviction is that this is an historical moment when the Resistance must make an intellectual leap and newly define its work on a multi-issue, multi-class basis. It cannot do that, so it seems to me, without some notion of the kind of society it ultimately wants to create, of the historical forces working for and against the attempt to achieve that vision, and of a coherent strategy, however tentative, for getting from here to there.

There is what might be termed a classical period in the history of draft resistance to the Vietnam war. This period began in April 1967, when about 150 young men burned their draft cards in Sheep's Meadow and, in the Bay Area, David Harris, Dennis Sweeney, Lenny Heller and Steve Hamilton named themselves The Resistance and in its name called for the mass return of draft cards on October 16. The classical period ended in April 1968, when within the space of a week Lyndon Johnson withdrew from the Presidential campaign and announced a partial bombing halt, a third day of card returns brought the number of noncooperators to perhaps 2500, and Martin Luther King was assassinated.

During that year, April 1967 to April 1968, there was an obvious answer to the question: What is a member of the Resistance? A member of the Resistance during this classic period was one who publicly and collectively noncooperated with the Selective Service System, or who advocated, aided and abetted that act.

Somehow the classic act of noncooperation with the Selective Service System has been permitted, to borrow from Karl Marx language which he borrowed from the anthropology of religion, to become a fetish, to be reified or thingified, so that an action which, after all, is only one way of resisting one form of repression, has come to define our movement as a whole.

The Resistance must grow beyond this classic definition of resistance. It must find its way behind the fetish on noncooperation with the Selective Service System to the spirit which prompted that act to begin with. To move forward from an ossified form is difficult, but a spirit can grow and take new forms. We need to do whatever has to be done so that, in a manner faithful to our original spirit, we can become a mass movement of resistance to all forms of repression.

How will we respond to this challenge? What is the future of the Resistance? Probably the history books of the next century will say something like this:

> After April 1968 the Resistance began to decline. High draft calls for college students in the summer of 1968 did not materialize. The war dragged on, even in some respects escalated, but in the absence of dramatic single acts of escalation the Resistance was unable to recapture its initial momentum. Factions crystallized into irreconcilable splinter groups. Some Resistance groups, impressed by the anti-imperialist analysis of SDS, began to demand a multi-issue program and a coherent long-run strategy for fundamental social change. Frustrated in their efforts to induce their fellow-resisters to develop such a perspective, those who felt this way drifted away from the Resistance, often into SDS, although not without occasional nostalgia for the consensus decision-making emotional openness, and decentralized structure of the resistance community. Among those who remained in the Resistance, concerns previously secondary to the war — drugs, diet, communes, the creation of nonviolence — became

more and more prominent; and this in itself had a fragmenting effect, as individuals began to put their main energies into coffee houses, free schools, and other enterprises distinct from draft resistance work. When the war finally ended, the Resistance, like other groups organized around the single issue of the war, disintegrated. Within six months of the signing of the Vietnam peace treaty, the Resistance was dead

This, I repeat, is what the history books will probably say. Now let me project another history, not probable, but I am convinced possible. Here is how that possible history goes:

After April 1968 the Resistance, like the larger movement, experienced the disorientation characteristic of Presidential election years. About a year later a new direction began to emerge. Despite the general confusion many Resistance groups had been patiently exploring forms of resistance beyond the draft, and conducting experimental joint actions with high-school, GI, and women's liberation groups, as well as with some local chapters of SDS. Internal tensions, a natural result of this exploration and experimentation, were fruitfully resolved at a national conference in Bloomington, Illinois. Work against the draft continued, of course. The draft itself continued, because American imperialsim required the flexible supply of manpower which the draft made available in order to fight more than one Third World insurrection simultaneously; and when, in the spring of 1969, it became clear that the war in Vietnam was far from over, the Resistance revived. But the Selective Service System was now viewed as a single facet of an illegitimate structure of power. Accordingly, many members of SDS, who had hitherto dismissed the Resistance as masochistic middle-class moralism, turned toward the draft resistance movement as a political vehicle which, in contrast to the polemical infighting dominant in SDS, combined sophisticated analysis with a humane spirit reminiscent of the movement in the early 1960s. As a result the Resistance found itself in a position to play a key role in building the broad liberation movement which organized the revolutionary general strikes of the next decade.

I don't have a formula for bringing to pass that second, merely possible history. No one does. I want to try to help us all think more creatively in that direction by examining two pieces of our common experience. First, the year prior to April 1967, during which we groped our way toward the act of public, collective card return; second, the year since April 1968, during which many Resistance groups have been revising their initial assumptions as they sought to relate to new issues and new social classes.

I

Several groups, several strains of thinking converged to produce the resistance actions of April 1967: the burning of draft cards in New York City, the call for October 16 from the Bay Area, and, lest we forget, the induction refusal of Muhammad Ali.

First there was a group of pacifists for whom dissociation from the draft expressed a more-than-political worldview. This group could trace its philosophy to A.J. Muste's essay on "holy disobedience." It included many members of the Committee for Nonviolent Action and the Catholic Worker community, such as Tom Rodd, David Miller and Tom Cornell. Meeting in New York City in October 1966, adherents of this approach issued the following "Statement of Non-cooperation with Military Conscription":

> We, the undersigned men of draft age (18-35), believe that all war is immoral and ultimately self-defeating. We believe that military conscription is evil and unjust. Therefore, we will not cooperate in any way with the Selective Service System.
>
> We will not register for the draft.
>
> If we have registered, we will sever all relations with the Selective Service System.
>
> We will carry no draft cards or other Selective Service certificates.
>
> We will not accept any deferment, such as 2-S.
>
> We will not accept any exemption, such as 1-O or 4-D.
>
> We will refuse induction in the armed forces.
>
> We urge and advocate that other young men join us in noncooperation with the Selective Service System.
>
> We are in full knowledge that these actions are violations of the Selective Service laws punishable by up to five years imprisonment and/or a fine of $10,000.

Near the opposite end of the political spectrum was a tendency illustrated by David Mitchell and, after the enunciation of Black Power in mid-1966, by SNCC. These resisters were not pacifist. Nor were they noncooperators, but they publicly refused induction. They were also explicitly anti-imperialistic, in David Mitchell's case since 1961. This tendency is represented in resistance work today by the Wisconsin Draft Resistance Union and the Boston Draft Resistance Group.

Between these two ideological extremes, pacifist noncooperation, and anti-imperialist induction refusal, fell the bulk of students opposed to the war. They expressed themselves in the spring of 1966 by sitting in against the sending of class ranks to draft boards, and in the fall of 1966 by signing We Won't Go statements. It is fashionable in the Resistance to deprecate such activities, since the students involved rarely grasped the nettle of induction refusal. But for many resisters, anti-rank and We Won't Go represented a stage in their development which they repudiated in moving on to resistance. Thus Michael Ferber, David Harris and Michael Cullen of the Milwaukee 14 signed We Won't Go statements; Kerry Berland, after taking part in an anti-ranking sit-in at Chicago, was shocked that after the sit-in many of the demonstrators took the test anyway.

I see the movement which became the Resistance emerging from certain groups of students who, as they moved beyond a We Won't Go position, sought to combine the insights of pacifist noncooperation with those of anti-imperialist induction refusal. No doubt the most significant of these student groups was that at Stanford, which included David Harris, Dennis Sweeney, Paul Rupert, Ira Arlook, and Joel Kugelmass. Here I would like to describe two East Coast groups, at Yale and Cornell.

In July 1966 there met in New Haven a group of young men who drew up the following statement:

> We men of draft age disavow all military obligations to our government until it ceases wars against peoples seeking to determine their own destinies. On November 16 (November 16, 1966, mind you) we will return our draft cards to our local boards with a notice of our refusal to cooperate until American invasions are ended. We fully realize that this action will be considered illegal and that we will be liable to five years imprisonment.

> We propose to develop our program August 25 and 26 prior to the SDS convention at Clear lake, Iowa. Of the eight men who signed that statement, one was longtime worker with CNVA. A second belonged to the self-styled anarchist wing of national SDS (I recall his saying at that meeting, "SDS members have never done anything."). A third had made a detailed proposal for anti-draft activity at the SDS National Council meeting the previous spring; his proposal, one of four, had been lost in rhetoric and he was ready to look elsewhere. Three of the others, as well as myself, had worked together in Mississippi in the summer of 1964. One had worked with Dennis Sweeney in McComb.

From that meeting in New Haven travellers fanned out across the country as far as the West Coast. I have a letter written from Madison on July 22, 1966 which began: "We've made our way to Chicago and on up to Madison, Wisc. The results of our probes into Detroit and Ann Arbor have been encouraging. Seven or eight of my close co-patriots in Detroit are gravitating very strongly. Ann Arbor folks, numbering five or six, are moving as well. We've been keeping the numbers small but discussions have been intense." This was exactly the process which Dennis Sweeney and David Harris would repeat the next summer on the West Coast. And already in mid-1966, the germs of the coming split between SDS and the Resistance were apparent. The letter goes on: "Discussion in Ann Arbor clarified another pattern of thinking; namely, that the idea and act were not political. Persons who say this attribute to this action a mere mechanical quality. For some people like Steve Weissman and Mike Goldfield, they had to see this idea as a comprehensive political program with organization 'guarantees' for its expansion into all levels of the student movement. Until that could be developed, they were unable to see it as a viable political movement. I come at the question from a different perspective."

On July 30, 1966 the travellers returned to New Haven for a second meeting. A report on that meeting included the following observations:

> Since the individual commitment to go to jail is the basis of the collective strength of the movement, we talked for a while about the kinds of reasons a person would take such an action. The two basic motivations are personal and political. In the case of the former, the person sees the draft situation as his personal climax with the system — he probably would have done a similar act anyway, but decides to do it with the group because of the strength that adds to him and the group. A large majority of us, however, would not have taken this act, at least not until after (being) confronted with induction itself. We are arriving at the decision because we feel that we have a political program we can make work.

The classic act of non-cooperation with the draft has been permitted to become a fetish — to be reified. The report laid out perspectives for organizing. "There was a very strong feeling that we have to organize by sending our field staff to places which are not normally reached by the movement, in addition to the usual centers of activity." The organizers, this report continued, "have to really go out and *work* to build strong democratic local organizations (or anti-draft struggle committees), that have a common relationship through this and other programs. In the case of existing organizations like SDS chapters, the idea would be to strengthen the movement and deepen the particular group's commitment to change. . . ." Further, "we have decided to reject the type of organizing that issues calls to do something, writes magazine articles and prints newspaper ads, and then expects people to act. . . . Only after the basic groundwork is laid over the next few months (i.e. building strong committed local groups by the field staff) will we pull out the stops of publicity. . . . Those of us who travelled west were awed by the size of the country and feel that if there is regional strength and unity this will help in the struggle that is to come."

The report on this meeting of July 30, 1966 went on to affirm that "the November launching date is seen as a *beginning*, not as a final goal. It is from this date that the important building has to be done with other constituencies and programs. It was generally agreed that the major *program* that would follow from the collective act of draft defiance would be the organizing" of "a broad range of forms of draft resistance." It was assumed that those who turned in their draft cards on November 16 would thereafter become organizers. Also discussed were adult support, that was to be my province, and the alternative merits of different kinds of legal defense: "We can take a civil liberties defense (claiming that we can advocate anything and also that the government is violating our liberties by drafting us to fight their war). We can take a Nuremburg defense (the war is immoral and unjust and it is our responsibility not to fight but to resist). We can also stand mute (and declare that the court is a political tool of the system and could not possibly grant us any justice)." Finally there was discussion of women's liberation: "It was noted that there was a vast potential for organizing young women since there was a vacuum now organizationally and programatically. WSP is mostly middle-aged and programatically fuzzy. SDS, despite occasional rhetoric to the contrary, remains a male-dominated organization. We agreed to a raise programmatic possibilities with women we know, but felt that it would be up to the women themselves to develop corollary programs to our draft resistance." There were women's workshops at the subsequent Des Moines meeting and at the We Won't Go conference in Chicago in December 1966. The first women's liberation groups in the country, organized by Heather Tobis Booth, Naomi Weinstein, Sue Munaker and others, grew directly from these workshops.

The Des Moines meeting in late August 1966 decided that the projected November 16 date was premature. Individuals were urged to return to their various communities and organize solid local groups. Perhaps the most important of these was at Cornell, for it was this group which called for the mass burning of draft cards in New York the following April. The organizer of the Cornell group was Tom Bell, who had attended the July 30 meeting in New Haven and the Des Moines conference. Tom has described in an article in *New Left Notes*, reprinted by my wife in *We Won't Go*, how he approached his task: in the characteristic Resistance manner, rather than calling a meeting he sought out an individual at a time. Characteristically, too, the call for mass draft card burning was stimulated by the decision of one person, Bruce Dancis, to burn his own card.

Bruce and Tom both illustrate the attempt to synthesize ethical and political insights which I have stressed as typical of these early resistance groups. Bruce Dancis was quite active in SDS as a Cornell freshman and at the time he burned his draft card was Cornell SDS president. The other side of his background is suggested by the fact that his father had been a CO in World War II, that he was raised in what he terms "an Ethical Culturist home," and that the summer before he went to college he met and was much influenced by David McReynolds of the War Resisters League.

The day he registered with the Selective Service System, in May 1966, Bruce Dancis also took part in a sit-in in the university president's office against the turning over of class ranks to that same system. At this time he told his draft board that he did not want a 2-S deferment, that he wanted 1-O status, but that if granted 1-O status he might not do alternative service. By the next fall (this is still 1966):

> I began to see that CO had the same things wrong with it that 2-S had. I saw that a guy from the streets of Harlem, who couldn't get a 2-S deferment since he wasn't in college, couldn't get a CO since it is such a difficult form to fill out. I couldn't see myself having to explain to a bunch of old men why I should be exempted from killing people. . . . In December, 1966 I finally decided that I must sever my ties with Selective Service. On December 14, outside a meeting of the Cornell faculty which was discussing the university's policy towards Selective Service, I read a statement to my local board before a crowd of 300 people and then ripped up my draft card.

The Cornell anti-draft union agonized for weeks over how to respond to Bruce's action. Finally on March 2 five men — Jan Flora, Burton Weiss, Robert Nelson, Michael Rotkin, Timothy Larkin — called on others to pledge to burn their draft cards April 15 if at least 500 people acted at the same time. The language of the call combined ethical and political arguments:

> The armies of the United States have, through conscription, already oppressed or destroyed the lives and consciences of millions of Americans and Vietnamese. We have argued and demonstrated to stop this destruction We have not succeeded. Murderers do not respond to reason. Powerful resistance is now demanded: radical, illegal, unpleasant, sustained.
>
> In Vietnam the war machine is directed against young and old, soldiers and civilians, without distinction. In our own country, the war machine is directed specifically against the young, against blacks more than against whites, but ultimately against all.
>
> Body and soul, we are oppressed in common. Body and soul, we must resist in common. The undersigned believe that we should begin this mass resistance by publicly destroying our draft cards at the Spring Mobilization.

The statement continued as follows:

The climate of anti-war opinion is changing. In the last few months student governments, church groups, and other organizations have publicly expressed understanding and sympathy with the position of individuals who refused to fight in Vietnam, who resist the draft. We are ready to put ourselves on the line for this position, and we expect that these people will come through with their support.

We are fully aware that our action makes us liable to penalties of up to five years in prison and $10,000 in fines. We believe, however, that the more people who take part in this action the more difficult it will be for the government to prosecute.

Even after the call had been issued, Tom Bell struggled with the question of whether the decision had been right. He wrote me on March 18, 1967:

I still have some pretty serious reservations about our action — especially as I see it at work. . . . What disturbs me is that almost fifty Cornellians have pledged to burn their draft cards and I am afraid for many of them the decision comes from the emotionalism of the moment. The sessions in the (student) union are very much like revival services (even including some of the rhetoric at times). We have speeches, a collection for the anti-war office and on the spot conversions — signing pledges, plus a lot of personal witnesses. I am going to try to get all the people who have signed pledges together for some collective thinking about what we are doing and I hope that we can get some things cleared up. There is a real agony for me in the dilemma presented by seeing this great opportunity for political organizing and action vs. the likelihood that a lot of people are going to be hurt (including myself) by the action being taken. I'm even more afraid when I think of the impersonal situation of sending out the calls. Don't really know why I am unloading all of this except that I feel caught — I don't like national actions but I do want to change America. I like a personal, deep communication type of politics but perhaps this is not really political. I don't want to manipulate anyone but I feel that it is essential for my own struggle and for the development of all of us as human beings that people change.

On April 2, less than two weeks away from April 15, Tom wrote again. "I've begun to feel better about the draft card burning, as a political act at least, but it looks like it will not come off. We have only about ninety pledges so far and the Spring Mobilization (Almighty Executive Board) has apparently refused to let us take the action as part of the April 15 action anyway." The rest is common knowledge. The evening of April 14 those who had signed the conditional pledge met and decided to go ahead if there were fifty persons who would burn their cards together. At that meeting just over fifty said, Yes. The next day three times that many acted.

What, besides nostalgia, ought we feel in recollecting these beginnings? What struck me most as I went over the documents again was the connection between noncooperation and the 2-S deferment. Those who chose noncooperation for philosophical reasons, such as the CNVA resisters, were a minority. For most resisters noncooperation was a means whereby students protected by 2-S deferments could make themselves vulnerable to induction and so compel the government, as Steve Hamilton put it, "to deal with us." Early leaflets of the Resistance make this motivation clear.

We wanted to get away from the role of auxiliary to a radicalism the center of gravity of which was in other peoples' lives. "An organization has been formed," began one, "of men preparing to jointly give up all deferments and refuse to serve." "THE RESISTANCE," another stated, "is a group of men who feel we can no longer passively accept our deferments so that others can go in our place." It would seem that had there been no 2-S deferment there would have been draft resistance, but it would have taken the form of mass induction refusal rather than mass noncooperation. And this is turn suggests that the division of the draft resistance movement into, on the one hand, a movement of induction refusal or resistance within the armed forces, and on the other hand, a movement characteristically expressing itself by the act of noncooperation, is itself a consequence of the class character of the Selective Service System, of channeling, of the success of the American governing class in dividiing the opposition.

The conclusion, if accurate, has implications for the current debate as to whether or not to give up draft card turn-ins. What it suggests to me is that noncooperation remains, as it has always been, an appropriate act of resistance for deferred college students and conscientious objectors; but that it is not now, nor should it ever have been regarded as, a likely form of resistance for the young man of draft age not so insulated; and that, therefore, on May Day for example, the form of ceremony which would most precisely reflect the fight relationship of noncooperation to other kinds of resistance would be a ceremony in which the noncooperator was one of several kinds of resisters each doing his thing.

II

There is, however, a further argument against the act of noncooperation which must be confronted. This is the argument first expressed (in my memory) by Carl Davidson in *New Left Notes* during the spring of 1967, and again by Steve Hamilton in the same journal when he broke with the

Resistance the next fall, namely, the contention that inviting imprisonment by noncooperation expressed a characteristically middle-class sentiment, of guilt, masochism, and would-be martyrdom. Davidson insisted that not only did permitting oneself to be imprisoned deprive the movement of a needed organizer, but that psychologically it weakened and emasculated, rather than strengthening, other young men of draft age. The implication of this criticism of the Resistance is that no one should return his draft card because the act is inherently apolitical and unhealthy.

Let me begin to respond to this criticism by recalling another strand of motivation which led to the Resistance. I have said that many of the proto-resisters whom I knew had worked together in Mississippi. For them, myself included, draft resistance was in complex ways a means of dealing with the psychological aftermath of that experience. As of spring 1966, with the articulation of Black Power, we were irrevocably excluded from the civil rights movement. I think it was more than the escalation of the Vietnam war which caused draft resistance to begin to take form the following summer. We were looking for something white radicals could do which would have the same spirit, ask as much of us, and challenge the system as fundamentally, as had our work in Mississippi.

Dennis Sweeny felt, he remembers, that while it was wrong to build a movement on risk-taking, still risk-taking was conspicuously missing from the movement in the North. Dennis never thought that the draft was the most important of all social issues or that the Resistance could end the draft. He considered the draft a particularly clear illustration of what was wrong with the system as a whole. He also wanted a means to pull together seriously-committed white radicals for longtime work. Draft resistance seemed to Dennis a kind of net (as he expressed it) which one could pull through the campuses of the country and thus collect the people with whom one really wanted to make a movement.

What did the South, in particular Mississipii, signify in the experience of former civil rights workers. Something we wanted to get away from, something else we wanted to keep. We wanted to get away from the role of white people helping black people, the role of missionary to the oppression of others, the role of auxiliary to a radicalism the center of gravity of which was in other people's lives. In the South many of us had drifted into administrative roles in the Atlanta SNCC office or the Jackson, Mississippi COFO office, not because we wanted to be leaders, but because we were obviously better able to write press releases and answer the telephone than to approach frightened black people in remote rural communities. The objective result, however, was that we made more decisions than we should have made, and black SNCC field secretaries had the experience of returning to their headquarters after beatings and imprisonments to find more white faces than black there. When the philosophy of control of black organizations by black people was announced our own experience made us recognize that, however painful for us personally, Black Power was right.

This time around, then, we did not want to manipulate the lives of others who ran risks which we did not share. In the words of the report of the New Haven meeting of July 30, 1966: "As organizers of draft resistance we must be the first to confront the government and to challenge its authority. We must be the first to confront the fear of long jail sentences." In the words of the call to the Sheep's Meadow card-burning: "We are ready to put ourselves on the line." As Paul Rupert puts the same feeling: It was a politics of risk. We had to be the first people to take the risk.

Was this a desire for martyrdom? Perhaps a politics of risk, but also a politics of guilt? Only in part. Insofar as noncooperation represented nothing more than a renunciation of a 2-S deferment it certainly resembled the impulse which sent white Northern students to the South. But noncooperation meant more than this. After publication of the channeling memorandum in January 1967 white radical students began to realize that "the club of induction" not only forced others into the army but forced themselves into a careerism and conformity which they abhorred. Hence in saying No to the draft one also said No to a grey-flannel image of one's future. In contrast to the role of the white student in the Southern civil rights movement, resistance to the draft and the war was resistance to an oppression which affected the non-student most severely but also oppressed oneself.

At this point the positive memory of the South, and particularly of Mississippi, came into play. Those of us who had worked with Bob Moses saw in him a model for the democratic organizer. It was not only that, in the fall of 1961, he had put his whole body on the line by going alone into Amite County to begin voter registration. It was also his rejection of the conventional leadership role: sitting in the back of the room at meetings, refusing to speak, when he spoke standing up in place rather than coming to the front of the meeting, when he came to the front asking questions rather than making a speech. When I first met David Harris at the ill-fated Madison, Wisconsin draft conference of August 1967, I was immediately struck by the similarity between David's reasons for resigning his position as student body president at Stanford and Bob's reasons for fiercely refusing the charisma thrust upon him. In each case, the motivation was not guilt, but the desire to enable others by removing the impediment of a dominant personality, to oblige others to improvise their own militancy rather than deferring to a leader.

The emotional thrust of the resistance movement is not masochistic self-denial but self-reliance, not emasculation but manhood. Guilt is so strong a strain in our authoritarian culture that we constantly betray and caricature our best impulses. Lenny Heller caricatured what resistance was about when he told all and sundry in the summer of 1967 that those unready to noncooperate and go to jail had no balls. David Harris may have permitted himself partially to betray his own initial understanding by playing the role of perpetual spokesman. But having spent two long nights recently exploring with David the genesis of West Coast Resistance, I am convinced that affirmation rather than self-denial was the emotional kernel of their call for October 16. David, who himself spent some time in Quitman County, Mississippi in the fall of 1964, believes the Resistance style of politics to have been a synthesis of the style developed in the South and what he terms an exploration of selfhood. Nietzsche was part of it; so was existentialism, and riding a motorcycle on the Sierras with the wind on one's face. The emotional overtones were, not asceticism, discipline, suffering, but endurance, going beyond one's limits, invulnerability, adventure. Running for Stanford student body president David's campaign buttons were "Home Rule" and "Community Not Colonialism." Their spirit anticipated the button with which SDS joined draft resistance in the spring of 1967, "Not With My Life You Don't." When David and Dennis went up and down the West Coast in the summer of 1967 seeking noncooperators, they, like Tom Bell before them sought out one individual at a time, spending time with him, getting to know all sides of him, playing guitar and dropping acid besides talking politics. The first leaflet of the Bay Area Committee for Draft Resistance was simply six individual statements of noncooperation. This "open style" of organizing, in which one man tells another why he has decided to do something, seems to me inherently life-affirming, as opposed to the style which asks others to immolate themselves in a collective, impersonal destiny.

Which brings me to an extraordinary coincidence. In February 1967, more or less at the same time that five men at Cornell called for draft card burning in Sheep's Meadow and that Steve Hamilton and Lenny Heller became acquainted with David Harris and Dennis Sweeney, the national secretary of SDS gave a speech at Princeton in which he described precisely that style of organizing, and that need to struggle for self-liberation, which were at the heart of the developing Resistance. Liberalism, Greg Calvert asserted, is based on the psychology of guilt and on the program of helping others to achieve what one already has. On the other hand, radicalism stems from "the perception of oneself as unfree, as oppressed" and expresses itself in "a struggle for collective liberation of all unfree, oppressed men." And Greg opened his speech with the following vignette of what, I submit, is resistance organizing at its best:

> It is said that when the Guatemalan guerillas enter a new village, they do not talk about the "anti-imperialist struggle" nor do they give

lessons on dialectical materialism — neither do they distribute copies of the "Communist Manifesto" or of Chairman Mao's "On Contradiction." What they do is gather together the people of the village in the center of the village and then, one by one, the guerrillas rise and talk to the villagers about their own lives: about how they see themselves and how they came to be who they are, about their deepest longings and the things they've striven for and hoped for, about the way in which their deepest longings were frustrated by the society in which they lived.

Then the guerrillas encourage the villagers to talk about their lives. And then a marvelous thing begins to happen. People who thought that their deepest problems and frustrations were their individual problems discover that their problems and longings are all the same — that no one man is any different than the others. That, in Sartre's phrase, "In each man there is all of man." And, finally, that out of the discovery of their common humanity comes the decision that men must unite together in the struggle to destroy the conditions of their common oppression.

That, it seems to me, is what we are about.

This speech suggests that protagonists on both sides of the debate between SDS and the Resistance should be careful not to deal in stereotypes abstrated from time and place. There was a period, roughly the years 1966-1967, when SDS and the tendencies which became the Resistance were very close to one another. One sees this not only in the speech just quoted, but in the further facts that Greg Calvert helped set up the Des Moines meeting of August 1966, that (as previously mentioned) Bruce Dancis was an SDS traveller, that Jeff Segal of SDS and later of Stop the Draft Week spoke at the Chicago We Won't Go Conference of December 1966, that in that same month the SDS National Council not only endorsed draft resistance, but condemned all military conscription, and finally, that at the 1967 SDS convention a resolution was passed supporting military desertion.

This was a period when draft resistance was a cutting-edge or growing-point for the movement as a whole. It developed for the most part outside SDS, but this was partly because of the size and heterogeneity of SDS; many people within SDS welcomed it.

What caused this happy state of things to deteriorate? It seems to me that the period when SDS and draft resistance were closest was also a period when white radicals, responding to their repudiation by SNCC, were asking how their own lives needed to be changed and whether it was possible to build a radical majority in white America. For white radicals it was a time of a politics of affirmation rather than a politics of guilt. With this in mind, perhaps one should turn the SDS critique of the Resistance inside out, and argue that during the past year SDS has been reverting to the very politics of middle-class self-flagellation which it charges to the Resistance; that is, that since the spring 1968 National Council meeting SDS has asked white people again to play the role of auxiliaries to other peoples' radicalism.

In this view, the psychological history of the movement falls into three periods. The first period, from 1960 roughly to 1965, is the period of orientation to the Southern civil rights movement. The intermediate period of non-vicarious politics found expression in the "student syndicalism" resolution at the SDS Clear Lake convention in August 1966, the draft resistance resolution adopted by the SDS National Council in December 1966, and the so-called "new working class" perspective developed by Carl Davidson, Greg Calvert, David Gilbert and others in the spring of 1967. The third period begins in April 1968, when the apparent deescalation of the Vietnam war and the riots following the assassination of Dr. King led SDS to drop the draft and turn to racism as the main issue.

To say this is not to deny that white radicalism in American history has been infected by racism, nor that the liberation front required to change America may have more black than white leaders. But the best way white radicals can contribute to that eventual coalition is by building a strong white radical movement. This movement must be free of racism, yet agitation against racism is not the best way to build it. For white radicals to make freeing Huey Newton or support for the demands of black students their primary political activity is to recreate at a higher level of struggle the friends-of-SNCC psychology of the early 1960s, and to program a new generation of activists into the functional equivalent of going South.

The problem about guilt which I see is not that in the past the Resistance built its politics on that emotion, but that, because so many people in the larger movement are not feeling guilty about being white and middle-class, we might at this point find it difficult to grow in a natural and relaxed way. Since April, 1968 the Resistance, like SDS, has been feeling its way beyond a middle-class constituency, and coming to the recognition that racism and capitalism as well as militarism must be resisted. Should this growth take place in an atmosphere of guilt, of repudiation of the past, of frenetic need for self-justification, of impatience for quick results because of fear of failing, then it *will* fail, and turn out to be not growth but disintegration. To be specific, I understand that there are Resistance groups which have involved themselves in university sit-ins and gone to pieces as a result; and it would be my guess, having been through an experience of that sort at the

University of Chicago, that the resisters involved lacked confidence that they could deal with this new kind of problem, failed to meet regularly during the course of the action, and so were overwhelmed and dispersed by the effort to move outside the draft issue. Again, I understand that there are those who feel that the New England Resistance hardly belongs to the Resistance any longer because it decided not to turn in draft cards on November 14. In contrast it seems to me that the experimental work with high-school students and GIs, which is the other side of that decision, should be a resource to all Resistance groups. The concern of many groups to develop educational programs about imperialism is another indication of new life which should be welcomed, not feared.

I am struggling to delineate and attitude which will permit growth to take place in oneself and in others. Is it correct not to cooperate with courts, or to try to transform them by asking juries to rule on law as well as fact? There is no correct line. Let's try both, and evaluate the outcome together. Is student power in the university desirable, or should students leave the university and resist it from the outside? Again, there seem to me arguments on both sides, and many more than two possible answers. Should a teacher go into the public schools or create a free school? We need both, and life may settle the issue by recruiting the staff for free schools from the teachers fired from the others. What is the proper relationship of resisters to SDS chapters, to women's liberation groups, to high-school students, to persons over draft age who want to be more than supporters? Once and for all, I say down with correct lines, and the structuring of situations as if only two choices were possible, and a politics which makes the participant live in fear of being wrong.

Lest I seem to have endorsed doing one's own thing *ad infinitum*, let me conclude by suggesting a few guidelines which I think can be helpful as we experiment and grow.

III

First, something specific. There are certain values which, it seems to me, have to be axiomatic in the movement, because it is precisely by these values that we define ourselves. One of these values is love and respect for all human beings. I can imagine a comrade who, feeling this love and respect, nevertheless kills someone. The attitude of the revolutionary Vietnamese as I experienced it comes very close to this. I cannot imagine a comrade who gratuitously vilifies and denigrates others. Hence, if I have explained myself at all clearly, I feel less separated from a person who in a moment of danger slugs a cop than I did from my friend Tom Hayden when, on the eve of the Democratic Convention, he wrote an article in which he called policemen "pigs." I am ashamed of a movement which calls policemen pigs. I don't want to belong to it. Similarly, I feel deeply troubled by the attitude that, since we are right, we can take away civil liberties from others which we insist on for ourselves. I preferred the New England Resistance when, in an instruction sheet for a spring 1968 demonstration, it said, "Everybody has a right to demonstrate: they have the right to yell at us," than when, in a fall 1968 issue of the *Journal of Resistance,* it tried to justify heckling Hubert Humphrey to the point that he was unable to speak. Morality aside, I consider this a suicidal attitude with which to approach politics in a period of increasing right-wing repression.

Nevertheless it would be the worst sort of dogmatic rigidity and parochialism, characteristic of the old middle-class pacifism which I am sure we all want to transcend, were we to permit even these fundamental questions of value to blind us to the many things we have to learn from the kind of thinking exemplified by the New England Resistance. Among such lessons are the following:

The Resistance should explicitly condemn capitalism as the ultimate source of America's aggressive foreign policy. I do not think this requires the theoretical overkill one finds these days in *New Left Notes.* I don't believe we need to take a position on, say, the relative importance of the stockpiling of weapons or the contrivance of unnecessary missile systems as devices to avoid depression, on the one hand, as over against, on the other hand, overseas private investment; nor do I think we need be unanimous as to whether overseas investment arises from a need for cheap foreign labor, a need to export surplus capital, or a need for new markets, or some combination of these, and if so, what combination; I do not think consensus is required as to the impact of imperialism on the wages of different sectors of the American working-class and finally, recognizing that existing American investment in Vietnam is slight, that the expectations of future investment is difficult to document and that quite apart from particular investments the people who run this country may wish to deny an area to Communism or demonstrate their power to crush Third World revolutions. I do not believe the Resistance should commit itself to a detailed explanation of the Vietnam war, which may not be possible for some time. In short, we do not need to lose ourselves in the theory of imperialism in order to condemn the capitalist economy and the imperialism to which, by whatever mechanisms, it indubitably gives rise. We must be very very clear that great power rivalry, the practice of conscription, and the sins of human nature, are not in themselves adequate explanations for American foreign policy; that the frantic character of American foreign policy is the other side of the ability of the peacetime domestic economy to maintain full employment and satisfactory profit margins; that to oppose Vietnam without opposing capitalism is to acquiesce in future Vietnams. I might add, taking note of the language of the conference agenda, that to oppose imperialism without opposing capitalism is also, in my opinion, to let the sickness spread while responding only to symptoms.

I don't see what sense it makes to talk about resisting capitalism without affirming an alternative. We should explicitly be socialists, or anarcho-syndicalists. The words are less important than the spirit. My intuition is that the movement will eventually come down on a political perspective intermediate between middle-class moralism, on the one hand, and Leninism, on the other, and that the Resistance, as a current in the movement intermediate between traditional pacifism and Marxism-Leninism is uniquely situated to affirm that perspective.

Let me give three illustrations of this perspective. Noam Chomsky, in his new book, speaks of "libertarian socialism," "anarchism," and "revolutionary pacifism." He illustrates what he has in mind by a long description of the revolution-from-below created by peasants and workers in the midst of the Spanish Civil War and uniformly neglected by the war's elitist historians.

Second, Daniel Cohn-Bendit, in his new book, criticizes Leninism in much the same terms and offers another illustration: the current within the Russian Revolution known as the "Workers Opposition" which insisted that socialism must mean workers' control, and which was crushed by the Bolshevik government at Kronstadt and elsewhere. Even in translation Cohn-Bendit evokes eloquently the vision of a revolution growing from decentralized resistance. What we need, he says, is "not organization with a capital O, but a host of insurrectional cells," "spontaneous resistance to all forms of domination," "the multiplication of nuclei of confrontation." And Cohn-Bendit is clear that this ultimate vision means that during the revolutionary process minorities within the revolution must have, not only the rights of free speech suppressed by the Bolsheviks, but the right to act out their minority convictions. Cohn-Bendit calls this "the right of independent action," a right, it seems to me, which the Resistance has hitherto practiced, and which it should not abandon in the quest for a more coherent political perspective.

Finally, there are the Wobblies, who wrote no books at all. At point after point, as we intuitively perceive, the spirit of the Resistance is akin to the spirit of the IWW. Their insight that change must come about through direct action at what they called "the point of production" is akin to the Resistance axiom that people must change the circumstances of their own daily lives. Their affirmation of the maxim that "an injury to one is an injury to all" is exactly the sense of solidarity with which the Resistance has sought to overcome the atomization created by the Selective Service System. Their belief in building "the new society within the shell of the old" overlaps what, in a more middle-class way, the Resistance has been feeling its way toward through alternative institutions.

This perspective is brilliantly laid out in an article by Dan Tilton in the *Journal of Resistance* for October 1968 entitled "Socialism and Human Freedom." Tilton asserts that "the time has come for the Resistance to seriously consider definite alternatives to capitalism. . . . It is time . . . for the Resistance to state clearly that not only is capitalism insane, but more importantly that socialism is the only possible alternative." What Tilton means by socialism, however, is libertarian socialism or anarcho-syndicalism. He feels that the Resistance should carry over into its new commitment to socialism its old awareness of the evils of militarism and the nation state.

> Our struggle in the Resistance has been up to now a struggle against governmental bureaucracy and illicit power. In this we have shown more wisdom than our Old Left counterparts with their ideas of nationalization of industry or the dictatorship of the proletariat. We have always realized that political power is suspect not just in capitalist nations but also in so-called socialist nations and that any solution to capitalism that involves socialism must answer the anarchist's questions concerning the nature of power and concerning its legitimacy. It must answer why "socialism" has not brought about human freedom.

Unlike many elements in the movement Tilton affirms rather than repudiates participatory democracy. "What needs to be done now," he writes, "is to carry the concept of participatory democracy to its ultimate conclusion."

Tilton's attitude toward participatory democracy is the attitude which people in the Resistance should have toward their original intentions. When we are told to abandon nonviolence so as to join in working-class struggle, we can respond that historically that struggle has expressed itself through the nonviolent means of strike, boycott, and sit-in. When advised to put away childish things and become politically "serious," we should remember that the characteristic Resistance conceptions of existential commitment, and the encounter between man and man, were created, not by armchair theorists, but by Albert Camus, Dietrich Bonhoeffer, Martin Buber, Ignazio Silone, in the furnace of resistance to fascism. I think it is possible to become politically serious without giving up the values which drew us into politics in the first place.

6

The Anarchist Revolution

Murray Bookchin

Fifth Estate: What is meant by anarchism? Why talk about anarchism today?

Murray Bookchin: Most people associate anarchists with traditional bomb-throwers and nonsense like that. Anarchism is something much larger than a particular set or a particular school.

Some thousands of years ago men lived in some kind of totality with nature. They were dominated by the natural world, but they also lived in harmony with the natural world.

Then there was a tremendous cleavage. Man's attempts to free himself from the domination of the natural world, to gain some type of security, resulted in the domination of man by man. It split man from nature, it split man from man, it brought about class society. It not only split man from man, it split man internally. It split his mind from his body. It split the concept of subject from object. It produced a whole logic of domination.

During this whole period in which man dominated man there was a gradual development of the technological forces. Slowly, bit by bit, in the course of this class society, in the course of propertied society, man began to develop his technology.

And for the first time over these thousands of years it's possible to see a unity restored again between man and nature, between man and man in which man will not so much dominate nature but will be secure, will be able to shape the natural world consciously.

Anarchism has always been a libidinal movement on the part of mankind to go back to that unity.

During all periods of great transition the masses of people have pressed against the system of domination that existed. They have seen it crumbling. They pressed against it and tried to restore this nonauthori-tarian, free world. But they haven't had the material conditions, the technology, to consolidate this. There has always been scarcity, always want. And the technology has opened up an entirely new vista of human liberation.

We're sort of returning to the old communism now but with an entirely new level, an entirely new possibility, an entirely new potential for human freedom. This potential can not only eliminate property, but might eliminate all those things which have kept man impoverished and divided between himself and the natural world. And this is what anarchism really means.

FE: What are the prospects of anarchy in the United States? How could anarchy come about?

MB: This is the country above all in which you have the highest development of technology. What is happening right now is this: Throughout the course of history these classes, the systems of class domination, while they dominated mankind still played a certain social function. The city played a certain social function. It has also been said that the State played a certain social function.

Class domination, according to Marx in particular, was supposed to have made it possible for mankind to develop a culture, to develop the science necessary to free himself from the domination of nature over man. The theory here is that the ruling classes, despite all the crimes that they inflict on humanity, nonetheless, had the leisure time to develop a literature, to develop mathematics, to develop a technology.

The city also has been described as the arena in which human culture developed. Men were brought together, removed from the land and brought into close proximity with each other to communicate ideas.

The State, despite the fact that it's always been an instrument of class domination according to Marx, has played the role of maintaining a certain amount of social peace.

These institutions have played a progressive role. Whether they did or not, the most striking thing that has happened is that now they all play a totally regressive role.

The state mobilizes the means of production in order to enforce the system of domination at a time when this could be eliminated. The economy is being used to impose domination, and to preserve domination; in fact, to preserve scarcity today artificially. The armaments industry is the most striking case in point here.

We have a tremendous productive capacity, but this productive capacity does not return to the people, it is not used to support them or to emancipate them. It is used to preserve scarcity artificially so that people have to go to work even when work is unnecessary.

The city today plays a totally regressive role. It no longer unifies people or brings them together. On the contrary, in the large cities today people are more alienated than ever before. This is an entirely new development historically. The city is no longer conceived as the arena of culture but at the arena of deculturation.

The contradiction between town and country has produced an enormous ecological crisis today. The city crawls over the land in the most destructive fashion. It is the center of air pollution, the arena in which most of the poisons are introduced into the human environment. And here again you have a very striking departure from all of the past.

Technology which should free men from toil actually becomes a means of imprisoning man. We have technological developments which are entirely destructive, which are entirely coercive.

The result is that you have a total exhaustion of all institutions, of time-honored property society. They no longer play even the progressive role that Marx imputed to them.

What is happening in the United States? Here more than any place else in the world we sense this. We sense on the one hand the enormous technological possibilities even if we sense them unconsciously. We sense on the other hand a condition that exists, a prevailing condition which imprisons man. The tension between what-could-be and what-is is now becoming excruciating in the United States.

A whole generation has emerged which senses this tension almost intuitively, and some people sense this consciously. The result is that you have a tremendous polarization of the new generation which has not been able to justify in its own mind the dominating role, sexually, psycho-logically, politically, institutionally, of all those forces which men in the past accepted.

With this generation you have a genuine generational conflict which cuts across all class lines. A very significant fact is that the youth revolt came from the middle classes, from those classes which were most affluent. What this youth revolt essentially expresses is a hatred of the whole quality and banality of life. All the old institutions can no longer be justified in their minds. They no longer make any sense in the face of the new possibilities that exist, in the face of the patent hypocrisy that exists in terms of the roles that these institutions profess to perform and the reality of the oppression which they create.

FE: In what sense is this youth revolt revolutionary?

MB: In the profoundest sense imaginable, class youth. You don't simply have a class war; more significantly you have a struggle of young people in all classes outside of the bourgeoisie (and in some cases even within the bourgeoisie) who fee that the present society can no longer be justified. These young people will not be satisfied merely with reforms of society, such as wage improvements, changes in hours, or an increase in the standard of living. They have rejected the American Dream itself.

This is the biggest thing that is happening. Over the past one hundred years you had building up in the United States, an American Dream, which in the 1920s was expressed by men like Hoover with his "two chickens in every pot, two cars in every garage." This involved the idea that commodities would raise the standard of living and provide a new sense of American life. A new dream would be realized through the productive capacities of the United States.

What we have found now is that for millions of people who had acquired this dream, life has become totally banal and meaningless. It has become senseless and pedestrian as well as vicious.

And the demand today gradually edges into a revolutionary dream, into a new sense of community to replace the exploitation of nature; into a new sense of sexual freedom to replace the patriarchal and even monogamous family; into a new sense of beauty of life itself, the idea that everyday life has to be liberated, that every moment has to be as marvelous as it possibly can.

These are entirely new conceptions. These notions which were once the property of a small handful of poets have now become increasingly general notions. And this represents an entirely new point of departure historically.

Nobody has brought forth this youth revolt. It has not been brought forth as such by the drug culture. It is something which rides on a new sense of technological possibility on the one hand and the absurdity of the whole past property culture on the other.

FE: Do you think this consciousness has an effect on the working class?

MB: I was personally a worker and I was even in the UAW, although not in Detroit. I remember the tradition of the working class at that time. The workers generally felt that they were anchored in the factories. They felt that the factory was their way of life, however much they disliked it. And young workers had a very fatalistic attitude about the job. This was, in a sense, their career and they took it awfully seriously. Bread and butter demands were the key demands of that period although union organization was also a very important demand.

Now what's happening is a young worker is beginning to emerge who does not regard the factory as his fate. This is the mentality of the most advanced sections of the workers today, particularly the young workers.

The feeling here is, in a sense, "What the hell am I doing here? I feel trapped." And there is a tendency to link up with the youth culture, to turn to dope, to turn to marijuana, to turn to rock music on an ever increasing scale, to feel even intuitively, although there's still a very deep suspicion between young workers and hippies, a greater kinship when the chips are down than there is to the older workers who come to counsel moderation, be cool, stick by the rules, bureaucracy, etc.

There is also a stronger tendency to flip out, which manifests itself in the wild-cat strikes and in a gross mistrust of the union bureaucracy; in the feeling that whatever they're going to do as workers, be it in the factory, or outside the factory, they want to control and they don't want things controlled for them.

I remember as a worker it could be said very legitimately by a Marxist that workers respect their leaders. This was in fact true. There was a tremendous personality cult and the tremendous respect for the union leadership.

Today this has disappeared to a very great extent. The most advanced of the workers feel that they don't want any bureaucracy; they mistrust leaders rather than revere them.

I feel that these are all very great points of departure. They reflect the entirely new possibilities that are emerging today. They reflect the idea that men can begin to think of a society in which there will be no leaders, in which they, themselves, will completely control the conditions of their lives.

FE: You have written in *Anarchos* several articles on the question of ecology, the relationship between man and his environment. Could you run this down a little?

MB: We have now a tremendous crisis in man's relationship with nature. There's a very strong chance that if we manage to survive all the other crises, this crisis will become almost insurmountable at the present rate that it's going.

It is not my opinion, but the opinion of many ecologists that we may not be able to get out of the Twentieth Century intact at the rate that we're despoiling the natural world. Not only is this a social crisis, it's one that the so-called left should be giving a great deal of attention to. Because this crisis can only be solved by what would be called a kind of anarcho-communism.

This crisis arises not only from the exploitation of the natural world for profit. It also emerges from the split between town and country. We haven't developed merely an urban civilization; we've developed a particularly destructive form of urban civilization. The fact that nearly sixty to seventy percent of the American population begins to move into immense cities and urban belts has a devastating effect upon the atmosphere.

We do not live in balance with the regions that we occupy. New York City or Detroit, for example, are no longer regional societies. They are really elements in a tremendous national division of labor in which vast areas such as the Mesabi range, such as certain farming districts, have to be despoiled, have to be exploited, in order to feed these immense populations.

The centralized nature of the societies today and the centralized natures of the cities today have turned the whole continent into a kind of factory. And this has had a destructive effect upon the natural ecology of every region in the United States, in fact, of every region in North America. The economy now organized on this centralized basis, organized on this national division of labor, has to override all the ecological distinctions, hydrological distinctions, atmospheric distinctions, climatic distinctions, differences in soil, differences in the ecology of animal and plant life to feed these immense giant centralized cities.

The results are likely to be catastrophic, if not in my generation, quite conceivably in yours or maybe in the generation shortly afterwards. At least we'll begin to feel the effects of it.

We have transportation systems today that are utterly destructive. The growth in the pollution of not simply the atmosphere but the soil, even up to the Greenland Ice Cap with lead deposits from our gasoline, is reaching appalling proportions. I think it's something we will have to contend with as a major health hazard in the not-too-distant future.

The spread of radioactivity, the spread of pesticides, not simply DDT, but a large spectrum of pesticides which are not receiving anywhere the attention that they should, are leading to massive pollution of the earth.

We are changing the whole carbon dioxide ratio in the atmosphere today, which may be leading to a warming up of the planet with all kinds of apocalyptic results in some distant future. We are polluting all the oceans on a massive scale, all the water-ways.

This is now becoming a problem, because what we are doing is undermining the complex biosphere, the complex world of life, on which an organism like man depends, not only for his health literally, but for his sanity. We are homogenizing the entire planet, we are turning it into a factory. And while man may be compelled to accept this kind of condition, nature will rebel against it.

We have to decentralize our cities now. This is an old and traditional anarchist demand and it was always seen as a dream. For the first time historically it has become not simply a dream but a necessity for human survival.

We have to eliminate the State which plays such a destructive role today not only in coercing people but in mobilizing the economy in the exploitation of resources. This is no longer merely a dream today, it has now become a necessity.

We have to eliminate property; we have to start using the earth as though it were a garden to satisfy human needs, material needs, instead of satisfying class interests. This today is no longer merely a dream. It, too, has become a necessity.

We have to start living in order to survive. That's the essence of the new situation which has arisen. In the past, everything was put this way: there is the dream, but we have to take care of survival first. The dream represented life, and survival represented economic necessity.

Now the whole question has been reversed. If we do not begin to live, we will be incapable of having any kind of reality at all.

For that reason the anarchist vision of a decentralized, propertyless, Stateless, communistic society, in which men will live not only in harmony with each other but in harmony with nature, are no longer really dreams. They have become preconditions, necessities for the survival of man on this planet.

7

The Red Flag and the Black

Emile Capouya

Nevertheless the people refused to obey the voice of Samuel; and they
said, Nay, but we will have a king over us;
That we also may be like all the nations; and that our king may judge
us, and go out before us, and fight our battles.

—I Kings 8

"I am the bloody man,
I have the bloody hand,
and I will have revenge."
So the mad mutineer,
anarch and parricide,
cried as he killed the state.

Old Song

Anarchism was dead and is alive. It exists once more as a political force,
though it is decried and praised with ignorant enthusiasm. Some who are
afraid of their own shadows, possibly with good reason, abuse as anarchy
any sign of life, any effort of renewal on the part of a social order that has
outlived its inspiration. Some who are incapable of a decent piety, since they
have never seen a man, and their young experience has shown them only the
scrimmage of appetite behind a hedge of official lies, exalt as anarchism

every trivial gesture of scorn for established ways. In anarchism the fearful and the foolhardy find a reciprocal myth. To do so, they agree to understand their own nature on the lowest possible terms, like those zealots who reduce Christianity to a feast for executioners and victims. Both parties compromise so far as they are able the chances of an idea that has found its time.

Despite its antagonists, despite its spokesmen, the spirit of anarchism breaks out irresistibly, everywhere, with its intrinsic ideal of brotherhood practically expressed. In Yugoslavia, the university students, who are members of the most favored, most privileged social class, demand that the sons and daughters of the poor be given stipends, so that their theoretical right of access to higher education can become a reality. In France, students represent it as an outrage that no more than six percent of those enrolled in the universities are children of working-class parents. In the United States, students have demanded for the admission of greater numbers of Negroes to the universities.

There was a time when "The poor you always have with you" was the expression of the highest morality, the recognition of a truth. Everywhere in the world, that time is past. Especially under the economy of plenty now enjoyed by the industrially advanced nations, the existence of what must seem immoral, the injustices of privilege unendurable. Brotherhood, in the spiritual and practical bearings of the conception, is felt to be not so much an ideal as a social necessity. It implies economic and political liberty for the individual, more control over his fate than the social order has permitted till now; for the wage-slave and the political helot are brothers to no one, even when they enjoy a "high standard of living," and are encouraged to ratify at the polls programs and policies that are irrelevant or inimical to their fortunes. Naturally, the despotisms and the managed democracies of East and West continue to regard as a provocation the demand for liberty, equality, fraternity. They are being provoked, and not be a hopeless Jacquerie but by the children of the dominant classes, the classes that manage their industries and armies, who are refusing to take up the social roles of their fathers and carry on the established order. A bad sign, that. In any widespread revolt, a government can no longer appeal to its classic means of self-defense. The rulers and managers and well paid technicians do not really want their sons and daughters shot by the police.

It is at this point that anarchist theory becomes relevant once again to our vision of a humane polity. Of all the socialist doctrines, anarchism has most consistently emphasized libertarian principles, uncoerced association and political revolution and renewal in accordance with the instincts of the mass of men rather than in response to the dictates of an elite. These ideas are coming forward once more because they are consistent with the awakened aspiration for brotherhood, and promise that our more generous impulses can be given concrete social expression in our conduct and our institutions. Wherever population presses against the limits of subsistence, anarchist ideas appear to have little chance of being translated into practical social programs — or so the historical record suggests. But in the advanced industrial societies that have so broad an economic margin to their lives, the reforms suggested by anarchist dogmas — decentralization of political decision, decentralization of industry, workers' control of their work and their tools, the abandonment of coercive institutions and sanctions — present themselves not merely as practicable alternative modes of social organization but as specific therapy for the characteristic troubles of regimented, routinized, demoralized, and heartless states. In the West, and probably in Soviet Russia as well, the natural direction of further development (natural in that the preconditions are already established) appears to be toward a form of social engineering that tries to administer populations as functions of computer technology. Now, the engineer's calculus of efficiency, just like the profit-and-loss account, is psychologically obtuse, morally blind, and politically illiterate. Since no new guiding animus would be introduced along with the computers, since in the nature of the case those clever machines would simply codify our unexamined current practice, we could look forward to a spectacular mess. It is absolutely safe to predict that the realization of the technocratic dream would worsen the conditions that are already destroying the internal cohesion of states, and intensify the struggle between the rich and the poor countries that is already threatening our prospects for survival. The reign of a computer technocracy a la Daniel Bell, the rule of programmer-kings, would certainly be short. But we might have little left to congratulate ourselves upon once the systems-engineers had departed.

The hints given us by anarchist doctrine are apposite here, surely. In a practical sense they are more than apposite, since anarchist moods, themes, and tactics are in fact being evoked every day in young radicals by the prospect of the further subordination of man to the machine. The advent of the technocratic society is being contested, then, by another "natural" development: the indifference of young people to the declared values of society, and their active contempt for the values it expresses in its practice.

Well and good. Anarchism has prescriptions for the humane ordering of social relations, and these might even be workable, given some dispensation other than the one we labor under. But there is no social process deducible from anarchist principles or actions that could help bring about that new dispensation. The piecemeal application of anarchist ideas, whether in so-called intentional communities or in individual gestures of disaffection and rebellion, amounts to that one roll of the dice that will never abolish chance. As for the theories of spontaneous revolution that have been associated with anarchism, these are especially puerile in the context of the modern state, more powerful and prepotent than those of the past, monopolizing the instruments of coercion.

Or thus, at any rate, the conventional argument against anarchism. Deferring in the most gentlemanly way all discussion of difficult assumptions such as the perfectibility of man, the instinct for cooperation, the desirability of community, these that are suspect as being sentimental, the conventional critic rests his case on the inadequacy of anarchism as a theory of social revolution. The conventional critic, however, is still living in the nineteenth century.

For our purposes, in the latter half of the twentieth, governments, like all other institutions, rest upon a system of emotional credit that undergoes fluctuations like those of the stock market. In the United States during the past few years, to take the nearest example, for the first time since the Civil War a significant number of young men have refused military service; there are organized movements within the armed forces themselves that are pledged to make life difficult for the idea of war-as-politics-by-other-means. A presidential election has just taken place, and it has provoked the largest number of refusals to vote in the history of the country. Public confidence in the major political parties is at a very low point, and it needs only the accidental shock of a balance-of-payments crisis, a stock market decline, or yet another obvious rebuke to the official goals of our foreign policy, for that lack of confidence to shift, as in 1929, from the political parties to our institutions as a whole. If this paradigm seems unlikely, call to mind the events in France last May as a test-case of the vulnerability of modern states to sudden changes in the popular sensibility.

No doubt what is being discussed here as a mysterious alteration in the public mood always has substantial causes, material and ideological. But since men are not entirely predictable in their reactions, such causes are more easily identified in the past than in the future, once the changes in popular psychology have actually taken place rather than when they have yet to manifest themselves. Thus, to all appearances France had been enjoying its share of the current prosperity, and if there was a good deal of grumbling at what Gaullism had done and left undone — built an atom bomb, for example, but only token stretches of the superhighways demanded by the newly available automobiles — well, the French admit to being a nation of grumblers. In any case, the Left could not organize effective opposition to the reigning General, and what that comes down to is the apparent absence of issues serious enough to stimulate political demands. Still, France was suffering from the distortions typical of late-capitalist economies administered to within an inch of their lives, but according to criteria that have onlya coincidental relation to well-being. One such distortion was the enormous overproduction of students in France, or the significant short fall, as economists say, of classrooms and professors — whichever way one looks at it. A part of the country's excess student capacity was being processed in a hastily constructed plant at Nanterre to prepare it for its ideological cadres that keep our societies humming. Nanterre was overcrowded, uncomfortable, and unattractive, but not intolerable. Nevertheless, some of the sociology students revolted.

French Sociology, like the American sociology it has come to resemble more and more, has two chief preoccupations. One is apologetics in the guise of social analysis, demonstrating that all is for the best in this best of all possible social worlds. That enterprise is best understood as an attempt on the part of living creatures to adapt themselves morally and psychologically to very trying conditions. The other specialty is the management of the masses, whether through labor relations, advertising, polling and sampling techniques, depth-psychology, density studies (optimal), or what have you — an effort to cope with the material basis of the life-processes as it is given in late-capitalist society. At Nanterre the sociology students complained about the overcrowding, the lack of amenity, and the parietal rules, but also about French sociology. They too the position that their science was making no serious attempt to gain insight into real problems; it was less the critic than the servant of a barbarous social order. So they placarded, picketed, and boycotted French sociology, and at last they disrupted its lectures.

This was, after all, the country of Voltaire, and, *pour encourager les autres,* the Dean called the police. His maneuver succeeded beyond his expectations: the students at the Sorbonne went on strike in support of their fellows at Nanterre. (The French Communist Party called the striking students "poor little rich boys.") The police were directed to occupy the Sorbonne, and the students built barricades in the streets of Paris. (The French Communist Party then called the students "provocateurs.") The residents of the Latin Quarter showed their sympathy by harboring injured students in their houses and by pelting the police from windows and rooftops. The students then appealed to various groups of industrial workers to join them in a general struggle against the government. (The Communist Party now told the members of its great labor union, the CGT, that the students were "counterrevolutionaries.") The workers at one large aircraft plant, including CGT members, were the first to respond to the students' appeal, and their example was followed within a week by very nearly the total industrial work force of France. Some ten million men and women walked off the job, or occupied their work-places. Incomparably the largest and most successful general strike in history.

During those stirring days, the French Communist Party had been living in parentheses — just as the ALF-CIO would do in this country if a general strike should happen along. For the French CP practices what is known in this country as business unionism. That is, it delivers disciplined labor, under contract, to the French employer. If its work force runs away, it loses all standing with the French employer. Naturally, the French Communist Party found such a state of affairs deplorable. Besides, General de Gaulle had for some time been sidling up to Brezhnev and Kosygin, effecting what in the language of diplomacy is called a *rapprochement*. Under the circumstances, for the French CP to countenance the overthrow of the De Gaulle government must appear very ill-bred. The revolutionary vanguard of the toiling masses was resolved not to lose standing with the French employer and not to open itself to reproach on the score of its manners.

Let us leave the vanguard in parentheses a moment longer. It is worth remarking on the process by which the sociology students of Nanterre managed to shake the De Gaulle government. First of all, they discovered that like Melisande they were not happy here. Instead of seeking the easily available remedies — psychoanalysis, television, cinema, stimulants, tranquilizers, or consciousness-expanders — they announced their discontent publicly and advanced some plausible reasons for it. The students of other faculties at Nanterre discovered that they, too, were unhappy, and then the students at the Sorbonne, and then the workers at Sud-Aviation, and finally the journalists and technicians of the state-controlled television network in revolt against their role of hired propagandists for the regime. Once they began to think it over and discuss it — they decided that what they were unhappy about was the quality of their lives, in France, in the second half of the twentieth century. Accordingly, the students did not stop short at demanding the abolition of parietal rules, or even the reorganization of the university. They demanded a change in the French way of life, to be brought about by their own more responsible participation in public decisions. The workers were not interested in higher wages. It was at this moment that the French Communist Party left its protective parentheses and started running at top speed in the hope of catching up with its rank and file. The CP negotiated a large wage increase with the frightened government as the price for ending the strike, but the workers refused the increase, saying, that's not what we meant at all, we want a change in the basic rules of the game.

This is all the vindication that the anarchist theory of spontaneous revolution requires. All genuine revolutions are spontaneous. They cannot be stage-managed, they do not respond to prayer. But no more than spontaneous combustion do they occur without a cause. These truths contradict the literalists of the imagination who suppose that the anarchist thesis amounts to an assertion that revolutions happen just anyhow. They give no comfort either to the ingenuous radicals who would act precisely in that spirit.

In France last May the revolution very nearly succeeded. Some commentators have denied that there was any revolution, since it did not succeed. That is quite like the common belief that there will be no revolution nor guerrilla war the length of the mountain chain that runs through South America, because Ernesto Guevara was killed last year in the Bolivian segment of it. But that is no more than wishful thinking. What would "success" have meant in terms of the May days in France? The fall of the De Gaulle government would have been success enough. With that accomplished, the political conditions for useful changes in the basic organization of French society would be present, or, to put it negatively, the barriers opposed to such changes would be down, in the sense that the order of society incarnated in the political structures of the De Gaulle regime would no longer be functioning. Every regime carries on, well or badly, the vital coordinative activities of social life. With the fall of the De Gaulle government brought about by a popular uprising, there would be a decent chance of reorganizing French society on a more democratic basis, for someone must govern, and in this case the people might decide to govern themselves. Now, in these terms the revolution in France was very nearly successful — but for the intervention of the Communist Party at one decisive moment, it would probably have overthrown De Gaulle — and it is the certain precursor of other uprisings. The cultures of all the advanced nations of the world are vulnerable to the very same criticisms as that of France. Their closely integrated economies are vulnerable as never before the the bloodless weapons of the boycott, the mass demonstration, and the general strike.

Faced with students and workers who demanded an end to Gaullism, and partnership in the state and in directing industry in some sense that might have meaning for their lives, De Gaulle abandoned the seat of government. It was assumed that he was retiring to his home in Colombey-les-Deux-Eglises. Instead, he slipped over to Germany, visited the French garrisons there, and pardoned a few senior officers who had been convicted of treason by his government. Thereafter, tanks paraded in Paris, followed the next day by a great Gaullist demonstration. The revolution had been arrested.

It is useful to pause here and subject this passage at arms to informal analysis, as we did the students' and workers' revolt. A reasonable reconstruction of the events might go like this: De Gaulle flies to Germany. Why? Are there no telephone lines between Paris and the outposts of French military power? There are, and De Gaulle has already made use of them. Clearly, before taking wing to Germany, the General has polled his favorite garrisons in France and elsewhere. And the response is, no, the officers are not anxious to flight and cannot answer for the attitude of their troops, who might refuse to fire on Frenchmen. Since the police had already protested against their own mission of provoking disorder by assaulting students and workers, the army's answer had to be taken as definitive. Thereupon De Gaulle prepares to withdraw to Colombey, for the game is up. But someone meanwhile has been busily telling the ten million strikers, who have already refused a wage increase and shouted down their leaders' pleas for compromise, that further intransigence would mean a bloodbath, a modern army massacring unarmed workers. That someone was undoubtedly the French Communist Party. So much is suggested by the very logic of their function in French society, and by the excuses made in their behalf by their warmest defenders in other countries, who have not yet tired of the bloodbath theme. It is ten to one that when the history of this period is established in detail, that egregious parenthetical party will prove to have played the decisive card of an imaginary threat of violence, preferring to chance the elections announced by De Gaulle rather than see a coalition of students and workers put forward a direct claim to power. And when the workers began to hesitate and vacillate, and their state of mind was reported to De Gaulle, he changed his travel plans. He goes to Germany partly to exert his personal force upon the army, partly perhaps to make it seem more likely that he is resorting to strong measures. Once there he revokes the sentences of the Rightist genrals — and even that gesture has more meaning for the Right in France itself than for the army. Finally, he tells the officers, "Who said anything about shooting? All you have to do is show the flag."

There is the point. On the conventional analysis, De Gaulle put down a revolution by a successful appeal to force. But the tanks that depolyed in Paris were not a usable weapon. Could they chase the workers back to their factories? Could they crush the bodies of boys and girls crowded together in the narrow streets of the Latin Quarter, and direct cannon and machine-gun fire on the shops and apartments of their middleclass sympathizers? They could do no such thing — not if the De Gaulle government meant to live a day longer. They could only provoke a Gaullist demonstration, the one kind of show of force that has any meaning in a complexly integrated modern industrial society. A million people come out upon the boulevards; their banners and shouted slogans make them clearly recognizable as a sample of the supporters of the status quo; the opposition loses heart and goes home.

Or, given the requisite temper and the necessary clearsightedness, it hold a counter-demonstration, reiterating its demands, formulating new ones, painting up-to-the minute witticisms on its placards. Whereupon the tanks go elsewhere — because their crews are working-class, too, like the French police, and may include students, and certainly include citizens. For all that General De Gaulle had done was to appeal with intelligent instinct to the sentiment of nationhood, as the students and workers had appealed to the sentiments of fraternity and self-respect. By many, perhaps by the majority everywhere, the patriotism that concerns itself with the actual condition of our physical and moral home, with the fate of our fellow citizens, and the level of their conversation. The patriotism that would cleanse our streams and the air over our cities, expend an equal measure of social tenderness on all our children, and educate all to be of some use to themselves and some interest to us, is a slower growth. However, that is the direction in which the race of man is growing. A decent respect for the earth, for ourselves, and for one another is a sentiment that may be appealed to with success someday. The revolt of the French students and workers tells us that the waste, injustice, and boredom of the consumer society has enlarged that sentiment.

The fact that the kind of demands set forth by the students and workers in France are being advanced in other places as well — in Germany, England, and the United States, and dramatically in Italy and Mexico —makes it especially important that we understand the anarchist impulse being expressed in those claims. Firstly, what it is not. It is not a view of life in society borrowed wholesale from the communist and socialist Left. Almost all the official varieties of those movements, the notable exceptions being Castroism and Maoism, are anathema to the young radicals in the universities of Western Europe and the Western Hemisphere. Wherever regimes calling themselves socialist or communist have actually been in power, they have either been weakly meliorist, amounting to a sort of enlightened welfare capitalism, or else radically egalitarian in theory and repressive in practice. If the students wanted no more than the official liberalism of America, Britain, Holland, or Scandinavia, they would not be restless. If they wanted government by murder, they would applaud the example afforded them by Russia and Eastern Europe, or by Greece. Castro is attractive to many among them because of the heroic legend of the Sierra Maestra, the improvisational character of his regime, and his tendencies toward populism. Mao Tse-tung also represents a well-founded legend of personal heroism as well as a puritanical dedication to revolution from below; and his country is conveniently distant. If the established parties of the traditional Left ever had a chance of capturing the allegiance of the young radicals, the performance of the French Communist Party during the May days would appear to have scotched it permanently. But even before that fiasco, what more than anything else united the young militants on campuses halfway round the world, and many of their fellow-students who were not radical in the least, was an instinctive revulsion to the way of life bequeathed them by their elders, and to its characteristic social structures and ideology. And in their eyes, communism in all its forms was a kind of postgraduate capitalism, rationalized still further in the interests of a religion of accumulation, dehumanized still further by the absence of amenity and civil liberty. The bureaucratic forms of organization shared by communism and capitalism were embodiments of insult to the ideals of individualism, spontaneity, mutual trust, and generosity that are the dominant themes of the new sensibility.

The disgust of the young radicals for the organizational arrangements prevailing in their unsatisfactory societies is easily, too easily, translated into disgust for organization as such. The anarchist movement itself has suffered throughout its history from its tendency toward an indiscrimi-nate condemnation of formal political structures out of a fear of the distortions and abuses to which they are subject. Modern societies at their most anodyne suffer from bureaucratism, which, with its callousness and lack of imagination, is an ever-present reminder of the possibility of oppressive social relations arising as unintended by-products of system order, and routine. Anarchism as a political force has often been brough to nothing by fanaticism on that point. In the name of liberty and spontaneity, anarchists have declined to compromise with their innter light to the extend required for carrying out a political program, or even for formulating political demands. But the core of anarachist doctrine is a common-sense assumption that men have a natural tendency to cooperate voluntarily, and that within the limits of their cultural and material resources they will spontaneously improvise such social arrangements as meet the case. For anarchists, in fact, man is defined by that very propensity to cooperative innovation — which explains the evolution of human culture, so mysterious on any other theory, like the popular one of natural antagonism associated with the names of such social philosophers as Robert Ardrey, Konrad Lorenz, and Desmond Morris. Yet the anarchist assumption, so reasonable when confronted with the facts of our common experience, is contradicted by the express policy of every government. Although each state owes its existence at any moment to the uncoerced collaboration of its citizens in a thousand and one relations, collaboration that could never be obtained through force or the threat of force, it acts habitually as if its sole guarantors were the sanctions of the criminal law. It is at least an open question how far that attitude has the effect of self-fulfilling prophecy; anarchists tend to assume that there is a cause-and-effect relation between the customary appeal to coercion and the existence of anti-social behavior. The argument can be made with a good deal of sophistication, and indeed in this century the development of theories and movements dealing with individual and social psychology, ranging from psychoanalysis to penology, has tended overwhemlingly to support it. As a general consequence of that development, our assumptions about human nature have changed radically. Anarchist teaching on the subject is much more congenial to contemporary ideas than are those survivals of a fearful and punitive social order that arrest our thoughts and actions just where they might stray toward more seemly customs or by a wider view.

The anarchists' faith in men's social inventiveness and in their ability to find solutions for their problems on their own, in the absence of lawgivers, kings, and commissars, has made them unpopular with the authoritarians on the Left. They are accused of infantilism, sentimentality, naivete. As the currents of history have run slower or faster, they have been ridiculed or shot. The truth about their role in the great crises of the century, as in the Russian Revolution or the Spanish Civil War, has been either suppressed or completely distorted, since their practical political successs are a direct affront to great leaders, petty bureaucrats, and authoritarian parties of the Right and Left. The argument against anarchism goes through three characteristic phases, corresponding to the level of social activity that its ideas or partisans may have reached at any given time. When anarchists because of the historical juncture must confine themselves to speculation and analysis, their theories are derided for having no relevance. When, in accordance with anarchist perspectives, social movements of protest and revolution arise to confound the cynics, those movements are denounced as premature, inchoate, and "objectively counter-revolutionary." When anarchists achieve political power, the forces of the Left no less than those of the Right combine to betray and crush them.

Yet they are a recurring phenomenon at the turning points of modern history, simply because the same unresolved issues bring to life again and again in men's minds the libertarian tradition as a tool for coping with social crisis. If it is a question of articulating the need of the hour, the anarchists are less constrained, by a bureaucratized system of intellectual categories, and less compromised by traffic with the established power. Moreover, their principles keep them constantly in mind of the primacy of genuine human needs where their colleagues of the Left are contemplating the architectonics of doctrines elaborated for generations with a fine regard for symmetry and proportion. The anarchists' direct preoccupation with homely concerns makes them appear provincial by the side of those princes of lucubration, but it favors their talent for effective social invention — and that in times of crisis, when the doctrinaires are paralyzed.

As the traditional Parties of the Left are subject to bureaucratism, and prone to rewrite all of history to justify changes of front that arise from nothing more profound than expediency, the anarchists exhibit the fecklessness that comes from the habit of being out of power. The Marxist parties see themselves as the natural inheritors of the machine civilization created by capitalism, and their critique of that civilization amounts to a quarrel over who shall enjoy its fruits, the plutocracy or the workers whose labor is the source of social wealth. Marx himself, a generous mind, could think of other objections, but his followers, like the capitalist ideologues, regard any more fundamental strictures on machine culture as sentimental nonsense, absolutely out of bounds. The anarchists, whose doctrines arose precisely as a reaction to the inherent vice of machine culture, alienation, were relegated to the margins of political thought and action while that culture was going through its most exuberant development phase. During that period, only its most ardent lovers, Marxists and capitalist managers, had much hope of playing an effective historical role. But now that the social costs of an uncriticized machine industry are becoming patently unbearable — in terms of the despoliation and pollution of the environment, and the spiritual destruction of human beings, not to mention technologically facilitated mass murder in wars—the village-atheist mentality of anarchism begins to look like a reservoir of social sanity. The attitudes that accompany it are reinvented every day by persons who have not developed political consciousness whatsoever. Besides, discipline developes naturally in political groups as the situation grows more serious, i.e., begins to offer the possibilities of political change. The *al fresco* manners of anarchist spokesmen and anarchizing students are a historical product; they can be expected to change as the times change, and as anarchism reverts to its essential preoccupation. And that, despite the equivocal name of the movement and the habits engrafted upon it by its history of being eternally in the opposition, is not fundamentally a doctrine of destruction but a doctrine of organic order, cooperative rather than competitive, libertarian rather than directive, creative rather than mechanical.

To assist this development, it is of the first importance to defend anarchism against the charge that it is not a political movement at all, but one that would do away with politics. That kind of stricture was never directed against the theorists of "the end of ideology," who richly deserved it. They were asserting just a few years ago, up to the very moment when the bottom fell out of that market, that the basic problems of capitalist society had already been solved, at least in theory, and that the task remaining was the intelligent administration of the human and material resources that would be made available through cybernetics. So painfully modest a vision of human possibilities was regarded as common-sensical by hard-headed intellectuals in this country, and an appropriate variant of that perspective was being celebrated in the Soviet Union, too. Anarchists, who conceive of politics as the life of common action, and reserve a share in that enterprise to every human being, never assented to these truly millennial pronouncements of the hierophants of corporate capitalism in the West and socialist bureaucratism in Russia. Politics is in fact the particular concern of anarchism, as accumulation and management are the special interests of the reigning ideologies. A consequence of this concern is that the anarchists have a theory of power which is cast in political terms rather than in terms of accumulation and management. This point calls for elaboration, since the critics of anarchism deny that its doctrines have any relevance to the problems of power. Even some anarchists, like Paul Goodman, are inclined to dismiss all theories of political power as unworthy, arising out of psychological deformation, or as a unhappy heritage of frozen theory and frozen institutions.

Those critics, inside and outside the anarchist movement, are under a misapprehension — whether essential or merely semantic has yet to be established, but unfortunate in any case. Power, on the part of an individual or a group, is simply an effective voice in ordering its life in society. (There are conceptual and practical ambiguities in proceeding from individual to group, but that's life; men feel pain and joy in their own persons, but since they are not biological solitaries like the members of some other animal species, the context for their lives is inevitably social. No conceivable social order can eliminate the tension between the individual and the collectivity. The humanly significant project is to make that relation creative rather than negative.) If a person or group has no such practical influence over its own fate, that person or group has the responsibility of achieving it. The attainment of an enlarged measure of self-determination is what is described in political terminology as the seizure of power.

This analysis can scarcely be expected to appeal to Marxist or capitalist ideologues, who inevitably conceive of the seizure of power in terms of the logistics of accumulation and management. What they forget is the ability of any class in revolt, any human collectivity, to reorganize those matters absolutely ad hoc. Such a failure of imagination has a practical bearing on the conduct of revolutionary movements before, during and after the seizure of power. Marxists, for example, have explained the abortive revolution in France last May as a consequence of the students and workers being technically unprepared to take over the management of state and industry from the capitalist class and its servants. Who would mine the coal, who would deliver the milk? The coal-miner and the milkman, said a little child. But Marxists do not trust those toilers to know how to carry on their functions without help from capitalists or commissars. In other words, they accept uncritically the capitalist myth that a peculiar virture is vested in managers and rulers, who provide the social nexus in which the miner and milkman exchange the products of their labor. That is mostly piffle, of course, a self-serving argument for professional managers, but only political geniuses on the level of a Kropotkin or a Lenin can see through the argument and hand down their insight to posterity. The requisite nexus need not be so expensive, so privileged, so overweeningly self-satisfied, so oppressive, and so destructive as it always turns out to be in the traditional capitalist and communist societies. The miner and milkman can hire the job done at a much cheaper rate, and get better service. Castroism and Maoism are attractive to young rebels precisely because they appear to deprecate the role of that precious nexus, whose natural evolution is toward a paralyzing tyranny over men's minds and liberties. A wheeze of Eve Merriam's is in point here. Those poor Chinese, she says, have no water power, no blast furnaces. All they have is Chinese water power and Chinese blast furnaces. In the same way, we needn't grieve that the workers have no middle-managers and no corporation heads.

As we have seen, the critically distinctive notion of power and the seizure of power that has been developed from anarchist perspectives focuses steadily on the enlargement of men's sphere of social action. Marxists have concentrated with nearsighted gravity on secondary considerations, and the further they get from Marx the more devotedly do they engage in time-and-motion studies of the functioning of the body politic. For anarchists, an enlarged opportunity to direct one's fate cannot in the nature of the case be received as a gift from above, from leaders, from the vanguard party, from the holy proletariat itself. Neither can it be delegated, and exercised in the individual's behalf on some theory like that of "virtual representation," or by representation of any kind. In an age of telecommunications, the anarchist demand for direct participation in public affairs is a chimera only to those who monopolize telecommunications for their own purposes, and to those who see no harm in letting them get away with it. For in this regard every man must do his own work, living in his own person the life of an emancipated social being. In passing we should notice the psychological acuteness of this prescription. It forestalls the rise of cults of personality, whether Eastern or Western, in that it minimizes the social role of vicarious satisfactions and exploits by proxy. In a free society, it is no good applauding astronauts; the citizen earns his self-esteem by taking charge of his own fate. The neurotic self-centeredness and self-pity of the modern personality, oppressively manifest in the art of the West during this century, is an outgrowth of a historically unique phenomenon. That is the effective social disfranchisement of an educated class. Never before has the class been so numerous, and never has it had less access to the levers of power. The Chekhovian diseases of the personality arising from civic unemployment are addressed directly by the voluntarist bias of anarchism and by its insistence on the right and the possibility of determining one's destiny.

At this stage in the evolution of society, the political problem is at bottom the problem of self-awareness, a winning free of the cramped imperatives of the traditional ideologies of Left and Right. In this country we poison all our streams and lakes; in the Soviet Union they have begun the deliberate pollution of Lake Baikal. Only a mature self-consciousness that understands and approves its own vital instincts and desires can advance the immediate project of the race, which must be to free mankind from the tyranny of a blind technology. The majority of men are a living sacrifice to the machine, and they may soon be a dead one. Neither capitalism nor socialism has any serious objection to our martyrdom by technology. That is what the young radicals everywhere have discovered, and what they mean when they erupt from the university with the black flag in their hands.

PART IV.

LIBERTARIANISM

Some anarchists may be liberals driven to despair. In 1849 Henry David Thoreau, while endorsing the notion that that government is best which governs least, pushed the argument to the conclusion that "that government is best which governs not at all." Libertarianism, in recent decades, has been used to describe an anti-statist philosophy that is profoundly individualistic and enamored of a (perhaps mythical) capitalist economic system which operates efficiently without the intervention of the state. Though a few libertarians have contested for elective office, most have repudiated "normal" politics and, like leftist anarchists, have argued for the dismantling of the state. At the root of libertarianism resides a common anarchist quest: for the freedom of the individual.

There were anarchists on the "right" in the late nineteenth and early twentieth centuries, particularly in an expanding capitalist America. Benjamin Tucker, for example, was a well-known pamphleteer and essayist who fought the state idea, whether socialist or not, in the name of liberty versus authority. But more recently, libertarians have emerged, with considerable sophistication and occasional polemical vehemence, from the conservative side of the political spectrum. The most articulate and comprehensive libertarian writer since World War II has been Murray N. Rothbard.

A widely read economist, Rothbard's libertarianism has moved beyond right-wing anti-state rhetoric to a position of principled belief in a *laissez-faire* system which rewards individual initiative and which, without the "unnatural" intervention of a protectionist authority, allows the free development of individual happiness. Rothbard reviews the emergence of a new Right in "The Transformation of the American Right." In "Why Be Libertarian?" he calls for a new justice which is abolitionist, abolishing all "invasions of liberty." Rothbard is self-consciously radical, that is he subjects the state idea to a thorough critique. Rothbard tries to solve the "problem" of the state from the libertarian viewpoint in "The Anatomy of the State."

In all his writings Rothbard — who, like many new leftists has tried to go beyond the tired distinctions of an earlier generation — is concerned with returning decision-making ability to the individual and the small group. His writing, and his publication of numerous broadsides and journals, is in the libertarian tradition of defying the state by attacking it at its ideological center.

8

The Transformation of the American Right

Murray N. Rothbard

In the spate of recent books and articles on the burgeoning conservative movement, little has been said of its governing ideas and its intellectual leadership. Instead, attention has been centered on the mass phenomena of the Right-wing: The Billy James Hargises, the Birchers, the various crusaders for god and country. And yet, the neglect of the ruling ideas of the Right-wing has obscured its true nature, and has hidden an enormous and significant change in the very nature of the Right that has taken place since World War II. In fact, due to the total absence of dialogue between various parts of the political spectrum in this country, both Right and Left are largely conducting their argument in what used to be called a severe "cultural lag"; both sides still mistakenly believe that the categories of the debate are the same as they were immediately after the war. In particular, under cover of a certain continuity of rhetoric, the intellectual content and goals of the Right-wing have been radically transformed in the last decade and a half, and this transformation has gone virtually unnoticed on either Right or Left.

The modern American Right began, in the 1930s and 1940s, as a reaction against the New Deal and the Roosevelt Revolution, and specifically as an opposition to the critical increase of statism and state intervention at home, and to war and state intervention abroad. The guiding *motif* of what we might call the "old American Right" was a deep and passionate commitment to individual liberty, and to the belief that this liberty, in the personal and the economic spheres, was gravely manaced by the growth and power of the Leviathan state, at home and abroad. As individuals and libertarians, the old Right felt that the growth of statism at home and abroad were corollaries: New Deal coercion, on behalf of an illusory domestic security, was matched by the ultimate coercion of war in pursuit of the illusion of "collective security" abroad; and both forms of intervention brought with them a swelling of state power over society and over the individual. At home, the Supreme Court was looked to for a "strict construction" of the Constitution to check governmental depredation of the liberty of the individual, and conscription was denounced as a return to an unconstitutional form of involuntary servitude.

As the force of the New Deal reached its heights, both foreign and domestic, during World War II, a beleagurered and tiny libertarian opposition began to emerge and to formulate its total critique of prevailing trends in America. Unfortunately, the Left, almost totally committed to the cause of World War II as well as to extensions of the domestic New Deal, saw in the opposition not a principled and reasoned stand for liberty, but a mere blind "isolationism" at best, and, at worst, a conscious or unconscious "parroting of the Goebbels line." It should not be forgotten that the Left, not so long ago, was not above engaging in its own form of plot-hunting and guilt-by-association. If the Right had its McCarthys and Dillings, the Left had its John Roy Carlsons.

Now it is certainly true that much of this nascent and emerging libertarian Right was tainted with blind chauvinsim, with scorn of "foreigners," etc., and that even then an unfortunate bent for plot-hunting was becoming evident. But still the prevailing trend, certainly among the intellectuals of the Right, was a principled and trenchant opposition to war and to its concomitant destruction of life and liberty, and of all human values. The Beardian ideal of abstention from European wars was essentially not a chauvinist scorn of the stranger, but a call for America to harken to its ancient aim of serving the world as a beacon-light of peace and liberty, rather than as master of a house of correction to set everyone in the world aright by force of bayonet. If the "isolationists" were not themselves libertarian, they were at least moving in that direction, and their ideas needed only refinement and systematization to arrive at that goal. In the devotion to peace, in the anxiety to limit and confine state military interventions and consequent wars, there was little difference between the Right-wing principle of neutrality of a generation ago, and the Left-wing principle of neutralism today. When we realize this, the essential obsolescence of the old categories of "Right" and "Left" begins to become clear.

The intellectual leaders of this old Right of World War II and the immediate aftermath were then and remain today almost unknown among the larger body of American intellectuals: Albert Jay Nock, Rose Wilder Lane, Isabel Paterson, Frank Chodorov, Garet Garrett. It almost takes a great effort of the will to recall the principles and objectives of the old Right, so different is the current Right-wing today. The stress, as we have noted, was on individual liberty in all its aspects as against state power: on freedom of speech and action, on economic liberty, on voluntary relations as opposed to coercion, on a peaceful foreign policy. The great threat to that liberty was state power, in its invasion of personal freedom and private property and in its burgeoning military despotism. Philosophically, the major emphasis was on the natural rights of man, arrived at by an investigation through reason of the laws of man's nature. Historically, the intellectual heroes of the old Right were such libertarians as John Locke, the Levellers, Jefferson, Paine, Thoreau, Cobden, Spencer, and Bastiat.

In short, this libertarian Right based itself on eighteenth and nineteenth century liberalism, and began systematically to extend that doctrine even further. The contemporary canon of the Right consisted of Nock's *Our Enemy the State* and *Memoirs of a Superfluous Man*, Paterson's *The God of the Machine* (the chapter, "Our Japanized Educational System" virtually launched the postwar reaction against progressive education), and H.L. Mencken's *A Mencken Chrestomathy*. Its organ of opinion was the now-forgotten monthly broadsheet *analysis*, edited by Nock's leading disciple, Frank Chodorov. The political thought of this group was well summarized by Chodorov: "the state is an anti-social organization, originating in conquest and concerned only with confiscating produc-tion....There are two ways of making a living, Nock explained. One is the *economic means*, the other the *political means*. The first consists of the application of human effort to raw materials so as to bring into being things that people want; the second is the confiscation of the rightful property of others."

The state is that group of people, who having got hold of the machinery of compulsion, legally or otherwise, use it to better their circumstances; that is the *political means*. Nock would hasten to explain that the state consists not only of politicians, but also those who make use of the politicians for their own ends; that would include those we call pressure groups, lobbyists and all who wangle special privileges out of the politicians. All the injustices that plague "advanced" societies, he maintained, are traceable to the workings of the state organizations that attach themselves to these societies.

When the cold war so swiftly succeeded World War II, the old Right was not bemused, let alone did it lead the war-cry. It is difficult to conceive now that the main political opposition to the cold war was led, not by the Left, then being brought into the war-camp by the ADA, but by the "extreme-Right-wing Republicans" of that era: by the Howard Buffetts and the Frederick C. Smiths. It was this group that opposed the Truman Doctrine, NATO, conscription and American entry into the Korean War — with little grateful acknowledgement by Left-wing peace groups then or now. In attacking the Truman Doctrine on the floor of Congress, Rep. Buffett, who was to be Taft's midwestern campaign manager in 1952, declared: "Even if it were desirable, America is not strong enough to police the world by military force. If that attempt is made, the blessings of liberty will be replaced by coercion and tyranny at home. Our Christian ideals cannot be exported to other lands by dollars and guns. Persuasion and example are the methods taught by the Carpenter of Nazareth, and if we believe in Christianity we should try to advance our ideals by his methods. We cannot practice might and force abroad and retain freedom at home. We cannot talk world cooperation and practice power politics."

Among the intellectual leadership of the old Right, Frank Chodorov vigorously set forth the libertarian position on both the cold war and the suppression of communists at home. The latter was summed up in the aphorism, "The way to get rid of communists in government jobs is to abolish the jobs." Or, more extensively:

> And now we come to the spy-hunt—which is, in reality, a heresy trial. What is it that perturbs the inquisitors? They do not ask the suspects: Do you believe in Power? Do you adhere to the idea that the individual exists for the glory of the state? . . . Are you against taxes, or would you raise them until they absorbed the entire output of the country? . . . Are you opposed to the principle of conscription? Do you favor more "social gains" under the aegis of an enlarged bureaucracy? . . . Such questions might prove embarrassing to the investigators. The answers might bring out a similarity between their ideas and purposes and those of the suspected. They too worship Power. Under the circumstances, they limit themselves to one question: Are you a member of the Communist Party? And this turns out to mean, have you aligned yourselves with the Moscow branch of the church? Power worship is presently sectarianized along nationalistic lines . . . each nation guards its orthodoxy . . . Where Power is attainable, the contest between rival sects is unavoidable. If, as seems likely, the American and Russian cults come into violent conflict, apostasy will disappear . . . War is the apotheosis of Power, the ultimate expression of the faith and solidification of its achievement . . .
>
> . . . The case against the communists involves a principle of freedom

that is of transcending importance. It is the right to be wrong. Heterdoxy is a necessary condition of a free society . . . The right to make a choice . . . is important to me, for the freedom of selection is necessary to my sense of personality; it is important to society, because only from the juxtaposition of ideas can we hope to approach the ideal of truth. Whenever I choose an idea or label it "right," I imply the prerogative of another to reject that idea and label it "wrong." To invalidate his right is to invalidate mine . . . If men are punished for espousing communism, shall we stop there? Once we deny the right to be wrong we put a vise on the human mind and put the temptation to turn the handle into the hands of ruthlessness.

And, in May 1940, Chodorov, praising a pamphlet on *The Militarization of America* issued by The National Council Against Conscription, wrote that "The state cannot intervene in the economic affairs of society without building up its coercive machinery, and that, after all, is militarism. Power is the correlative of politics."

The Old Right reached its full flower in devotion to peace during the Korean War, which provoked several trenchant efforts during the early 1950s. The Foundation for Economic Education, generally concerned with free-market econonomics, devoted several studies to the problem. Thus, Leonard E. Read wrote in *Conscience on the Battlefield* (1951): "It is strange that war, the most brutal of man's activities, requires the utmost delicacy in discussion . . . War is liberty's greatest enemy, and the deadly foe of economic progress . . . To fight evil with evil is only to make evil general." In the same year, Dr. F.A. Harper published an FEE pamphlet, *In Search of Peace,* in which he wrote:

> Charges of pacifism are likely to be hurled at anyone who in troubled times praises any question about the race into war. If pacifism means embracing the objective of peace, I am willing to accept the charge. If it means opposing all aggression against others, I am willing to accept the charge also. It is now urgent in the interest of liberty that many persons become "peacemongers . . ."
> So the nation goes to war, and while war is going on, the real enemy (the idea of slavery)—long ago forgotten and camouflaged by the processes of war—rides on to victory in both camps . . . Further evidence that in war the attack is not leveled at the real enemy is the 'fact that we seem never to know what to do with "victory." . . . Are the "liberated" peoples to be shot, or all put in prison camps, or what? Is the national boundary to be moved? Is there to be further destruction of the property of the defeated. Or what? . . . False ideas can be attacked only with counter-ideas, facts, and logic . . . Nor can the

ideas of [Karl Marx] be destroyed today by murder or suicide of their leading exponent, or of any thousands or millions of devotees . . . Least of all can the ideas of Karl Marx be destroyed by murdering innocent victims of the form of slavery he advocated, whether they be conscripts in armies or victims caught in the path of battle.

Ideas must be met by ideas, on the battlefield of belief. And, as late as May 1955, Dean Russell wrote, in FEE's *The Conscription Idea:*

Those who advocate the "temporary loss" of our freedom in order to preserve it permanently are advocating only one thing: the abolition of liberty . . . However good their intentions may be, those people are enemies of your freedom and my freedom; and I fear them far more than I fear any potential Russian threat to my liberty. These sincere but highly emotional patriots are clear and present threats to freedom; the Russians are still thousands of miles away . . . The Russians would only attack us for either of two reasons: fear of our intentions or retaliation to our acts . . . As long as we keep troops in countries on Russia's borders, the Russians can be expected to act somewhat as we would act if Russia were to station troops in Guatemala or Mexico . . . I can see no more logic in fighting Russia over Korea or Outer Mongolia, than in fighting England over Cyprus, or France over Morocco . . . The historical facts of imperialism . . . are not sufficient reasons to justify the destruction of freedom within the United States by turning ourselves into a permanent garrison state . . . We are rapidly becoming a caricature of the thing we profess to hate.

There is no need to multiply examples. Frank Chodorov consistently worked against the war drive in analysis and later, in 1954, as editor of the *Freeman.* The Right-wing libertarian journal *Faith and Freedom* featured, in April, 1954, an all-peace issue, with contributions by Garet Garrett, Robert LeFevre, the industrial Ernest T. Weir, and the present writer. We might elaborate here on two neglected contributions in that period. One was an essay by Garrett ("The Rise of Empire," 1952, reprinted in *The People's Pottage,* 1953) which pinpointed the main issue of our time as the rise of a deplorable American imperialism: "We have crossed the boundary that lies between Republic and Empire." The other was a relatively unnoticed book by Louis Bromfield, *A New Pattern for a Tired World* (1954) which decried statism, war, conscription, and imperialism. Bromfield wrote with conviction of imperialism and of the revolution of the undeveloped countries:

One of the great failures of our foreign policy throughout the world arises from the fact that we have permitted ourselves to be identified everywhere with the old, doomed, and rotting colonial-imperialist small European nations which once imposed upon so much of the world the pattern of exploitation and economic and political domination ... None of these rebellious, awakening peoples will ... trust us or cooperate in any way so long as we remain identified with the economic colonial system of Europe, which represents, even in its capitalistic pattern, the last remnants of feudalism ... We leave these awakening peoples with no choice but to turn to Russian and communist comfort and promise of Utopia.

And on American cold-war policy, Bromfield charged:

Our warmongers and the military apparently believe ... that all other nations are unimporant and can be trampled under foot the moment either Russia or the U.S. sees fit to precipitate a war ... To this faction (the warmongers and the military) it seems of small concern that the nations living between us and Russia would be the most terrible sufferers ... The growing "neutralism" of the European nations is merely a reasonable, sensible, and civilized reaction, legitimate in every respect when all the factors from Russia's inherent weaknesses to our own meddling and aggressiveness are taken into consideration ... The Korean situation ... will not be settled until we withdraw entirely from an area in which we have no right to be and leave the peoples of that area to work out their own problems.

These quotations give the flavor of an era that is so remote as to make it seem incredible that such views should have dominated the American Right-wing. To the current Right-wing, which has virtually obliterated its own former position from its memory, such views today would be branded, at the very least, as "soft on communism." The radical transformation of the Right-wing can even be seen in the fate of something like the Bricker Amendment. Only a decade ago, the Bricker Amendment was the number one foreign-policy plank of the Right-wing, dear to all the "little old ladies in tennis shoes" that used to form its mass base. And the reason the resurgent conservative movement, and its political embodiment in the Goldwater movement, have entirely buried the Bricker Amendment is because that Amendment, while defining not the most important or the most idealistic foreign-policy stance, was an expression of the "isolationism," or the fear of the effects of big government upon the individual, that bears no relation to today's new Right.

Much of the Left, however, still writes as if the main trouble with today's Right is its "isolationism," its wish to withdraw from foreign aid or international commitments. Others on the Left claim that the Right's anticommunism is a mere cloak for *laissez-faire* economic views. There could not be a more mistaken analysis of the essence of the current position of the American Right. For that position is virtually the reverse: today's Right-wing is directed, with passion, dedication, and even fanaticism to one overriding goal, to which all other possible goals are totally subordinate. And that goal is the nuclear annihilation of the Soviet Union. Here is the essence of the new Right, the gauge of the totality of its transformation. As one of its major theoreticians likes to put it: "I have a vision, a great vision of the future—a totally devastated Soviet Union." Here, in brief, is the vision that animates the conservative revival.

For the blight that destroyed the libertarianism of the Right-wing and effected its transformation was nothing less than hysterical anticommunism. It began with this kind reasoning: there are two "threats" to liberty: the "internal" threat of domestic socialism, and the "external" threat of Soviet Russia. The external threat is the most important. *Therefore,* all energies must now be directed to battling and destroying that "threat." In the course of this shift of focus from statism to communism as the "enemy," the Right-wing somehow failed to see that the real "external" threat was not Soviet Russia, but a warlike foreign policy of global intervention, and especially the nuclear weapons of mass destruction used to back such a policy. And they failed to see that the main architect in organizing a foreign policy of global nuclear intervention was the United States. In short, they failed to see that both the "external" and "internal" threats of statism to liberty were essentially domestic.

Under pressure of anticommunist hysteria, the Right-wing, despite its fondness for quasi-theological or moral cant, has imitated the communists themselves in virtually abandoning all moral principles except one: in this case, the destruction of all opposition, foreign and domestic. For the immorality of communism is not uniquely diabilic; it stems from the fact that for communists, *all other* moral principles are expendable before the overriding end of the maintenance and advance of the communist system. But, the Right-wing has similarly erected as its sole, overriding end the destruction of communists and communist countries, and all other considerations are scrapped to attain that end. There seems to be one crucial difference, however; the communists are more convinced than ever that nuclear weapons of annihilation make imperative peaceful coexistence between states, and that social change must come about through internal changes within each state, where conflict would be relatively small-scale and confined. But the Right-wing has not only failed to learn this lesson; on the contrary, the more terrible modern weaponry has become, the more fanatically determined upon total war has the Right-wing grown. This seems to be a lunatic position, and undoubtedly it is, but it is *precisely* the position of the present-day Right.

Now, of course, no one has every wanted war per se; Hitler would not have attacked Soviet Russia, for example, if Russia had agreed to surrender unconditionally without war. And neither would the Right-wing launch an H-bomb attack on Russia if Khrushchev and his government were to resign and turn over the Soviet Union to, let us say, an American army of occupation. But that is the point: that nothing short of unconditional surrender would satisfy the Right-wing, or would deflect it from nuclear attack. How does the Right-wing justify a position that is *prima facie* monstrous and even crazed? The essential justification is, curiously enough, theological and Christian. It is even Catholic, for while the mass base of the Right-wing, apart from the Eastern cities, is fundamentalist-Protestant, the intellectual leaders are almost all either Catholic or "proto-Catholic."[1] The justification is a willingness to destroy the world, and the human race along with it, for matters of high principal. The highest principle, as we have seen above, is the destruction of communists, who are, at least implicitly and sometimes explicitly, identified with the devil and his agents upon earth. And, after all, what does the destruction of the world matter when men's immortal souls will continue in eternal life: As the leading publicist of the new Right has said: "If I had to 'push the button,' I would push it unswervingly, in the firm knowledge that I am in the right." Those who may balk at this blithe attitude toward world destruction are accused of being cowards, and atheistic cowards at that, for only atheists would cling so adamantly to "mere biological life" when great principle is at stake. (Not being a Catholic, I will have to leave the theological refutation of this position to others; I am surprised, however, to hear that mass suicide and mass murder are looked upon approvingly by the Church.)

Another curious justification is the famous "red or dead" dichotomy. But in fact the stark choice of "red or dead" is just as unrealistic an alternative for America as the old "communist or fascist" choice posed by many of the Left in the 1930s. There is at least one other choice: peaceful coexistence and joint nuclear disarmament. Moreover, choosing death over redness is suicide, and one would have thought that suicide was a grave sin for Christians. And finally this dichotomy allows no reference to the fact that approximately one billion people, now living in communist countries throughout the world, are choosing redness every day, by not committing suicide. Is there no lesson here? Does it make any sense, furthermore, to destroy these people, and untold Americans along with them, thus to "liberate" those who have made their own personal choice for redness over death? Is it moral, or Christian, to change their choice from life to death by force? In short, is it moral, or Christian, for American conservatives to annihilate millions of Russians, Poles, etc., to "liberate" through murder those who have already made their choice for life?

Also implicit in the Right-wing thesis is the view that the devil is omnipotent; that once communism "takes over" a country, it is doomed, and its population might as well be written off to the eternal abyss. That this is a starkly pessimistic view of mankind is obvious; and this is all the more curious in the light of the demonstrations by libertarian economists that socialism cannot provide a viable economic system for an industrial society. It also studiously ignores the enormous changes that have taken place within communist countries since World War II, the considerable liberalization and even increased emphasis on private enterprise in Russia and many of the countries of eastern Europe. Communist China's recent expression of concern as to whether Yugoslavia is a socialist country is evidence enough of the alarm felt by communist fundamentalists at the unwilling but headlong retreat from socialism in that communist land. It is also significant that not one Right-wing economist or strategist has taken the trouble to consider the surely important question of how one would decommunize Russia if it should surrender to the American army — now or at any other time? I believe that de-communization could be achieved and in a way similar to, though much more thoroughgoing than, the path of Yugoslavia; but the point is that the indifference to this problem on the Right is another indication of its central concern: nuclear war. De-communization is to come about, not through a change in the ideas and actions of the Russian and other peoples, but, according to the Right, through their liquidation.

Evidence of the Right-wing subordination of all its other goals and principles to nuclear war against communists is overwhelming, and at every hand. It lies at the root of the obscene eagerness with which the Right hurries to embrace every dictator no matter how fascistic or blood-stained, who affirms his "anti-communism." William F. Buckley's "libertarian" apologia for the fascist regime of South Africa in the pages of *National Review* is a case in point. So is the enormous enthusiasm for Chiang-kai-Shek, for Franco, for Syngman Rhee, and, most recently, for Mme. Nhu. It is not simply that these dictators are welcomed reluctantly, for expendiency's sake in the "war against communism." The Right has proceeded, in its war hysteria, far beyond that point. For now these dictators are *better* since their policy is evidently far "harder" on communists and suspected communists than the policy of the democracies. Mme. Nhu, as a Catholic as well as a totalitarian, has touched the heart of every Right-wing publicist. There can be nothing "harder" on one's subjects than repressing a religious majority and herding the peasants of the country into concentration camps in order to stave off "communism." The fact that this is hardly a better policy than communism itself makes no imprint whatever on a Right-wing which often likes to boast of itself as a "conservative-libertarian" movement. It is tragically ironic and almost incredible that a movement which began, not too many years ago, in a passionate commitment to human liberty, should end as the cheering squad for a Mme. Is it really too impolite to wonder how the Right-wing would now regard the man who was, in his day, the "hardest" and the "toughest" anticommunist of them all: Adolf Hitler?

In domestic affairs, the free-market rhetoric has become simply that: after dinner talk carrying no enthusiasm or true conviction. Indeed, the promise of *laissez-faire* now performs the same function for the new American Right as the promise of unlimited abundance under commu-nism did for Stalin. While enslaving and exploiting the Soviet people, Stalin held out a splendid *future* of utopian abundance that would make current sacrifices worthwhile. The present-day Right hold out the eventual promise of freedom and the free-market *after* communists shall have been exterminated. If there are any survivors emerging from their civil-defense shelters after the holocaust, they will presumably be allowed to engage in free-market activities, provided, of course, that some other "enemy" shall not have raised its head in the meanwhile.

This total subordination of all concerns to anticommunism accounts for all the otherwise inexplicable reversals on the Right. Thus, the Supreme Court is now bitterly attacked for the opposite reasons as in the 1930s: because it *prevents* infringements of the state on the liberties of the person. Justice Frankfurter, once assailed as a virtual advocate of tyranny, is now hailed by the Right for his sound, pragmatic conservatism in not interfering with anticommunist persecutions — the fruits, of course, of the self-same juridical philosophy. Social Democrats and New Dealers, such as the *New Leader*, Sidney Hook, Senator Dodd, George Meany, and others are embraced for their "hard anticommunism." The *New Leader's* collaboration with the Right-wing in publishing a pro-Chiang propaganda article is indicative of this change in atmosphere, a change that alters all the old categories of "right" and "left" that are still unthinkingly used in political discourse.

It is instructive, finally, to consider the political concerns of the Young Americans for Freedom, virtually the political action arm of National Review. To my knowledge, not one political action drive of YAF has been directed to an increase of individual liberty or of the free-market; stressed instead have been such items as perpetuating and strengthing HUAC, calls for blockade, and more, of Cuba, opposition to the test-ban treaty, restoring prayer to the public school, and advocacy of local ordinances and "card-parties" coercively interfering with the right of stores to sell goods from communist countries — hardly a contribution to a free market. I believe there is only one exception to this generalization: an eager enthusiasm for the Mitchell program to reduce relief payments in Newburgh, New York, an enthusiasm that may not have been unrelated to the racial issue involved.

Coterminous with the *political* transformation of the American Right has come a *philosophical* transformation, and I do not believe that the two are unconnected. The latter greatly bolsters and perpetuates the former. The positive positions of the various conservative thinkers vary greatly; but they all unite in determined opposition to human reason, to individual liberty, to separation of church and state, to all the things that characterized the classical liberal position and its modern extension. There is, unfortunately, no space here for a full discussion of the current conservative position: but basically it is a return to the essential principles of early nineteenth century conservatism. We must realize that the great fact of modern history was the classical liberal revolution against the old order, a "revolution" that expressed itself in many forms: *laissez-faire* economics, individual liberty, separation of church-and-state, free trade and international peace, opposition to statism and militarism. Its great embodiments were the three great revolutions of the late eighteenth century: the Industrial Revolution, the American Revolution, and the French Revolution. Each, in its way, was part of the general classical liberal revolt against the old order.

Conservatism emerged, in France, Britain, and elsewhere in Europe, as a conscious reactionary attempt to smash this revolution and to restore the old order even more systematically than it had been installed before. The essence of that order may be summed up in the famous phrase "Throne-and-Altar." In short, the old order consisted of a ruling oligarchy of church, Anglican or Gallican. It was an order, as explicated by conservatives, that stressed the overriding importance of "community"—as embodied in the state, of theocratic union of church and state, of the virtues of nationalism and war, of coerced "morality" and of the denigration of the individual subject. And philosophically, reason was derided in behalf of pure faith in ruling tradition.

At first it might seem that this old conservatism is irrelevant to American conservatism today, but I do not believe this to be true. It is true that an American conservative has difficulty finding a legitimate monarch *in America.* But he does the best he can; the current American Right-wing is, for one thing, highly enamoured of European monarchy, and there is much enthusiasm for restoration of the Hapsburgs. One leading proto-Catholic conservative still toasts "the King over the water," and Frederick Wilhelmsen apparently regards the Crown of St. Stephen as the summit of Western civilization. Russel Kirk, in turn, seems to prefer the Tory squirearchy of Anglican England. At every hand, Metternich, the Stuarts, and the later Burke have replaced libertarians as historical heroes. But a king for the United States is, of course, a bit difficult, and conservatives have had to content themselves with makeshifts: with the resotration to historiographical favor, for example, of such statists as Alexander

Hamilton, and of solicitude for the peculiar institution of slavery in the South. Willmoore Kendall has found in Congress the apotheosis of conservatism, and asserts not only the right, but the duty of the Greek community to preserve itself from the irritating probing of Socrates. Everywhere on the Right the "open society" is condemned, and a coerced morality affirmed. God is supposed to be put back into government. Free speech is treated with suspicion and distrust, and the military are hailed as the greatest patriots, and conscription strongly upheld. Western imperialism is trumpeted as the proper way to deal with backward peoples, and pilgrimages are made to Franco's Spain for inspiration in governmental forms. And, at every side, reason is denigrated, and faith in tradition and custom held up as the proper path for man.

It is true that most modern conservatives do not, like their forebears, wish to destroy the industrial system and revert to small farms and happy handicraftsmen — although there is a strong strain of even this idea in contemporary conservatism. But, basically, the current conservatives are supremely indifferent to a free-market economy; they do not blanch at the vast economic distortions imposed by arms contracts or at crippling restrictions on foreign trade, and they could not tolerate a budget cut that would reduce America's military posture in the world. In fact, such leading conservatives as Ernest van den Haag and Willmoore Kendall have been frankly Keynesian in economics. In the end, all must be subordinated to the state; as William F. Buckley has affirmed: "Where reconciliation of an individual's and the government's interests cannot be achieved, the interests of the government shall be given exclusive consideration." One observer of the conservative movement has commented, "How's that for laissez-faire?" Indeed. Above all, the modern conservative program reduces to dragooning the American people, under the control of the current American version of Throne-and-Altar, into lockstep uniformity and a closed society dedicated to the overriding end of destroying communism, even at the expense of nuclear annihilation.

What of the old liberatrian segment of the Right? Largely they have been submerged in the transformation of the Right-wing, generally because they have not had articulate spokesmen explaining to them the nature and magnitude of what has taken lace. They have largely been bemused by the pervasive idea that there is, in some strong sense, a joint "conservative-libertarian movement," and that no matter how much conservatives may diverge from liberty, they are the libertarian's natural allies — at the same end of the spectrum, and at the polar opposite from socialism. But this idea suffers from the "cultural lag" that we have observed. The old Right may have been the natural ally of the *laissez-faire* libertarian, but this is not at all true of the new.

The libertarian needs, perhaps most of all, to be informed by history, and to realize that conservatism was always the polar opposite of classical liberalism. Socialism, in contrast, was not the polar opposite of either, but rather, in my view, a muddled and irrationally contradictory mixture of both liberalism and conservatism. For socialism was essentially a movement to come to terms with the industrial revolution, to try to achieve *liberal ends* by the use of collectivistic, *conservative means*. It tried to achieve the ideals of peace, freedom, and a progressing standard of living by using the collectivist, organicist, hierarchical means of conservatism as adapted to industrial society. As a middle-of-the-road doctrine, it is easy for socialism, once it abandoned the liberal ideals of peace and freedom, to shift completely to the conservative pole in the many varying forms of "national socialism."

Mr. Frank S. Meyer, the leading proponent of a fused "conservative-libertarian movement," has called upon us to ignore the nineteenth century, "heir to the disruption of the French Revolution," and to go back beyond "the parochial disputes of the nineteenth century." Such a course would indeed be convenient for Meyer's thesis, as it would sweep the whole meaning of the liberal and conservative movements. For the point is that both liberalism and conservatism (and socialism as well) found their form and their doctrine precisely in the nineteenth century, as a result of the struggles between the old order and the new. It is precisely by focussing on the history of the nineteenth century that we learn of the true origins of the various "isms" of our day, as well as the illogical and mythical nature of the attempted "conservative-libertarian" fusion.

There are some signs, indeed, that from various sides, thinkers are beginning to apprehend the dissolution of the old forms, the obsolescence of the old "left" and "right" stereotypes in American politics, and the invalidity of a fusion of libertarians with an old conservatism *redivivus*. Libertarians are beginning to protest; in the pages of *New Individualist Review*, the outstanding student journal of the Right, Ronald Hamowy, one of its editors-in-chief, has, in a well-known article, bitterly attacked the conservative philosophy and politics of Buckley and *National Review*. Dean Benjamin Rogge of Wabash College has contributed a thoughtful critique of the new conservatism, and Howard Buffett has called for an end to conscription. But *New Individualist Review* was basically founded in commitment to the conservative-libertarian mythos, and it clearly suffers from being mired in this inner contradiction. Robert LeFevre, head of the libertarian Freedom School, in a trenchant leaflet, *Those Who Protest*, has pointed out and attacked the transformation of the Right-wing. And from a different direction, the noted critic Edmund Wilson has now raised his powerful voice to protest both *The Cold War and the Income Tax*.

Perhaps indeed, the country is ripe for a fundamental ideological realignment.

NOTES

1. "Proto-Catholic" is an important category which seems to have gone unnoticed — of intellectuals who write and speak in a Catholic vein, who are almost more ardently Catholic and impatient of heresy than Catholics themselves, and who yet have somehow never found their way into the Church.

9

The Anatomy of the State

Murray N. Rothbard

What the State Is Not

The State is almost universally considered an institution of social service. Some theorists venerate the State as the apotheosis of society; others regard it as an amiable though often inefficient organization for achieving social ends; but almost all regard it as a necessary means for achieving the goals of mankind, a means to be ranged against the "private sector" and often winning in this competition of resources. With the rise of democracy, the identification of the State with society has been redoubled, until it is common to hear sentiments expressed which violate virtually every tenet of reason and common sense; such as "we *are* the government." The useful collective term "we" has enabled an ideological camouflage to be thrown over the reality of political life. If "we are the government," then anything a government does to an individual is *not only* just and untyrannical; it is also "voluntary" on the part of the individual concerned. If the government has incurred a huge public debt which must be paid by taxing one group for the benefit of another, this reality of burden is obscured by saying that "we owe it to ourselves"; if the the government conscripts a man, or throws him into jail for dissident opinion, then he is "doing it to himself" and therefore nothing untoward has occurred. Under this reasoning, any Jews murdered by the Nazi government were *not* murdered; instead, they must have "committed suicide," since they *were* the government (which was democratically chosen), and therefore anything the government did to them was voluntary on their part. One would not think it necessary to belabor this point, and yet the overwhelming bulk of the people hold this fallacy to a greater or less degree.

We must therefore emphasize that "we" are *not* the government; the government is not "us." The government does *not* in any accurate sense "represent" the majority of the people,[1] but even if it did, even if seventy percent of the people decided to murder the remaining thirty percent, this would still be murder, and would not be voluntary suicide on the part of slaughtered minority.[2] No organicist metaphor, no irrelevant bromide that "we are all part of one another," must be permitted to obscure this basic fact.

If, then, the State is not "us," if it is not "the human family" getting together to decide mutual problems, if it is not a lodge meeting or country club, what is it? Briefly, the State is that organization in society which attempts to maintain a monopoly of the use of force and violence in a given territorial area; in particular, it is the only organization in society that obtains its revenue not by voluntary contribution or payment for services rendered, but by coercion. While other individuals or institutions obtain their income by production of goods and services, and by the peaceful and voluntary sale of these goods and services to others, the State obtains its revenue by the use of compulsion, i.e., by the use and the threat of the jailhouse and the bayonet.[3] Having used force and violence to obtain its revenue, the State generally goes on to regulate and dictate the other actions of its individual subjects. One would think that simple observation of all States through history and over the globe would be proof enough of this assertion; but the miasma of myth has lain so long over State activity that elaboration is necessary.

What the State Is

Man is born naked into the world, and needing to use his mind to learn how to take the resources given him by nature, and to transform them (i.e., by investment in "capital") into shapes and forms and places where the resources can be used for the satisfaction of his wants and the advancement of his standard of living. The only way by which man can do this is by the use of his mind and energy to transform resources ("production") and to exchange these products for products created by others. Man has found that, through the process of voluntary, mutual exchange, the productivity, and hence the living standards, of all participants in exchange may increase enormously. The only "natural" course for man to survive and to attain wealth, therefore, is by using his mind and energy to engage in the production-and-exchange process. He does this, first by *finding* natural resources, and then by transforming them (by "mixing his labor" with them, as Locke puts it), to make them his individual property, and then by exchanging this property for the similarly obtained property of others. The social path dictated by the requirements of man's nature, therefore, is the path of "property rights" and the "free market" of gift or exchange of such rights. Through this path, men have learned how to avoid the "jungle" methods of fighting over scarce resources so that A can only acquire them at the expense of B, and, instead, to multiply those resources enormously in peaceful and harmonious production and exchange.

The great German sociologist Franz Oppenheimer pointed out that there are two mutually exclusive ways of acquiring wealth; one, the above way of production and exchange, he called the "economic means." The other way is simpler in that it does not require productivity; it is the way of seizure of another's goods or services by the use of force and violence. This is the method of one-sided confiscation, of theft of the property of others. This is the method which Oppenheimer termed "the political means" to wealth. It should be clear that the peaceful use of one's reason and energy in production is the "natural" path for man: the means for his survival and prosperity on this earth. It should be equally clear that the coercive, exploitative means is contrary to natural law; it is *parasitic*, for instead of adding to production, it subtracts from it. The "political means" siphons production off to a parasitic and destructive individual or group; and this siphoning not only subtracts from the number producing, it also lowers the producer's incentive to produce beyond his *own* subsistence. In the long run, the robber destroys his won subsistence by dwindling or eliminating the source of his own supply. But not only that; even in the short run, the predator is acting contrary to his own true nature as a man.

We are now in a position to answer more fully the question: what *is* the State? The State, in the words of Oppenheimer, is the "organization of the political means"; it is the systematization of the predatory process over a given territory.[4] For crime, at best, is sporadic and uncertain; the parasitism is ephemeral, and the coercive, parasitic life-line may be cut off at any time by the resistance of the victims. The State provides a legal, orderly, systematic channel for the predation of private property; it renders certain, secure, and relatively "peaceful" the lifeline of the parasitic caste in society.[5] Since production must always precede predation, the free market is anterior to the State. The State has never been created by a "social contract"; it has always been born in conquest and exploitation. The classic paradigm was a conquering tribe pausing in its time-honored method of looting and murdering a conquered tribe, to realize that the time-span of plunder would be longer and more secure, and the situation more pleasant, if the conquered tribe were allowed to live and produce, with the conquerors settling among them as rulers exacting a steady annual tribute.[6] One method of the birth of a State may be illustrated as follows: in the hills of southern "Ruritania," a bandit group manages to obtain physical control over the territory, and finally the bandit chieftain proclaims himself "King of the sovereign and independent government of South Ruritania," and, if he and his men have the force to maintain this rule for a while, lo and behold! a new State has joined the "family of nations," and the former bandit leaders have been transformed into the lawful nobility of the realm.

How the State Preserves Itself

Once a State has been established, the problem of the ruling group or "caste" is how to maintain their rule.[7] While force is their *modus operandi,* their basic and long-run problem is ideological. For in order to continue in office, *any* government (not simply a "democratic" government) must have the support of the majority of its subjects. This support, it must be noted, need not be active enthusiasm; it may well be passive resignation as if to an inevitable law of nature. But support in the sense of acceptance of some sort it must be; else the minority of State rulers would eventually be outweighed by the active resistance of the majority of the public. Since predation must be supported out of the surplus of production, it is necessarily true that the class constituting the State, the full-time bureaucracy (and nobility), must be a rather small minority in the land, although it may of course purchase allies among important groups in the population. Therefore, the chief task of the rulers is always to secure the active or resigned acceptance of the majority of the citizens.[8]

Of course, one method of securing support is through the creation of vested economic interests. Therefore, the King alone cannot rule; he must have a sizable group of followers who enjoy the perquisites of rule, i.e., the members of the State apparatus, such as the full-time bureaucracy or the established nobility.[9] But this still secures only a minority of eager supporters, and even the essential purchasing of support by subsidies and other grants of privilege still does not obtain the consent of the majority. For this essential acceptance, the majority must be persuaded by *ideology* that their government is good, wise, and, at least, inevitable, and certainly better than other conceivable alternatives. Promoting this ideology among the people is the vital social task of the "intellectuals." For the masses of men do not create their own ideas, or indeed think through these ideas independently; they follow passively the ideas adopted and disseminated by the body of intellectuals. The intellectuals are therefore the "opinion-moulders" in society. And since it is precisely a moulding of opinion that the State almost desperately needs, the basis for age-old alliance between the State and the intellectuals becomes clear.

It is evident that the State needs the intellectuals; it is not so evident why intellectuals need the State. Put simply, we may state that the intellectual's livelihood in the free market is never too secure; for the intellectual must depend on the values and choices of the masses of his fellow-men, and it is precisely characteristic of the masses that they are generally uninterested in intellectual matters. The State, on the other hand, is willing to offer the intellectuals a secure and permanent berth in the State apparatus: and thus a secure income, and the panoply of prestige. For the intellectuals will be handsomely rewarded for the important function they perform for the State rulers, of which group they now become a part.[10]

The alliance between the State and the intellectuals was symbolized in the eager desire of professors at the University of Berlin, in the nineteenth century, to form the "intellectual bodyguard of the House of Hohenzollern." In the present day, let us note the revealing comment of an eminent Marxist scholar concerning Professor Wittfogel's critical study of ancient Oriental despotism: "The civilization which Professor Wittfogel is so bitterly attacking was one which could make poets and scholars into officials."[11] Of innumerable examples, we may cite the recent development of the "science" of strategy, in the service of the government's main violence wielding arm, the military.[12] A venerable institution, furthermore, is the official or "court" historian, dedicated to purveying the rulers' views of their own and their predecessors' actions.[13]

Many and varied have been the arguments by which the State and its intellectuals have induced their subjects to support their rule. Basically the strands of argument may be summed up as follows: (a) the State rulers are great and wise men (they "rule by divine right," they are the "aristocracy" of men, they are the "scientific experts"), much greater and wiser than the good but rather simple subjects, and (b) rule by the extant government is inevitable, absolutely necessary, and far better than the indescribable evils that would ensue upon its downfall. The union of Church and State was one of the oldest and most successful of these ideological devices. The ruler was either anointed by God or, in the case of the absolute rule of many Oriental despotisms, was himself God; hence, any resistance to his rule would be blasphemy. The State's priestcraft performed the basic intellectual function of obtaining popular support and even worship for the rulers.[14]

Another successful device was to instill fear of any alternative systems of rule or nonrule. The present rulers, it was maintained, supply to the citizens an essential service for which they should be most grateful:

protection against sporadic criminals and marauders. For the State, to preserve its own monopoly of predation, did indeed see to it that private and unsystematic crime was kept to a minimum; the State has always been jealous of its own preserve. Especially has the State been successful in recent centuries in instilling fear of *other* State rulers. Since the land area of the globe has been parcelled out among particular States, one of the basic doctrines of the State was to identify *itself* with the territory it governed. Since most men tend to love their homeland, the identification of that land, and its people, with the State, was a means of making natural patriotism work to the State's advantage. If "Ruritania" was being attacked by "Walldavia," the first task of the State and its intellectuals was to convince the people of Ruritania that the attack was really upon *them,* and not simply upon the ruling caste. In this way, a war between *rulers* was converted into a war between *peoples,* with each people coming to the defense of its rulers in the erroneous belief that the rulers were defending *them.* This device of "nationalism" has only been successful, in Western civilization, in recent centuries; it was not too long ago that the mass of subjects regarded wars as irrelevant battles between various sets of nobles.

Many and subtle are the ideological weapons that the State has wielded through the centuries. One excellent weapon has been *tradition.* The longer that the rule of a State has been able to preserve itself, the more powerful this weapon; for then, the X-Dynasty or the Y-State has the seeming weight of centuries of tradition behind it.[15] Worship of one's ancestors then becomes a none-too-subtle means of worship of one's ancient rulers. The greatest danger to the State is independent intellectual criticism; there is no better way to stifle that criticism than to attack any isolated voice, any raiser of new doubts, as a profane violator of the wisdom of his ancestors. Another potent ideological force is to deprecate the *individual* and exalt the collectivity of society. For since any given rule implies majority acceptance, any ideological danger to that rule can only start from one or a few independently thinking individuals. The new idea, much less the new critical idea, must needs *begin* as a small minority opinion; therefore, the State must nip the view in the bud by ridiculing any view that defies the opinions of the mass. "Listen only to your brothers" or "adjust to society" thus become ideological weapons for crushing individual dissent.[16] By such measurers, the masses will never learn of the non-existence of their Emperor's clothes.[17]

It is also important for the State to make its rule seem inevitable; even if its reign is disliked, it will then be met with passive resignation, as witness the familiar coupling of "death and taxes." One method is to induce historiographical determinism, as opposed to individual freedom of will. If the X-Dynasty rules us, this is because the Inexorable Laws of History (or the Divine Will, or the Absolute, or the Material Productive Forces) have so decreed, and nothing any puny individuals may do can change this inevitable decree. It is also important for the State to inculcate in its subjects an aversion to any "conspiracy theory of history"; for a search for "conspiracies" means a search for motives, and an attribution of responsibility for historical misdeeds. If, however, any tyranny imposed by the State, or venality, or aggressive war, was caused *not* by the State rulers but by mysterious and arcane "social forces," or by the imperfect state of the world, or, if in some way, *everyone* was responsible ("We Are All Murderers," proclaims one slogan), then there is no point to the people's becoming indignant, or rising up against such misdeeds. Furthermore, an attack on "conspiracy theories" means that the subjects will become more gullible in believing the "general welfare" reasons that are always put forth by the State for engaging in any of its despotic actions. A "conspiracy theory" can unsettle the system by causing the public to doubt the State's ideological propaganda.

Another tried and true method for bending subjects to one's will is inducing guilt. Any increase in private well-being can be attacked as "unconscionable greed," "materialism," or "excessive affluence," profit-making can be attacked as "exploitation" and "usury," mutually beneficial exchanges denounced as "selfishness," and somehow with the conclusion always being drawn that more resources should be siphoned from the private to the "public sector." The induced guilt makes the public more ready to do just that. For while individual persons tend to indulge in "selfish greed," the failure of the State's rulers to engage in exchanges is supposed to signify *their* devotion to higher and nobler causes — parasitic predation being apparently morally and esthetically lofty as compared to peaceful and productive work.

In the present more secular age, the Divine Right of the State has been supplemented by the invocation of a new god, Science. State rule is now proclaimed as being ultra-scientific, as constituting planning by experts. But while "reason" is invoked more than in previous centuries, this is not the true reason of the individual and his exercise of free will; it is still collectivist and determinist, still implying holistic aggregates and coercive manipulation of passive subjects by their rulers.

The increasing use of scientific jargon has permitted the State's intellectuals to weave obscurantist apologia for State rule that would have only met with derision by the populace of a simpler age. A robber who justified his theft by saying that he really helped his victims by his spending giving a boost to retail trade would find few converts; but when this theory is clothed in Keynesian equations and impressive references to the "multiplier effect," it unfortunately carries more conviction. And so the assault on common sense proceeds, each age performing the task in its own ways.

Thus, ideological support being vital to the State, it must unceasingly try to impress the public with its "legitimacy," to distinguish its activities from those of mere brigands. The unremitting determination of its assaults on common sense is no accident, for as Mencken vividly maintained:

> The average man, whatever his errors otherwise, at least sees clearly that govenment is something lying outside him and outside the generality of his fellow men — that it is a separate, independent, and hostile power, only partly under his control, and capable of doing him great harm. Is it a fact of no significance that robbing the government is everywhere regarded as a crime of less magnitude than robbing an individual, or even a corporation? . . . What lies behind all this, I believe, is a deep sense of the fundamental antagonism between the government and the people it governs. It is apprehended, not as a committee of citizens chosen to carry on the communal business of the whole population, but as a separate and autonomous corporation, mainly devoted to exploiting the population for the benefit of its own members. . . . When a private citizen is robbed, a worthy man is deprived of the fruits of his industry and thrift; when the government is robbed, the worst that happens is that certain rogues and loafers have less money to play with than they had before. The notion that they have earned that money is never entertained; to most sensible men it would seem ludicrous. . . .[18]

How the State Transcends Its Limits

As Bertrand de Jouvenel has sagely pointed out, through the centuries men have formed concepts designed to check and limit the exercise of State rule; and, one after another, the State, using its intellectual allies, has been able to transform these concepts into intellectual rubber stamps of legitimacy and virtue to attach to its decrees and actions. Originally, in Western Europe, the concept of divine sovereignty held that the kings may rule only according to divine law; the kings turned the concept into a rubber stamp of divine approval for any of the king's actions. The concept of parliamentary democracy began as a popular check upon absolute monarchial rule; it ended with parliament being the essential part of the State and its every act totally sovereign. As de Jouvenel concludes: "Many writers on theories of sovereignty have worked out one...of these restrictive devices. But in the end every single such theory has, sooner or later, lost its original purpose, and come to act merely as a springboard to Power, by providing it with the powerful aid of an invisible sovereign with whom it could in time successfully identify itself."[19]

Similarly with more specific doctrines: the "natural rights" of the individual enshrined in John Locke and the Bill of Rights, became a statist "right to a job"; utilitarianism turned from arguments for liberty to arguments against resisting the State's invasions of liberty, etc.

Certainly the most ambitious attempt to impose limits on the State has been the Bill of Rights and other restrictive parts of the American Constitution, in which written limits on government became the Fundamental Law to be interpreted by a judiciary supposedly independent of the other branches of government. All Americans are familiar with the process by which the construction of limits in the Constitution has been inexorably broadened over the last century. But few have been as keen as Professor Charles Black to see that the State has, in the process, largely transformed judicial review itself from a *limiting* device to yet another instrument for furnishing ideological legitimacy to the government's actions. For if a judicial decree of "unconstitutional" is a mighty check to government power, an implicit or explicit verdict of "constitutional" is a mighty weapon for fostering public acceptance of ever-greater government power.

Professor Black begins his analysis by pointing out the crucial necessity of "legitimacy" for any government to endure, this legitimation signifying basic majority acceptance of the government and its actions."[20] Acceptance of legitimacy becomes a particular problem in a country such as the United States, where "substantive limitations are built into the theory on which the government rests." What is needed, adds Black, is a means by which the government can assure the public that its increasing powers are, indeed, "constitutional." And this, he concludes, has been the major historic function of judicial review.

Let Black illustrate the problem:

> The supreme risk (to the government) is that of disaffection and a feeling of outrage widely disseminated throughout the population, and loss of moral authority by the government as such, however long it may be propped up by force or inertia or the lack of an appealing and immediately available alternative. Almost everybody living under a government of limited powers, must sooner or later be subjected to some governmental action which as a matter of private opinion he regards as outside the power of government or positively forbidden to government. A man is drafted, though he finds nothing in the Constitution about being drafted.... A farmer is told how much wheat he can raise; he believes, and he discovers that some respectable lawyers believe with him, that the government has no more right to tell

him how much wheat he can grow than it has to tell his daughter whom she can marry. A man goes to the federal penitentiary for saying what he wants to, and he paces his cell reciting . . . "Congress shall make no laws abridging the freedom of speech". . . . A businessman is told what he can ask, and must ask, for buttermilk.

The danger is real enough that each of these people (and who is not of their number?) will confront the concept of governmental limitation with the reality (as he sees it) of the flagrant overstepping of actual limits, and draw the obvious conclusion as to the status of his government with respect to legitimacy.[21]

This danger is averted by the State's propounding the doctrine that *some one* agency must have the ultimate decision on constitutionality, and that this agency, in the last analysis, must be *part of* the federal government.[22] For while the seeming independence of the federal judiciary has played vital part in making its actions virtual Holy Writ for the bulk of the people, it is also and ever true that the judiciary is part and parcel of the government apparatus, and appointed by the executive and legislative branches. Black admits that this means that the State has set itself up as a judge in its own cause, thus violating a basic juridical principle for aiming at just decisions. He brusquely denies the possibility of any alternative.[23]

Black adds: "The problem, then, is to devise such governmental means of deciding as will (hopefully) reduce to a tolerable minimum the intensity of the objection that government is judge in its own cause. Having done this, you can only hope that this objection, *though theoretically still tenable* (italics mine), will practically lose enough of its force that the legitimating work of the deciding institution can win acceptance."[24]

In the last analysis, Black finds the achievement of justice and legitimacy from the State's perpetual judging of its own cause as "something of a miracle."[25]

Applying his thesis to the famous conflict between the Supreme Court and the New Deal, Professor Black keenly chides his fellow pro-New Deal colleagues for their shortsightedness in denouncing judicial obstruction:

> The standard version of the story of the New Deal and the Court, though accurate in its way, displaces the emphasis. . . . It concentrates on the difficulties; it almost forgets how the whole thing turned out. The upshot of the matter was (and this is what I like to emphasize) that after some twenty-four months of balking . . . the Supreme Court, without a single change in the law of its composition, or, indeed, in its actual manning, placed the affirmative stamp of legitimacy on the New Deal, and on the whole new conception of government in America.[26]

In this way, the Supreme Court was able to put the quietus on the large body of Americans who had had strong constitutional objections to the New Deal:

> Of course, not everyone was satisfied. The Bonnie Prince Charlie of constitutionally commanded laissez-faire still stirs the hearts of a few zealots in the Highlands of choleric unreality. But there is no longer any significant or dangerous public doubt as to the constitutional power of Congress to deal as it does with the national economy. We had no means, other than the Supreme Court, for imparting legitimacy to the New Deal.[27]

As Black recognizes, one major political theorist who recognized, and largely in advance, the glaring loophole in a constitutional limit on government of placing the ultimate interpreting power in the Supreme Court was John C. Calhoun. Calhoun was not content with the "miracle," but instead proceeded to a profound analysis of the constitutional problem. In his *Disquisition,* Calhoun demonstrated the inherent tendency of the State to break through the limits of such a constitution:

> A written constitution certainly has many and considerable advantages, but it is a great mistake to suppose that the mere insertion of provisions to restrict and limit the power of the government, without investing those for whose protection they are inserted with the means of enforcing their observance will be sufficient to prevent the major and dominant party from abusing its powers. Being the party in possession of the government, they will, from the same constitution of man which makes government necessary to protect society, be in favor of the powers granted by the constitution and opposed to the restrictions intended to limit them. . . The minor or weaker party, on the contrary, would take the opposite direction and regard them (the restrictions) as essential to their protection against the dominant party. . . . But where there are no means by which they could compel the major party to observe the restrictions, the only resort left them would be a strict construction of the constitution. . . . To this the major party would oppose a liberal construction. . . . It would be construction against construction —the one to contract and the other to enlarge the powers of the government to the utmost. But of what possible avail could the strict construction of the minor party be, against the liberal construction of the major, when the one would have all the power of the government to carry its construction into effect and the other be deprived of all means of enforcing its construction? In a contest so unequal, the result would not be doubtful. The party in favor of the

restrictions would be overpowered.... The end of the contest would be the subversion of the constitution... the restrictions would ultimately be annulled and the government be converted into one of unlimited powers.[28]

One of the few political scientists who appreciated Calhoun's analysis of the Constitution was Professor J. Allen Smith. Smith noted that the Constitution was designed with checks and balances to limit any one governmental power, and yet had then developed a Supreme Court with the monopoly of ultimate interpreting power. If the federal government was created to check invasions of individual liberty by the separate states, who was to check the federal power? Smith maintained that implicit in the check-and-balance idea of the Constitution was the concomitant view that no one branch of government may be conceded the ultimate power of interpretation: "It was assumed by the people that the new government could not be permitted to determine the limits of its own authority, since this would make it, and not the Constitution, supreme.[29]

The solution advanced by Calhoun (and seconded, in this century, by such writers as Smith) was, of course, the famous doctrine of the "concurrent majority." If any substantial minority interest in the country, specifically a state government, believed that the federal government was exceeding its powers and encroaching on that minority, the minority would have the right to veto this exercise of power as unconstitutional. Applied to state governments, this theory implied the right of "nullification" of a federal law or ruling within a state's jurisdiction.

In theory, the ensuing constitutional system would assure that the federal government check any state invasion of individual rights, while the states would check excessive federal power over the individual. And yet, while limitations would undoubtedly be more effective than at present, there are many difficulties and problems in the Calhoun solution. If, indeed, a subordinate interest should rightfully have a veto over matters concerning it, then why stop with the *states*? Why not place veto power in counties, cities, wards? Furthermore, interests are not only sectional, they are also occupational, social, etc. What of bakers, or taxi drivers, or any other occupation? Should *they* not be permitted a veto power over their own lives? This brings us to the important point that the nullification theory confines its checks to *agencies of government itself*. Let us not forget that federal and state governments, and their respective branches, are still States, are still guided by their own State interests rather than by the interests of the private citizens. What is to prevent the Calhoun system from working in reverse: with states tyrannizing over *their* citizens, and only vetoing the federal government when it tries to intervene to *stop* that state tyranny? Or for states to acquiesce in federal tyranny? What is to prevent federal and state governments from forming mutually profitable alliances for the joint exploitation of the citizenry? And even if the private occupational groupings were to be given some form of "functional" representation in government, what is to prevent them from using the State to gain subsidies and other special privileges for themselves, or from imposing compulsory cartels on their own members?

In short, Calhoun does not push his path-seeking theory on concurrence far enough: he does not push it down *to the individual* himself. If the individual, after all, is the one whose rights are to be protected, then a consistent theory of concurrence would imply veto power by every individual, i.e., some form of "unanimity principle." When Calhoun wrote that it should be "impossible to put or to keep it (the government) in action without the concurrent consent of all," he was, perhaps unwittingly, implying just such a conclusion.[30] But such speculation begins to take us away from our subject, for down this path lie political systems which could hardly be called "States" at all.[31] For one thing, just as the right of nullification for a state logically implies its right of secession, so a right of individual nullification would imply the right of any individual to "secede" from the State under which he lives.[32]

Thus, the State has invariably shown a striking talent for the expansion of its powers beyond any limits that might be imposed upon it. Since the State necessarily lives by the compulsory confiscation of private capital, and since its expansion necessarily involves ever-greater incursions on private individuals and private enterprise, we must assert that the State is profoundly and inherently *anti*-capitalist. In a sense, our position is the reverse of the Marxist *dictum* that the State is the "executive committee" of the ruling class — in the present day, supposedly the capitalists. Instead, the State — the organization of the political means — constitutes, and is the source of, the "ruling class" (rather, ruling *caste*), and is in permanent opposition to *genuinely* private capital. We may therefore say, with De Jouvenel:

> Only those who know nothing of any time but their own, who are completely in the dark as to the manner of Power's behaving through thousands of years, would regard these proceedings (nationalization, the income tax, etc.) as the fruit of a particular set of doctrines. They are in fact the normal manifestations of Power, and differ not at all in their nature from Henry VIII's confiscation of the monasteries. The same principle is at work; the hunger for authority, the thirst for resources; and in all of these operations the same characteristics are present, including the rapid elevation of the dividers of the spoils. Whether it is socialist or whether it is not, Power must always be at war with the capitalist authorities and despoil the capitalists of their accumulated wealth; in doing so it obeys the laws of its nature.[33]

What the State Fears

What the State fears above all, of course, is any fundamental threat to its own power and its own existence. The death of a State can come about in two major ways: (a) through conquest by another State, or (b) through revolutionary overthrow by its own subjects — in short, by war or revolution. War and revolution, as the two basic threats, invariably arouse in the State rulers their maxium efforts and maximum propaganda among the people. As stated above, any way must always be used to mobilize the people to come to the State's defense in the belief that they are defending themselves. The fallacy of that idea becomes evident when conscription is wielded against those who refuse to "defend" themselves and are therefore forced into joining the State's military band: needless to add, no "defense" is permitted them against this act of "their own" State.

In war, State power is pushed to its ultimate, and, under the slogans of "defense" and "emergency," it can impose a tyranny upon the public such as might be openly resisted in time of peace. War thus provides many benefits to a State, and indeed every modern war has brought to the warring peoples a permanent legacy of increased State burdens upon society. War, moreover, provides to a State tempting opportunities for conquest of land areas over which it may exercise its monopoly of force. Randolph Bourne was certainly correct when he wrote that "war is the health of the State," but to any particular State a war may spell either health or grave injury.[34]

We may test the hypothesis that the State is largely interested in protecting *itself* rather than its subjects by asking: which category of crimes does the State pursue and punish most intensely — those against private citizens or those against *itself*? The gravest crimes in the State's lexicon are almost invariably not invasions of private person or property, but dangers to its *own* contentment, e.g., treason, desertion of a soldier to the enemy, failure to register for the draft, subversion and subversive conspiracy, assassination of rulers, and such economic crimes against the State as counterfeiting its money, or evasion of its income tax. Or compare the degree of zeal devoted to pursuing the man who assaults a policeman, with the attention that the State pays to the assault of an ordinary citizen. Yet, curiously, the State's openly assigned priority to its own defense against the public strikes few people as inconsistent with its presumed *raison d' être*.[36]

How States Relate to One Another

Since the territorial area of the earth is divided among different States, inter-State relations must occupy much of a State's time and energy. The natural tendency of a State is to expand its power, and, externally, such expansion takes place by conquest of a territorial area. Unless a territory is stateless or uninhabited, any such expansion involves an inherent conflict of interest between one set of State rulers and another. Only one set of rulers can obtain a monopoly of coercion over any given territorial area at any one time; complete power over a territory by State X can only be obtained by the expulsion of State Y. War, while risky, will be an ever-present tendency of States, punctuated by periods of peace and by shifting alliances and coalitions between States.

We have seen that the "internal" or "domestic" attempt to limit the State, in the seventeenth through nineteenth centuries, reached its most notable form in constitutionalism. Its "external," or "foreign affairs," counterpart was the development of "international law," especially such forms as the "laws of war" and "neutrals' rights."[36] Parts of international law were originally purely private, growing out of the need of merchants and traders everywhere to protect their property and adjudicate disputes. Examples are admiralty law and the law merchant. But even the governmental rules emerged voluntarily, and were not imposed by any international super-State. The object of the "laws of war" was to limit inter-State destruction *to the State apparatus itself*, thereby preserving the innocent "civilian" public from the slaughter and devastation of war. The object of the development of neutrals' rights was to preserve private civilian international commerce, even with "enemy" countries, from seizure by one of the warring parties. The overriding aim, then, was to limit the extent of any war, and particularly to limit its destructive impact on the private citizens of the neutral, and even the warring, countries.

The jurist F.J.P. Veale charmingly describes such "civilized warfare" as it briefly flourished in fifteenth-century Italy:

> The rich burghers and merchants of medieval Italy were too busy making money and enjoying life to undertake the hardships and dangers of soldiering themselves. So they adopted the practice of hiring mercenaries to do their fighting for them, and, being thrifty, business-like folk, they dismissed these mercenaries immediately after their services could be dispensed with. Wars were, therefore, fought by armies hired for each campaign. . . . For the first time, soldiering became a reasonable and comparatively harmless profession. The generals of that period maneuvered against each other, often with consummate skill, but when one had won the advantage, his opponent generally either retreated or surrendered. It was a recognized rule that a town could only be sacked, if it offered resistance: immunity could always be purchased by paying a ransom. . . . As one natural consequence, no town ever resisted, it being

obvious that a government too week to defend its citizens had forfeited their allegiance. Civilians had little fear from the dangers of war which were the concern only of professional soldiers.[37]

The well-nigh absolute separation of the private civilian from the State's wars in eighteenth-century Europe is highlighted by Nef:

> Even postal communications were not successfully restricted for long in wartime. Letters circulated without censorship, with a freedom that astonishes the twentieth-century mind. . . . The subjects of two warring nations talked to each other if they met, and when they could not meet, corresponded, not as enemies but as friends. The modern notion hardly existed that . . . subjects of any enemy country are partly accountable for the belligerent acts of their rulers. Nor had the warring rulers any firm disposition to stop communications with subjects of the enemy. The old inquistorial practices of espionage in connection with religious worship and belief were disappearing, and no comparable inquisition in connection with political or economic communications was even contemplated. Passports were originally created to provide safe-conduct in time of war. During most of the eighteenth century it seldom occurred to Europeans to abandon their travels in a foreign country which their own was fighting.[38]
>
> And trade being increasingly recognized as beneficial to both parties, eighteenth-century warfare also countenanced a considerable amount of "trading with the enemy."[39]

How far States have transcended rules of civilized warfare in this century needs no elaboration here. In the modern era of total war combined with the technology of total destruction, the very idea of keeping war limited to the State apparati seems even more quaint and obsolete than the original Constitution of the United States.

When States are not at war, agreements are often necessary to keep frictions at a minimum. One doctrine that has gained curiously wide acceptance is the alleged "sanctity of treaties." This concept is treated as the counterpart of the "sanctity of contract." But a treaty and a genuine contract have nothing in common. A contract transfers, in a precise manner, titles to private property. Since a government does not, in any proper sense, "own" its territorial agea, any agreements that it concludes do not confer titles to property. If, for example, Mr. Jones sells or gives his land to Mr. Smith, Jones' heir cannot legitimately descend upon Smith's heir and claim the land as rightfully his. The property title has already been transferred. Old Jones' contract is automatically binding upon Young Jones, because the former had already transferred the property; Young Jones, therefore, has no property claim. Young Jones can only claim that which he has inherited from Old Jones, and Old Jones can only bequeath property which he still owns. But if, at a certain date, the government of, say, Ruritania, is coerced or even bribed by the government of Walldavia, it is absurd to claim that the governments or inhabitants of the two countries are forever barred from a claim to reunification of Ruritania on the grounds of the sanctity of a treaty. Neither the people nor the land of North-west Ruritania are *owned* by either of the two governments. As a corollary, one government can certainly not bind, by the dead hand of the past, a later government through treaty. A revolutionary government which overthrew the king of Ruritania could, similarly, hardly be called to account for the king's actions or debts, for a government is not, as is a child, a true "heir" to its predecessor's property.

History As a Race Between State Power and Social Power

Just as the two basic and mutually exclusive inter-relations between men are peaceful cooperation or coercive exploitation, production or predation, so the history of mankind, particularly its economic history, may be considered as a contest between these two principles. On the one hand, there is creative productivity, peaceful exchange and cooperation; on the other, coercive dictation and predation over those social relations. Albert Jay Nock happily termed these contesting forces: "social power" and "State power."[40] Social power is man's *power over nature*, his cooperative transformation of nature's resources and insight into nature's laws, for the benefit of all participating individuals. Social power is the power over nature, the living standards, achieved by men in mutual exchange. State power, as we have seen, is the coercive and parasitic seizure of this production — a draining of the fruits of society for the benefit of non-productive (actually *anti*-productive) rulers. While social power is over nature, State power is *power over man*. Through history, man's productive and creative forces have, time and again, carved out new ways of transforming nature for man's benefit. These have been the times when social power has spurted ahead of State power, and when the degree of state encroachment over society has considerably lessened. But always, after a greater or smaller time lag, the State has moved into these new areas, to cripple and confiscate social power once more.[41] If the seventeenth through the nineteenth centuries were, in many countries of the West, times of accelerating social power, and a corollary increase in freedom, peace, and material welfare, the twentieth century has been primarily an age in which State power has been catching up — with a consequent reversion to slavery, war and destruction.[42]

In this century, the human race faces once again the virulent reign of the State — of the State now armed with the fruits of man's creative powers, confiscated and perverted to its own aims. The last few centuries were times when men tried to place constitutional and other limits on the State, only to find that such limits, as with all other attempts, have failed. Of all the numerous forms that governments have taken over the centuries, of all the concepts and institutions that have been tried, none has succeeded in keeping the State in check. The problem of the State is evidently as far from solution as ever. Perhaps new paths of inquiry must be explored, if the successful, final solution of the State question is ever to be attained.[43]

NOTES

1. We cannot, in this paper, develop the many problems and fallacies of "democracy." Suffice it to say here that an individual's true agent or "representative" is always subject to that individual's orders, can be dismissed at any time, and cannot act contrary to the interests or wishes of his principal. Clearly, the "representative" in a democracy can never fulfill such agency functions, the only ones consonant with a libertarian society.

2. Social democrats often retort that democracy—majority choice of rulers— logically implies that the majority must leave certain freedoms to the minority, for the minority might one day become the majority. Apart from other flaws, this argument obviously does not hold where the minority cannot become the majority, e.g., when the minority is of a different racial or ethnic group from the majority.

3. "The friction or antagonism between the private and the public sphere was intensified from the first by the fact that . . . the State has been living on a revenue which was being produced in the private sphere for private purposes and had to be deflected from these purposes by political force. The theory which construes taxes on the analogy of club dues or of the purchase of the services of, say, a doctor only proves how far removed this part of the social sciences is from scientific habits of mind." Joseph A. Schumpeter, *Capitalism, Socialism, and Democracy* (New York: Harper and Bros., 1942), p. 198. Also see Murray N. Rothbard, "The Fallacy of the 'Public Sector,' " *New Individualist Review* (Summer 1961): 3 ff.

4. "There are two fundamentally opposed means whereby man, requiring sustenance, is impelled to obtain the necessary means for satisfying his desires. These are work and robbery, one's own labor and the forcible appropriation of the labor of others. . . . I propose in the following discussion to call one's own labor and the equivalent exchange of one's own labor for the labor of others, the 'economic means' for the satisfaction of needs, while the unrequited appropriation of the labor of others will be called the 'political means'. . . . The State is an organization of the political means. No State, therefore, can come into being until the economic means has created a definite number of objects for the satisfaction of needs, which objects may be taken away or appropriated by warlike robbery." Franz Oppenheimer, *The State* (New York: Vanguard Press, 1926), pp. 24-27.

5. Albert Jay Nock wrote vividly that "the State claims and exercises the monopoly of crime. . . . It forbids private murder, but itself organizes murder on a colossal scale. It punishes private theft, but itself lays unscrupulous hands on anything it wants, whether the property of citizen or of alien." Nock, *On Doing the Right Thing, and Other Essays* (New York: Harper, 1928), p. 143;

quoted in Jack Schwartzman, "Albert Jay Nock—A Superfluous Man," *Faith and Freedom* (December 1953): p.11.

6. "What, then, is the State as a sociological concept? The State, completely in its genesis . . . is a social institution, forced by a victorious group of men on a defeated group, with the sole purpose of regulating the dominion of the victorious group of men on a defeated group, and securing itself against revolt from within and attacks from abroad. Teleologically, this dominion had no other purpose than the economic exploitation of the vanquished by the victors." Oppenheimer, *op. cit.*, p. 15. And De Jouvenel has written: "the State is in essence the result of the successes achieved by a band of brigands who superimpose themselves on small, distinct societies. . . ." Bertrand De Jouvenel, *On Power* (New York: Viking Press, 1949), pp.100-1.

7. On the crucial distinction between "caste", a group with privileges or burdens coercively granted or imposed by the State, and the Marxian concept of "class" in society, see Ludwig von Mises, *Theory and History* (New Haven: Yale University Press, 1957), pp.122 ff.

8. Such acceptance does not, of course, imply that the State rule has become "voluntary"; for even if the majority support be active and eager, this support is not unanimous by every individual. That every government, no matter how "dictatorial" over individuals, must secure such support has been demonstrated by such acute political theorists as Etienne de la Boétie, David Hume, and Ludwig von Mises. Thus, cf. David Hume, "Of the First Principles of Government", in *Essays, Literary, Moral and Political* (London: Ward, Locke, and Taylor, n.d.), p.23; Etienne de la Boétie, *Anti-Dictator* (New York: Columbia University Press, 1942), pp.8-9; Ludwig von Mises, *Human Action* (New Haven: Yale University Press, 1949), pp.188 ff. For more on the contribution to the analysis of the State by La Boétie, see Oscar Jaszi and John D. Lewis, *Against the Tyrant* (Glencoe, Ill.: The Free Press, 1957), pp.55-57.

9. ". . . whenever a ruler makes himself dictator . . . all those who are corrupted by burning ambition or extraordinary avarice, these gather around him and support him in order to have a share in the booty and to constitute themselves petty chiefs under the big tyrant." La Boétie, op. cit., pp.43-44.

10. This by no means implies that all intellectuals ally themselves with the State. On aspects of the alliance of intellectuals and the State, cf. Bertrand de Jouvenel, "The Attitude of the Intellectuals to the Market Society," *The Owl* (January, 1951), pp.19-27; de Jouvenel, "The Treatment of Capitalism by Continental Intellectuals," in F. A. Hayek, ed., *Capitalism and the Historians* (Chicago: University of Chicago Press, 1954) pp.93-123, reprinted in George B. De Hussar, *The Intellectuals* (Glencoe, Ill.: The Free Press, 1960), pp.385-399; and Schumpeter, op. cit., pp.143-55.

11. Joseph Needham, "Review of Karl A. Wittfogel, *Oriental Despotism,*" *Science and Society* (1958): 65. Needham also writes that "the successive (Chinese) emperors were served in all ages by a great company of profoundly human and disinterested scholars." Ibid., p.61. Wittfogel notes the Confucian doctrine that the glory of the ruling class rested on its gentleman-scholar-bureaucrat officials, destined to be professional rulers dictating to the mass of the populace. Karl A. Wittfogel, *Oriental Despotism* (New Haven: Yale University Press, 1957), pp.320-21 and passim. For an attitude contrasting to Needham's, cf. John Lukacs, "Intellectual Class or Intellectual Profession?" in de Huzzar, op. cit., pp.521-22.

12. "Strategists insist that their occupation deserves the dignity of 'the academic counterpart of the military profession.'" Jeanne Riha, "The War Plotters," *Liberation* (August 1961): 13. Also see Marcus Raskin, "The Megadeath Intellectuals," *New York Review of Books* (November 14, 1963): 6-7.

13. Thus, the historian Conyers Read, in his presidential address, advocated the suppression of historical fact in the service of "democratic" and national values. Read proclaimed that "total was, whether it is hot or cold, enlists everyone and calls upon everyone to play his part. The historian is not freer from this obligation than the physicist..." Read, "The Social Responsibilities of the Historian," *American Historical Review* (1951): 283 ff. For a critique of Read and other aspects of court history, see Howard K. Beale, "The Professional Historian: His Theory and Practice," The *Pacific Historical Review* (August 1953): 227-55. Also cf. Herbert Butterfield, "Official History: Its Pitfalls and Criteria," in *History and Human Relations* (New York: Macmillan, 1952), pp.182-224; and Harry Elmer Barnes, *The Court Historians Versus Revisionism* (n.d.), pp. 2 ff.

14. Cf. Wittfogel, op. cit., pp.87-100. On the contrasting roles of religion vis-á-vis the State in ancient China and Japan, see Norman Jacobs, *The Origin of Modern Capitalism and Eastern Asia* (Hong Kong: Hong Kong University Press, 1958), pp.161-94.

15. "The essential reason for obedience is that it has become a habit of the species ... Power is for us a fact of nature. From the earliest days of recorded history it has always presided over human destinies . . . the authorities which ruled (societies) in former times did not disappear without bequeathing to their successors their privilege nor without leaving in men's minds imprints which are cumulative in their effect. The succession of governments which, in the course of centuries, rule the same society may be looked on as one underlying government which takes on continuous accretions." De Jouvenel, *On Power, op. cit.*, p.22.

16. On such uses of the religion of China, see Jacobs, passim.

17. "All [government] can see in an original idea is potential change, and hence an invasion of its prerogatives. The most dangerous man, to any government, is the man who is able to think things out for himself, without regard to the prevailing superstitions and taboos. Almost inevitably he comes to the conclusion that the government he lives under is dishonest, insane and intolerable, and so, if he is romantic, he tries to change it. And even if he is not romantic personally he is very apt to spread discontent among those who are." H. L. Mencken, *A Mencken Crestomathy* (New York: Knopf, 1949), p.145.

18. Ibid., pp.146-47.

19. De Jouvenel, *On Power, pp.27 ff.*

20. Charles L. Black, Jr., *The People and the Court* (New York: Macmillan, 1960), pp.35 ff.

21. Ibid., pp.42-43.

22. "The prime and most necessary function of the (supreme) Court has been that of *validation,* not that of invalidation. What a government of limited powers needs, at the beginning and forever, is some means of satisfying the people that it has taken all steps humanly possible to stay within its powers. This is the condition of its legitimacy, and its legitimacy, in the long run, is the condition of its life. And the Court, through its history, has acted as the legitimation of the government." Ibid., p.52.

23.	To Black, this "solution," while paradoxical, is blithely self-evident: "the final power of the State . . . must stop where the law stops it. And who shall set the limit, and who shall enforce the stopping, against the mightiest power? Why, the State itself, of course, through its judges and its laws. Who controls the temperate? Who teaches the wise?" Ibid., pp.32-33. And: "Where the questions concern governmental power in a sovereign nation, it is not possible to select an umpire who is outside government. Every national government, so long as it is a government, must have the final say on its own power." Ibid., pp.48-49.

24.	Ibid., p.49.

25.	This ascription of the miraculous to government is reminiscent of James Burnham's justification of government by mysticism and irrationality: "In ancient times, before the illusions of science had corrupted traditional wisdom, the founders of cities were known to be gods or demigods. . . . Neither the source nor the justification of government can be put in wholly rational terms . . . why should I accept the hereditary or democratic or any other principle of legitimacy? Why should a principle justify the rule of that man over me? . . . I accept the principle, well . . . because I do, because that is the way it is and has been." James Burnham, *Congress and the American Tradition* (Chicago: Regnery, 1959), pp.3-8. But what if one does *not* accept the principle? What will "the way" be then?

26.	Black, op. cit., p.64.

27.	Ibid., p.65.

28.	John C. Calhoun, *A Disquisition on Government* (New York: Liberal Arts Press, 1953), pp.25-27. Also cf. Rothbard, "Conservatism and Freedom: A Libertarian Comment," *Modern Age* (Spring 1961): 219.

29.	J. Allen Smith, *The Growth and Decadence of Constitutional Government* (New York: Holt, 1930), p.88. Smith added: "It was obvious that where a provision of the Constitution was designed to limit the powers of a governmental organ, it could be effectively nullified if its interpretation and enforcement were left to the authorities it was designed to restrain. Clearly, common sense required that no organ of the government should be able to determine its own powers." Ibid., p.87. Clearly, common sense and "miracles" dictate very different views of government.

30.	Calhoun, op. cit., pp.20-21.

31.	In recent years, the unanimity principle has experienced a hightly diluted revival, particularly in the writings of Professor James Buchanan. Injecting unanimity into the present situation, however, and applying it only to *changes* in the *status quo* and not to existing laws, can only result in another transformation of a limiting concept into a rubber stamp for the State. If the unanimity principle is to be applied only to *changes* in laws and edicts, the nature of the initial "point of origin" then makes all the difference. Cf. James Buchanan and Gordon Tullock, *The Calculus of Consent* (Ann Arbor: University of Michigan Press, 1962), passim.

32.	Cf. Herbert Spencer, "The Right to Ignore the State," in *Social Statics* (New York: Appleton, 1890), pp.229-39.

33.	De Jouvenel, *On Power*, p.171.

34.	We have seen that essential to the State is support by the intellectuals, and this includes support against their two acute threats. Thus, on the role of American intellectuals in America's entry into World War I, see Randolph Bourne, "The

War and the Intellectuals," in *The History of a Literary Radical and Other Papers* (New York: Russell, 1956), pp.205-22. As Bourne states, a common device of intellectuals in winning support for State actions, is to channel any discussion within the limits of basic State policy, and to discourage any fundamental or total critique of this basic framework.

35. As Mencken puts it in his inimitable fashion: "This gang ['the exploiters constituting the government'] is well-nigh immune to punishment. Its worst extortions, even when they are baldly for private profit, carry no certain penalties under our laws. Since the first days of the Republic, less than a few dozen of its members have been impeached, and only a few obscure understrappers have ever been put into prison. The number of men sitting at Atlanta and Leavenworth for revolting against the extortions of the government is always ten times as great as the number of government officials condemned for oppressing the taxpayers to their own gain." Mecken, op., cit., pp.147-48. For a vivid and entertaining description of the lack of protection for the individual against incursion of his liberty by his "protectors," see H. L. Mencken, "The Nature of Liberty," in *Prejudices: A Selection* (New York: Vintage Books, 1958), pp. 138-43.

36. This is to be distinguished from modern international law, with its stress on maximizing the extent of war through such concepts as "collective security."

37. F. J. P. Veale, *Advance to Barbarism* (Appleton, Wisc.: Nelson, 1953), p.63. Similarly, Professor Nef writes, of the War of Don Carlos, waged in Italy between France, Spain, and Sardinia against Austria, in the eighteenth century: "at the siege of Milan by the allies and several weeks later at Parma . . . the rival armies met in a fierce battle outside the town. In neither place were the sympathies of the inhabitants seriously moved by one side or the other. their only fear was that the troops of either army should get within the gates and pillage. The fear proved groundless. At Parma the citizens ran up to the town walls to watch the battle in the open country beyond . . . " John U. Nef., *War and Human Progress* (Cambridge: Harvard University Press, 1950), p.158. Also cf. Hoffman Nickerson, *Can We Limit War?* (New York: Stoke, 1934).

38. Nef, op. cit., p.162.

39. Ibid., p.161. On advocacy of trading with the enemy by leaders of the American Revolution, see Joseph Dorfman, *The Economic Mind in American Civilization* (New York: Viking Press, 1946), I, 210-11.

40. On the concepts of State power and social power, see Nock, *Our Enemy the State* (Caldwell, Idaho: Caxton, 1946). Also see Nock, *Memoirs of a Superfluous Man* (New York: Harpers, 1943), and Frank Chodorov, *The Rise and Fall of Society* (New York: Devin-Adair, 1959).

41. Amidst the flux of expansion or contraction, the State always makes sure that it seizes and retains certain crucial "command posts" of the economy and society. Among these command posts are a monopoly of violence, monopoly of the ultimate judicial power, the channels of communication and transportation (post office roads, rivers, air routes), irrigated water in Oriental despotisms, and education—to mold the opinions of its future citizens. In the modern economy, *money* is the critical command post.

42. This parasitic process of "catching up" has been almost openly proclaimed by Karl Marx, who conceded that socialism must be established through seizure of capital *previously accumulated* under capitalism.

43. Certainly, one indispensable ingredient of such a solution must be the sundering of the alliance of intellectual and State, through the creation of

centers of intellectual inquiry and education, which will be independent of State power. Christopher Dawson notes that the great intellectual movements of the Renaissance and the Enlightenment were achieved by working outside of, and sometimes against, the entrenched universities. These academies of the new ideas were established by independent patrons. See Christopher Dawson, *The Crisis of Western Education* (New York: Sheed and Ward, 1961).

10.
Why Be Libertarian?

Murray N. Rothbard

Why be libertarian, anyway? By this we mean: what's the point of the whole thing? Why engage in a deep and lifelong commitment for the principle and goal of individual liberty? For such a commitment, in our largely unfree world, means inevitably a radical disagreement with, and alienation from, the *status quo,* an alienation which equally inevitably imposes many sacrifices in money and prestige. When life is short and the moment of victory far in the future, why go through all this?

Incredibly, we have found among the increasing number of libertarians in this country many people who come to a libertarian commitment from one or another extremely narrow and personal point of view. Many are irresistibly attracted to liberty as an intellectual system or as an aesthetic goal, but liberty remains for them a purely intellectual and parlor game, totally divorced from what they consider the "real" activities of their daily lives. Others are motivated to remain libertarians solely from their anticipation of their own personal financial profit. Realizing that a free market would provide greater opportunities for able, independent men to reap entrepreneurial profits, they become and remain libertarians solely to find larger opportunities for business profit. While it is true that opportunities for profit will be far greater and more widespread in a free market and a free society, placing one's *primary* emphasis on this motivation for being a libertarian can only be considered grotesque. For in the often tortuous, difficult and gruelling path that must be trod before liberty can be achieved, the libertarian's opportunity for personal profit will far more often be negative than abundant.

The consequence of the narrow and myopic vision of both the gamester and the would-be profitmaker is that neither group has the slightest interest in the work of building a libertarian movement. And yet it is only through building such a movement that liberty can be achieved. Ideas, especially radical ideas, do not advance in the world in and by themselves, as it were in a vacuum; they can only be advanced by *people,* and therefore the advancement and development of such people—and therefore of a "movement"—becomes a prime task for the libertarian who is really serious about advancing his goals.

Turning from these men of narrow vision, we must also see that utilitarianism, the common ground of free-market economists, is unsatisfactory for developing a flourishing libertarian movement. While it is true and valuable to know that a free market would bring far greater abundance and a healthier economy to everyone, rich and poor alike, a critical problem is whether this knowledge is enough to bring many people to lifelong dedication to liberty. In short, how many people will man the barricades and endure the many sacrifices that a consistent dedication to liberty entails, merely so that umpteen percent more people will have better bathtubs? Will they not rather settle for an easy life and forget the bathtubs? Ultimately, then, utilitarian economics, while indispensable in the developed structure of libertarian thought and action, is almost as unsatisfactory a basic groundwork for the Movement as those opportunists who simply seek a short-range profit.

It is our lifelong view that a flourishing libertarian movement, a lifelong dedication to liberty, can only be grounded on a passion for justice. Here must the mainspring of our movement drive, the armor that will sustain us in all storms ahead; not the search for a quick buck the playing of intellectual games, or the cool calculation of general economic goals. And to have a passion for justice one must have a *theory* of what justice and injustice are— in short, a set of ethical principles of justice and injustice which cannot be provided by utilitarian economics. It is because we see the world reeking with injustices pile one on another to the very heavens that we are impelled to do all that we can do to seek a world in which these and other injustices will be eradicated. Other traditional radical goals—such as the "abolition of poverty" are, in contrast to this one, truly Utopian; for man, simply by exerting his will, cannot abolish poverty. Poverty can only be abolished through the operation of certain economic factors, notably the investment of savings in capital, which can operate only by transforming nature over a long period of time. In short, man's will here is severely limited by the workings of, to use an old-fashioned but still valid term, natural law. But *injustices* are deeds that are inflicted by one set of men on another; they are precisely the actions of men, and hence they and their elimination are subject to man's instantaneous will.

Let us take an example: England's centuries-long occupation and brutal oppression of the Irish people. Now if, in 1900, we had looked at the state of Ireland, and we had considered the poverty of the Irish people, we would have had to say: that poverty could be improved by the English getting out and removing their land monopolies, but that the elimination of poverty in Ireland, under the best of conditions, would have to take time and would be subject to the workings of economic law. But the goal of ending English oppression—that *could* have been done by the instantaneous action of men's will: by the English simply deciding to pull out of the country. The fact that of course such decisions do not take place instantaneously is not the point; the point is that the very failure is an injustice that has been decided upon and imposed by the perpetrators of injustice: in this case the English government. In the field of justice, man's will is all: men *can* move mountains, if only enough men so decide. A passion for instantaneous justice—in short, a radical passion—is therefore not Utopian, as would be a desire for the instant elimination of poverty or the instant transformation of everyone into a concert pianist. For instant justice *could* be achieved if enough people so willed.

A true passion for justice, then, must be *radical*—in short, it must at least *wish* to attain its goals radically and instantaneously. Leonard E. Read, President of the Foundation for Economic Education, expressed this radical spirit twenty years ago when he wrote a pamphlet, *I'd Push the Button.* The problem was what to do about the network of wage and price controls then imposed on the economy by the Office of Price Administration. Most economic liberals were timidly or "realistically" one or another form of gradual or staggered decontrols; at that point Mr. Read took an unequivocal and radical stand on principle: "If there were a button on this rostrum," he began his address, "the pressing of which would release all wage and price controls instantaneously, I would put my finger on it and push!"[1] The true test then, of the radical spirit, is the button-pushing test: if we could push the button for the instantaneous abolition of unjust invasions of liberty, would we do it? If we would *not* do it, we could scarcely call ourselves libertarians, and most of us would only do it if primarily guided by a passion for justice.

The genuine libertarian, then, is, in all senses of the word, an "abolitionist", he would, if he could, abolish instantaneously all invasions of liberty; whether it be, in the original coining of the term, slavery, or it be the manifold other instances of State oppression. He would, in the words of another libertarian in a similar connection: "blister my thumb pushing that button!" The libertarian must perforce be a "button-pusher and an "abolitionist." Powered by justice, he cannot be moved by amoral utilitarian pleas that justice cannot come about until the criminals are "compensated." Thus, when in the early nineteenth century, the great abolitionist movement arose, voices of moderation promptly appeared counselling that it would only be fair to abolish slavery if the slave masters were financially compensated for their loss. In short, after centuries of oppression and exploitation, the slave masters were supposed to be further rewarded by a handsome sum mulcted by force from the mass of innocent taxpayers! The most apt comment on this proposal was made by the English Philosophical Radical Benjamin Pearson, who remarked that "he had thought it was the slaves who should have been compensated;" clearly, such compensation could only have come from the slaveholders themselves.[2]

Anti-libertarians, and anti-radicals generally, characteristically make the point that such "abolitionism" is "unrealistic;" by making the charge that they are hopelessly confusing the desired goal with a strategic estimate of the probable outcome. In framing principle, it is of the utmost importance *not* to mix in strategic estimates with the forging of desired goals. *First,* one must formulate one's goals, which in this case would be the instant abolition of slavery or whatever other statist oppression we are considering. And we must first frame these goals without considering the probability of obtaining them. The libertarian goals are "realistic" in the sense that they *could* be achieved if enough people agreed on their desirability, and that if achieved they would bring about a far better world. The "realism" of the goal can only be challenged by a critique of the goal itself, not in the problem of how to attain it. Then, *after* we have decided on the goal, we can have the entirely different strategic question of how to obtain that goal as rapidly as possible, how to build a movement to attain it, etc. Thus, William Lloyd Garrison was not being "unrealistic" when, in the 1830s, he raised the glorious standard of the immediate emancipation of the slaves. His goal was the proper one; and his strategic realism came in the fact that he did not *expect* his goal to be quickly reached. Or, as Garrison himself distinguished: "Urge immediate abolition as earnestly as we may, it will, alas! be gradual abolition in the end. We never said that slavery would be overthrown in a single blow; that it ought to be, we shall always contend."[3]

Actually, in the realm of the strategic, raising the banner of pure and radical principle is generally the fastest way of arriving at radical goals. For if the pure goal is not brought to force, there will never be any momentum developed for driving toward it. Slavery would never had been abolished at all if the abolitionists had not raised the hue and cry thirty years earlier; and, as things come to pass, the abolition was at virtually a single blow rather than gradual or compensated.[4] In his famous editorial that launched The *Liberator* at the beginning of 1831, William Lloyd Garrison repented his previous adoption of the doctrine of gradual abolition: "I seize this opportunity to make a full and unequivocal recantation, and thus publicly to ask the pardon of my God, of my country, and of my brethren, the poor slaves, for having uttered a sentiment so full of timidity, injustice and absurdity." Upon being reproached for the habitual severity and heat of his language, Garrison retorted: "I have need to be all on fire, for I have mountains of ice about me to melt." It is this spirit that must mark the man truly dedicated to the cause of liberty.[5]

Notes

1. Leonard E. Read, *I'd Push the Button* (New York: McGuire, 1946), p.3.
2. William D. Gramp, *The Manchester School of Economics* (Stanford, California: Stanford University Press, 1960), p.59.
3. Quoted in William H. and Jane H. Pease, eds., *The Antislavery Argument* (Indianapolis: Bobbs-Merrill, 1965), p.xxxv.
4. At the conclusion of a brilliant philosophical critique of the charge of "unrealism" and its confusion of the good and currently probable, Professor Philbrook declares: "Only one type of serious defense of a policy is open to an economist or anyone else: he must maintain that the policy is good. True 'realism' is the same thing men have always meant by wisdom: to decide the immediate in the light of the ultimate." Clarence Philbrook, "Realism in Policy Espousal," *American Economic Review* (December 1953): 859.
5. For the quotes from Garrison, see Louis Ruchames, ed., *The Abolitionists* (New York: Capricorn Books, 1964), p.31, and Fawn M. Brodie, "Who Defends the Abolitionists?" in Martin Duberman, ed., *The Antislavery Vanguard* (Princeton: Princeton University Press, 1965), p.67. The Duberman work is a storehouse of valuable material, including refutations of the common effort by those committed to the status quo to engage in psychological smearing of radicals in general and abolitionists in particular. See especially Martin Duberman, "The Northern Response to Slavery," in Ibid., pp.406-13.

PART V.

DOING ANARCHISM

Much anarchist writing, past and present, has a "Russian" character. The sense of urgency in anarchist propaganda derives from the anarchists' constant desire to ask the question posed by so many 19th century Russian radicals: what is to be done? The moral, sometimes moralizing, tone of anarchist pamphlets and broadsides, usually composed swiftly and on the spot, reflects the deeply held conviction that society is in the midst of a moral and political emergency. As Peter Kropotkin put it in an 1873 essay: "activists cannot . . . calmly bear the injustice surrounding them, and they inevitably strive to enter the battle against this injustice, in whatever form it appears."

The "feel" of anarchist defiance can be sensed through reading the weekly and monthly radical press. Rarely are full-scale analytic essays to be found; rather, a burst of passionate protest combined with a detailed indictment of authority is experienced. Anarchist writing cannot be equated with other forms of agitation. A mass meeting, a strike, a fast or a confrontation in the streets has an energy and "reality" which can never be replicated in words or proclamations.

But, as Emma Goldman, one of the best anarchist agitators and a unequalled platform speaker, once said: "oral propaganda is at best but a means of shaking people from their lethargy; it leaves no lasting impression." Anarchist writing, still passionate and engaged, has longer and deeper effects.

Most of the pieces included in this section come from unique sources. The British anarchist paper, *Freedom,* has published continuously since 1886, when Kropotkin settled in England. During the 1960s and early 1970s its pages were filled with the best anarchist prose, written by Americans and Europeans as well as by British anarchists. The Freedom Press, since 1961, issued a monthly journal, *Anarchy,* which published longer and more sustained anarchist analyses. For an immersion into the concerns and activities of anarchists during the recent revival, there are not any better sources.

The diversity of anarchists becomes apparent in reading the articles in *Freedom* and *Anarchy.* Individualists and collectivists are represented. Arguments about tactical issues abound; for example, over the uses and abuses of violence and terrorism. The anarchist writers often present a penetrating critique not only of the state but of other radicals as well. Marxists and other leftists are not spared. At all times, the old question — what is to be done? — is asked and, often temporarily, answered. The anarchist beacon shines into unexpected places. For example, after the New York City power blackout of 1965 an anarchist analyses the spontaneous generation of mutual aid and claims that such altruism proves the anarchist contention that man is inherently sociable and freedom-loving.

Though anarchists are often engaged in the problems of daily life, they are also seekers after a better future. The utopian element in anarchism is undeniable. The search for a just social order through non-violent means is charted, at the end of this section, by George Lakey, the American Quaker pacifist and author, in "Manifesto for a Nonviolent Revolution." Lakey's analysis would not meet the approval of all anarchists. Most likely no analysis would. But his decentralism, his ecological awareness, his moral partisanship and his emphasis upon human interdependence speak clearly in the anarchist idiom.

11.
Anarchists—And Proud of It

George Cairncross

ANARCHIST! The very word conjures up visions of dangerous men in black cloaks with bombs, wild acts of uncontrolled violence, bloody insurrection, rape, looting and the complete breakdown of imposed law and order; causing the mass of the people to shy away as though it were some incurable disease. Yet how wrong is the popular image. It is true that acts of violence have been committed in the name of Anarchism, it is true that wild statements have been issued. Yet who are the greatest perpetrators of crimes against humanity on untold scales? It is governments who drop tons of explosives on defenseless people, it is governments who have been responsible for the massacres of countless millions throughout history. Governments who supposedly represent law and order and all that is supposed to be peace loving in society.

Contrary to popular belief, the majority of anarchists, though certainly not pacifists, are neither inclined to violence, mostly being peace-loving persons who want no more than to live in a truly free society, where men treat men with respect for human dignity. Why does the popular image remain so vivid? Its basic cause lies in the fact that the anarchist movement is dedicated to the overthrow of government in any form, thus promoting the idea that it is a philosophy based on lawlessness. Nothing could be further from the truth. Anarchism is possibly the most highly organised form of society in that, in such a society, every man would live in mutual harmony with his fellow man in a situation where individuals would live in voluntary co-operation with other individuals. It holds to the self-evident truth that, until man is responsible for and in control of his own life, then society's ills will not be cured. It is the only political movement that has this idea to offer. All other political movements are based on the assumption that a government must exist to organize society, thus anarchists are opposed to any form of political grouping that has the formation of another government as its basic aim. The abolition of the state and all its apparatus is one of the basic and original tenets of Anarchism.

In our present society and that of the communist world, we find that the whole economy is geared to profit-making. Everything that is produced must make a profit whether that item is necessary or not. Thus the quality of life is immediately reduced to the level of sordid materialism. The anarchist wants a society in which production is geared to need and not to profit. A society in which the population itself controls its own means of production. For centuries the working man has been robbed of the reward of his own labor. It is a hard fact of life that a very small minority control the destiny of the majority purely through economic dominance. yet the very ones who produce that wealth are the ones who are exploited. Thus the capitalist, whether state or private, joins with the government in a hatred of the anarchist movement.

Popular Myths

The popular image of the bomb-throwing anarchist is that which is perpetuated by the National Press. Every outrage that cannot be explained is immediately tagged with the label "Anarchy." Every breakdown of law and order threatens to produce Anarchy and thus the myth goes on. Yet these very papers which do so much to spread anti-anarchist propaganda are themselves owned by those who have a vested interest in keeping society as it is. Little wonder that they attack and libel Anarchism at every possible moment. To them, the success of such a movement would mean, in real terms, a loss of the privileges which they do so much to retain.

Our democratic society is supposedly based on equality, yet thousands live in conditions which would bring down the wrath of the RSPCA if applied in a zoo. Many are homeless. Yet huge office blocks stand empty for lack of prospective tenants due to high rents; empty blocks whose value increases daily to provide huge profits for land speculators. Many people actually owning more than one house, government ministers, and often socialist at that, not least amongst them. The anarchist wants an end to this situation, he wants to see all property held in common through such means as Tenants' Associations or perhaps Federated Estates, where all the housing belongs to all those within the Federation and not any individual or council. A society in which everyone is well housed in conditions amenable to human dignity, where people no longer have to squat to find a roof, where exorbitant rents, or indeed any rents are non-existent, where a man can tend his garden and watch his children grow up in health and happiness in conditions fit for all human beings, and not the privileged few.

Education?

One of the chief propagators of our myth of democracy is the educational system which is founded on class distinctions and prejudice. The whole system is repressive and is used as a cog in the machinery of conformity, where children are moulded through various nefarious methods, into accepting a society of exploitation. An obnoxious examination system creams off those of academic achievement to serve as the management of society, whilst the remainder are left as fodder to serve them. A system controlled by discipline and competition designed to repress the individual into a conforming mass. Obviously an education system which exists for the enlightenment of the individual cannot be allowed to prosper, as any form of government just cannot afford to allow a society of free thinking, enlightened individuals to grow, as such a society would spell doom for that government. Anarchism insists that education, particularly higher education, is a right of all and not a privilege for those of the monied classes or for those with establishment-backed qualifications. The educational system should be used to propagate the ideals of freedom and self-reliance which in turn would lead to and reinforce a free society. But no government in existence would allow this to happen as it would imply self-extinction because people would soon realize that government was completely unnecessary.

How is it that governments can continue to blithely mislead the people they govern so easily? The governments effectively control all the means of communication and media from newspapers, as already mentioned, to TV and radio. The people are only told what the government wishes them to know. Our so-called free press and communications system is only free in that it must comply within certain insidious boundaries. The only alternative is the free presses of the anarchist movement and the like and their propagation. But prosecution on some pretext or another, will always lie just around the corner if ever these alternative news media become too much of a menace to the established way of things. It is not for nothing that the government exercises a strict monoply of the radio and TV service.

The government has a strong ally in the support of a large middle-class which aspires to attain a status of sober respectability, where false values are inflated beyond all reason and a philosophy of trying to be somebody is all-important. Anarchism to the vast proportion of these people is complete anathema, creating visions of everything they fear. They are too afraid of losing what little they have, not realizing that their small loss is everybody's greater gain, and gaily supporting a corrupt system that gives them little handouts to keep them satisfied.

The State Is Evil

Meanwhile the anarchist revolution continues. Each year the movement finds more adherents. revolution takes place not only on the streets but also in the mind, although it may well be on the streets where the actual revolution is decided. To become a conscious anarchist is in itself a revolution in thought and philosophy, it is a philosophy that once grasped makes nonsense of any other political thought. Anarchism is varied, each anarchist is an individual and they often differ on many aspects of the philosophy, but all are agreed on the important and basic issues, chief amongst them that the state is evil and has to be dismantled. As more people become more individually conscious, it is reasonable that more people will join the movement. The spread of its literature over recent years has brought the movement to more people. Recent events, such as blocking motorways, have brought more people into conflict with the authorities than at previous times. It is true that many of these people are not anarchists, but the actions they have taken are the direct action methods advocated by anarchists, which in itself is a step forward. Once people reject leaders, then leaders will cease to exist. The decline in figures at the polling booths at recent elections seems to indicate that more people have had more than enough of politicians, a trend which if it increases could have serious connotations for any government.

None of us know what the future anarchist society will be like, we can only point to various aspects of it that we would like to see. There has never been an actual anarchist society to use as a pointer, apart from areas of Spain during the Spanish Civil War where much was achieved in a very short time. One thing is certain. In an anarchist society everyone will be anarchists. Anarchists first and carpenters, builders, poets, etc., second. It will be a society where people do the work they like best and are best fitted for. Work will be pleasure, not a labor of toil for some unspecified reason other than to make a meagre living to continue what one is doing for another week, and to produce profit for some privileged group. Work is the stuff of life, but work of a creative nature, not employment which is what passes for work in our repressive society. It will be a society in which everyone is useful to themselves and others. It will be based on harmony, voluntary co-operation, peace, happiness and freedom of the individual both politically and economically, social sciences which will cease to exist.

12.

Why Terror Is Not an Anarchist Means

M. C.

When a terrorist act is done, the concerted expressions of horror and unqualified condemnation from all quarters are likely to cause in anarchists a dulling of the shock, a seeking for excuses and justifications in reaction against the presentation of the total blamelessness of the victim and the absolute lack of grounds for the violent act of the perpetrators. It is a reaction we should guard against; not to let our judgement, moral and political, be betrayed by sympathy for the doers who, being hunted by the police then become victims, or by the need for solidarity should they turn out to be anarchists or others opposing the unjust arrangement of society which we are opposed to.

This is of course evoked by the bomb attack on the home of the Minister for Employment. We don't yet know who thought it up or carried it out, or how serious they intended the result to be, or how they hoped it would affect the man concerned, the present Government, the members of the trades unions, the general public, and the "Revolutionary Left" in general and the anarchists in particular, if the bombers are anarchists.

The police appear to have made anarchists their first guess; the *Evening Standard* (14.1.71) described an unnamed anarchist 'leader' in his twenties

163

strongly suspected of plotting other bomb attacks in London, and said detectives believed the date—the day of protests against the Govenment's Industrial Relations Bill—significant, but *not* the choice of the Employment Minister (my italics), and filled most of the rest of the story with details of attacks on the Spanish Embassy and bombs placed on Iberia Airlines' planes last year in London, Paris and elsewhere (that in London was found before exploding, I do not remember whether any at Continental airports exploded). The report also referred to the questioning of a man and the holding for forty-eight hours of a girl-friend of his after the Iberian Airlines incident, which coincide with a report from Anarchist Black Cross printed in FREEDOM (20.6.70) of police attentions paid to equally unnamed anarchists.

What we can try to assess, and for this it does not matter whether or not this particular act was the work of anarchists, is the value of this kind of act in attaining the ends desired by anarchists, its rightness or wrongness in any context, and whether it fits any interpretation of anarchist philosophy.

Because I am setting out from the premise of the specific attack on Robert Carr's home, let me state that I am not suggesting it was intended, or thought possible, to cause death or injury to any occupant of the house. But any attack on property using explosives is liable to cause injury to a living being if anyone is there, and death if the amount of explosive used or damage caused is great enough; therefore it becomes a terrorist act against people. And, although anarchists have a lesser record of killings and terrorism than adherents of other political creeds, and immeasurably less than any government one might select unless one could exclude the smallest republics and newest-established states, assassination and terror are historical ingredients of anarchist activity. Is it essential to anarchism, or alien, or irrelevant?

As a Means to an Anarchist End

Plainly, it is not essential to anarchism, since the essence of anarchism is that it is possible and desirable for human beings to provide each other with all the physical and cultural necessities of life, no individual or group having power to deprive others of these and thereby forcing by fear and necessity those others to provide them with an unjust share and by a form of work and style of life they have not chosen. The obstacles to this are the absence of a lively enough sense of injustice, a passion for freedom and awareness of possible alternatives on the part of the subjugated, and the all-too-lively consciousness of the value of privilege and the sweets of power on the part of those who hold wealth and wield power. How are these obstacles to be removed?

Of the two, the first seems to be the heaviest to shift. It is not even possible to guess its weight. The fact that about half the adults in this country voted Conservative seven months ago, the fact that the proliferation of rebellious and protesting movements of the last few years have been peopled by a minority of the population, and that even the plight of the squatting homeless did not stir to compassionate help or self-help any numbers of those in the same need or in a position to help, all combine to give an oppressive feeling that the weight is leaden and dead. Yet this is belied by the amount of mental breakdown, the unremitting industrial unrest and unofficial strikes, and the critical attitude to some of the present Government's approaches and the sympathetic coverage given to minority movements and their self-protective organisations in the "establishment" press; all indications that all is not for the best in the best of all possible worlds. The effect of continued activity and withholding of consent and cooperation by the disparate dissenting elements must be to modify the pattern the present Government seeks to impose. We have yet to see what the only widespread and powerful section, the trade unions, will do when the provisions of the Industrial Relations Bill are imposed by law; to make any change more fundamental than putting the Labour Party back in the next election, requires, if the change is to be in a libertarian direction, a vastly greater spreading and acceptance of libertarian ideas and programs among the people who appear to be unsatisfied but unaware of alternatives. The sporadic bomb attack seems to have little connection with or effect on this. In the absence of mass support, when it would be unnecessary, it is merely a demonstration that somebody, somewhere has stronger feelings on the subject or a larger portion of hate in his make-up than other people, which seems to qualify the act as irrelevant.

Terrorism Right or Wrong?

Is it a proper or successful means of removing the second obstacle, the desire to hold on to power? This is more problematical, as there are no recorded instances to my knowledge of despots resigning or secret police desisting from torture because they were asked. In Czarist Russia despotism was tempered with dynamite for many years but the revolution did not occur until external factors changed circumstances and a very large number of people were possessed of similar or related ideas and desires. In Cyprus British soldiers went in terror and eventually the British left, but the majority of the predominant population wanted independence. It is not proven that the terrorism was a necessary expression of the will. The killing of the police chief which resulted in the persecution of the six Basques who recently aroused the sympathy of nearly the whole world can be clearly understood as a rational act, if he was in fact killed by a political opponent, because this was a particular man who was persecuting and torturing people who had no hope of his removal by any other means. Maybe this kind of terror does work by imposing some restraints on the behavior of successors. What thirty years of guerilla action and attentats have not done is to remove the hated *regime*. Even supported by the most courageous strikes by quite numerous sections of workers such as the Asturian miners. Why? Is it only because the regime has sufficiently large regiments of armed soldiers and police? Or is it in addition that a large section of the population is doing well enough under the regime, having regained their pre-revolutionary status, and an even larger section had enough of blood and terror during the revolution and civil war, and would rather settle for a degree of "liberalization" and "prosperity," drawing nearer to that of the rest of capitalist Europe?

And Spain has a heritage of anarchist thought and aspiration (as well as aristocracy and political communism). "Accepted" as anarchism has become here in recent years, and real as the anarchistic rejection of our tawdry material society has been on the part of so many young people, we are a long way from an understanding and acceptance of anarchist ideas by a large enough number of people to make them work. We know the workers could run their factories and produce food and decide what are our real needs without a Minister of Employment; the task is to pass on our confidence to them—adding shareholders and bosses to the list. Surely no one imagines that even if one Minister could be terrified out of his job there wouldn't be another to follow, or that the Government would fold up the Ministry and their Industrial Relations Bill under anything less than massive, concerted pressure from the workers and trade union members affected by it. The official protest of the Trades Union Congress and the Labour Party might have rung a bit hollow on Tuesday, January 12; the marches and rallies of several thousand trade unionists held in working hours and in rejection of the TUC advice may have had more reality but indicated that really determined militancy was not evident throughout the millions of trade unionists of the country; the bombs directed at the Minister of Employment seem to demonstrate only that a few people have left the world and taken up residence in a bad television film.

13

Black Anarchy in New York

H. W. Morton

On November 9, 1965, shortly after 5 P. M., at the Sir Adam Beck No. 2 Distribution Plant at Queenston, Ontario, a little four-inch-square electric relay took it upon itself to illuminate a number of anarchist principles. In doing so it selected a method which in and of itself is anarchistic: direct action. Certainly it was far and away the all-time world's champion blown fuse, in that it blacked out 80,000 square miles of the U. S. and Canada, leaving about thirty million people in total darkness. This was an electronic *Attentat*—and on a scale one is hard put to overlook. Yet through the darkness, like a beacon, shone such anarchist truisms as decentralism, mutual aid, direct action, and the like.

On the individual level we found people acting so beautifully that even Kropotkin might have been impressed. Naturally there were instances of people acting like capitalists—selling candles at $1.50 (11/-) each, charging up to fifty dollars (£18) for a taxicab ride, gouging pounds of flesh for flashlights, etc. However, as *Newsweek* (11.11.65) pointed out, the "real keynote" was struck by a Negro cleaning woman who led a Manhattan career girl up ten flights of stairs to her apartment, gave her two candles, and then waved away a five dollar tip. "It's O.K., honey, tonight everyone helps everyone."

Somehow it seemed as if the whole crazy city had read *Mutual Aid* the night before. Remember, New York is notorious for being this planet's biggest cut-throat rat-race. Furthermore it was not only the town longest hit by the blackout, it was also by far the most vulnerable area. The blackout struck in the middle of the rush hour, hence there were probably 800,000 people stranded in subways and/or subway trains when the power failed. Another 100,000 were stranded waiting for commuter trains. Thousands more were trapped on the upper floors of skyscrapers. Undoubtedly the worst off were the hundreds upon hundreds who were trapped in elevators. Yet there was no panic! Everyone was calm and patient. Neither was there any crime wave or looting—of course for this we have to thank the fact that the police were kept too busy with the rescue work and other emergency activities. It was estimated that $100 million (£36 million) was lost in revenue. Certainly one of the hardest hit business interests was the New York Police Force. Therefore I have to give them credit for coming through in the pinch, although several cops of the twenty-forth Precinct failed to appreciate my concern when I walked by in the darkness explaining to my companions in stentorian tones of commiseration that the poor guys were beating their brains out and "all on straight salary for a change". (The Twenty-forth Precinct specializes in shooting fourteen-year-old Puerto Ricans.) All in all some 5,000 off-duty policemen were called up to join the 7,000 already on duty. The Fire Department brought in their off-duty personnel also.

Yet although these men all performed beautifully at tasks of supererogation, the real stars of the show were the people. Piecing together various contemporary reports (cf. *Life, Time, Newsweek, U. S. News and World Report, New York Times*, and *Post*) many people actually enjoyed the situation. There was drinking, singing, and necking in the streets. Parties of Frenchmen and U. S. Southerners stuck on the eighty-sixth floor observation roof of the Empire State building chorused each other alternately with "La Marseillaise" and "Dixie," though how many hours they kept this up was not reported. A church sexton handed out free votive candles—even God lost money—while a blind woman led passengers out of a subway station. One nineteen-year-old girl said: "They should do this more often; everyone is much more friendly. It's a big community again— people have time to stop and talk."

Volunteers directed traffic with flashlights and handkerchiefs. Home transistor radio listeners pitched in to report on developments and incidents so that helpful information could be shared with everyone else. Drivers shared cars with pedestrians. People quietly queued up at pay telephones, restaurants and saloons. They gathered on street corners to listen together to portable radios. One shoeshine boy completed his task by his customer's matches.

There was incident upon incident: the whole situation was fantastic. *Time* later mentioned a "crisis-born spirit of camaraderie and exhilaration" and a very prevalent view was that "it brought out the best in people." Of course the fact is that our authoritarian social system cannot help but bring out the worst in people, hence its removal, and bear in mind that the state had well-nigh disappeared, merely allowed them to act as free human beings. After the blackout various politicians, officials, and kindred parasites delivered encomia to the splendid behaviour of their "fellow citizens," never realizing how completely superfluous this splendid behavior proved their own functions to be. Somehow or other the ruling class is incredibly fortunate: people often see through individual leaders, but rarely through leadership *per se*. One woman said that she had received "so many singular courtesies" during the power failure that her "faith in mankind had been restored." Tragically she didn't say she had received so many that her faith in authority based on force had been lost. Yet that power failure was nearly a power vacuum: we were closer to a true anarchy for those few hours than anything most of us will ever be lucky enough to see again. Incidentally, the Statue of Liberty, because it draws its current from New Jersey, remained lighted throughout the blackout. For the first time in her life "that old bitch" here, was almost telling the truth.

To some extent there was a Dionysian quality reminding one observer of VE or VJ Day "when everybody loved everybody." Another commented on "the same air of revelry that often accompanies a heavy snowstorm." A lawyer in his thirty-second-floor office said, "first we just sat around having drinks. Now we're having a seance to communicate with the spirit that caused this bliss. We could have walked down, but it's about 600 steps, so we're staying, and we're all getting to know each other." Someone else confessed: "It's a big pain and all, but I sort of hate to see it over. Tomorrow will be just another working day." But the following day, and several thereafer, there was a continued elan as people exchanged anecdotes of courage, kindness and adventure. There was something to talk about and we were impressed by one another. Cab drivers, waitresses, secretaries, truck drivers, grandmothers, teenagers, lawyers and bellhops interviewed by the *New York Post* all remarked on the "calm, cheerful, considerate attitude the majority of people maintained." Yet, by way of contrast, there were the inevitable exceptions: an elderly woman paused diffidently trying to cross Fifth Avenue and instantly acquired a four-man escort; meanwhile a panhandler continued to intercept passers-by, concentrating on his own version of mutual aid.

Naturally, the transportation hang-up, vertical as well as horizontal, posed the biggest problem. There were 600 stalled subway trains containing some 800,000 commuters, hundreds of whom were trapped for as long as eight hours, and sixty of whom stayed on for over fourteen hours. Furthermore in New York City there were hundreds of elevators stalled between floors in apartment and office buildings, which meant several thousand additional victims requiring rescue.

Nonetheless even in these untoward circumstances the leitmotif was solidarity. As one housewife put it after a six-hour stay in a subway car, "I never thought New Yorkers could be that way. I mean everybody seemed to lose his anger." In one car a passenger was leading people in Calypso songs and handclapping. Couples were dancing when the conductor arrived to lead them out of an emergency stairwell to the surface. The universal report was that there was no panic. As one woman said, "Our conductor would pop in every once in a while and ask 'How's everybody?', and everybody would say 'Fine'. We really weren't worried at all." Some good samaritans left one train and walked along catwalks to find emergency exits. But then, instead of going safely home, they returned to lead their fellow passengers out. On other trains, talented victims entertained their fellows: in one car there was a tenor; in another, an harmonica player; but the *piece de resistance* was a bagpiper. Many cars featured communal singing. The most common thing, however, was light conversation interspersed with sardonic humour. Men gave up their seats to ladies who frequently offered them back. In one car a woman fainted but word was transmitted from person to person until someone was located with smelling salts. Thereupon these were passed back up hand to hand.

Those who had long waits on their hands exchanged whatever comestibles they had in pockets or pocket books: peanuts, wild cherry drops, assorted goodies, or even antacid tablets. One group shared a combination of doughnuts and salami which had been sliced with a nailfile. At midnight the Transit Authority sent in food to those who had't yet been extricated. The food-bearers were greeted with a tableau of people sleeping with their arms draped about other people who had been complete strangers five hours previously, and nary a cop in sight!!!

Meanwhile those unfortunates trapped in elevators, ninety-six in the Empire State Building alone, were enduring their plight with the same sort of equanimity exhibited in the subways. Here too the people entertained one another with improvised games, such as the unlikeliest partners for stalled elevators. This was readily won with the combination of Defense Secretary MacNamara and a draft card burner. In an elevator in the RCA Building one gentleman gave a course in Yoga positions. When firemen chopped their way into one immobilised car, they asked: "Are there any pregnant women in here?" They were answered: "We've hardly met!"

Surface transportation reflected the same of co-operation and solidarity. Even though the Transit Authority was running 3,500 of its 4,000 buses it could barely make a dent. Therefore countless thousands hiked home across the bridges or up the avenues. Others waited calmly in line at the bus stops, with no pushing or shoving. Nobody seemed to take advantage of the confusion to avoid paying fares, although some passengers couldn't have paid if they'd tried—they were riding on the rear bumpers. Bus drivers themselves were inordinately accommodating, calling out each stop as they approached. In New York this comes under the heading of *mirabile dictu*. At the same time, dozens of private automobiles were loading up at every intersection with absolute strangers,

On the other hand all was not sweetness and light during the darkness. Some people capitalized on others' vulnerability. About 100 windows were smashed in, and about forty-one looters were arrested (none in blue uniform). All told perhaps a dozen stores were looted, which is absolutely negligible in a city of over eight million. Even Police Commissioner Broderick conceded that both the crime and the casualty rates for the night were far below normal. (So who needs him?) One enterprising gunman held up a rare-coin dealer by the flickering light of the shop's only candle— a touching vignette to be sure. There were a total of sixty-five persons arrested for burglary, larceny, or felonious assault—as opposed to a typical 380 for a comparable sixteen hour stretch. The sum total of arrests for all crimes was only twenty-five percent of what it would have been during an ordinary night. There were very few shoplifters reported, which is nothing short of miraculous considering the open-house policy of the department stores (cf. infra). Moreover there were only thirty-three vehicle accidents involving injuries, and forty-four involving property damage— and this in the world's largest city, completely devoid of traffic lights! There was one bus that ploughed into a crowd of people in Queens knocking down thirty-eight person, some of whom were seriously injured. The driver, evidently in complete consternation, jumped out and fled. Yet his actions must be viewed in context with the fact that his was only one out of 3,500 buses operating under these weird conditions.

Somewhere along the line a subway motorman found himself facing charges of rape for flashing a badge and leading a young lady to the ostensible safety of his room. Yet later in court he contended that on any number of previous occasions he had led the same young lady to a similar lair to similarly lay her, so who knows. . . .Progressing from debatably to unquestionably false alarms, we find that the Fire Department reported a much higher incidence than usual: 227 rather than the typical fifty. this is totally irreconcilable with anarchist theory, so I've decided not to mention it at all.

Easily offsetting those relatively few human beings who acted like capitalists were the many capitalists who acted like human beings. For example many department stores flirted with free access for the evening. Macy's played host to an estimated 5,000 customers and employees for the night—inviting one and all to make themselves comfortable, and serving them all coffee, sandwiches, cookies, and candy. Needless to say, the furniture department on the ninth floor was the best spot for comfort. Meanwhile, across the street, Gimbels was featuring a guitar-playing salesman for the entertainment of its customer/guests. One of the songs they reportedly joined in on was the old wartime favorite, "When the Lights Go on Again All Over the World." Evidently no one was familiar with "We Shall Overcome." Lord and Taylor's turned over its entire second floor to customers for the duration of the blackout, while B. Altman's turned over its first. Altman's incidentally, has its own power generator, so there was some light by which to enjoy the caviare and specially blended coffee which were among the imported delicacies provided by the gourmet department and served to shoppers and employees. Five hundred stayed there overnight, evidently being unable to tear themselves away from all that caviare. Bloomingdales turned over its home furnishings department to strandees— one woman slept on an $800 (£287) sofa—and then capped it off by having its staff serve breakfast to everyone the next morning. Fina Company had a combination sales meeting and dinner scheduled for that evening, but they catered it to customers instead. Bonwit Teller chartered two buses to get its employees home, and suggested that they hold hands leaving the store so that none would get lost. Indicative of the prevailing mood was the fact that the employees danced out of the store together because "someone thought it would be fun." Meanwhile forty people were bedded down for the night in the showroom of the Simmons Mattress Co.

The city's hotels came through in grand style. The Commodore set up 150 cots in a banquet room. Both the Roosevelt and the Algonquin switched elderly guests and those with heart conditions to the lower floors. At the Stanhope the manager gave up his own room, and an assistant manager carried a crippled woman up the sixteenth floor. On arrival, she said, "Now I'd like a glass of water," so he procured one. At the Statler Hilton two bellmen carried a crippled guest to the seventh floor, but it was not reported what his needs were on arrival. The Americana passed out blankets and pillows to the 200 occupants of its plush lobby—most of the other hotels merely provided their lobbies as free space. The Sheraton-Atlantic, whose lobby was occupied by some 2,000 people, considered the evening somewhat less than a total loss, because as one manager pointed out, "The bar is doing a land-office business." That hotel's report seemed typical: ninety-nine percent of the people were "terrific" but a few guests tried to sublet their rooms at double the rate.

Unfortunately, utopian free access was much less prevalent in food than it was in shelter. Nevertheless one meat market in Brooklyn donated a whole pig to a neighbouring convent thereby providing roast pork snacks to everybody for blocks around. Two numerically named restaurants, 21 and Four Seasons, adopted a policy dangerously akin to "from each according to his ability; to each according to his need." The 21 passed out steak sandwiches and free drinks without limit, while Four Seasons ladled out free soup. Fully to appreciate the enormity of this, reflect on the following: in 1960, when prices persumably were lower, an acquaintance of mine told me that two friends of his went to Four Seasons for luncheon. Including drinks and tip it cost them nearly sixty dollars (over £21) while the band played "Nearer my Veblen to Thee." My wife and I didn't happen to go there that night so we missed out on the free soup, but we did enjoy knishes by candlelight at our expense in a nearby delicatessen. Many other restaurants, although they didn't give away food, stayed open all night to provide free shelter.

Most downtown offices close at five P. M. and were empty when the blackout struck. Those still occupied did whatever they could. Revlon, for example, gave its girls couches in the executive offices and then told them to take the next day off. One of their secretaries, stuck on the twenty-seventh floor, ate crabmeat and graham cracker sandwiches, and described her experience with a wistful: "I had a great time." Whether she was alluding the crabmeat or the couches was not made clear.

All sorts of institutions opened their doors, or in some instances dropped their gangways, as a free public service during the emergency. Final estimates included well over 400 people who had been put up for the night in staterooms of ships in port when the lights went out. Armories were thrown open to all comers, while railroad stations, airlines terminals, and churches sheltered countless thousands.

The Thirty-Forth Street Armory alone accommodated 1,500 refugees, offering wooden chairs and what illumination could be furnished from the headlights of a few jeeps parked in the middle of the drill floor. For some unexplained reason no cots were available. Naturally Rockefeller had immediately called out the National Guard, which is always a good safe ploy for masking gubernatorial inutility. According to the *New York Post* the Guardsmen were armed with rifles "unloaded but impressive." To complete the farce they wore packs containing ponchos and gas masks, perhaps out of fear that someone would fart. The Guard's major contribution seems to have been scouring the area around Thiry-Fourth Street and Park Avenue until 1:30 a.m.—a full eight hours after the attentat—at which point they finally came up with coffee and French bread for the beseiged. Compare this forlorn, dilatory effort on the part of the military to the ingenuity of the prostitutes in their quest for bread. *Life* magazine pointed out that these ladies "were among the first to procure flashlights," indicating that the yen is still mightier than the sword.

At the Central Commercial High School, a double session school, the second session runs from 12:30 to 5:50 p.m. Thus there were 1,000 students being subjected to obfuscation when the blackout struck. Some 400 of these left during the course of the evening as parents arrived to pick them up, but the school officials kept the other 600 in the classrooms all night. These joked, sang, and later put their heads on their desks and slept—readily taking the crisis in stride. Of course they were nowhere near as comfortable as the lucky ones who spend the night cardled in luxurious barber chairs, but they were infinitely better off than the hundreds who sought sanctuary in St. Patrick's Cathedral. These were huddled in the pews without even a hair shirt for warmth, and worst of all, no bogs. Msgr. McGovern later confessed, "We've been sending people over to the New Western Hotel for eighty years," which tends to confirm something many of us have long suspected: God's up shit creek.

Of far more serious import was the situation in hospitals. Here, too, people improvised brilliantly in the emergency. At Bellevue a delicate cornea transplant was under way when the lights went out, but was successfully completed by battery-operated floodlights. At St. John's, under similar conditions, emergency surgery was peformed on two people whose spleen had been ruptured in the previously mentioned bus accident. In another hospital a five-hour craniotomy was performed by makeshift light. Final reports indicated at least five dozen babies delivered by candle or otherwise. One man died tragically in the emergency room at Flushing Hospital. He had been in an automobile accident prior to the blackout and was already under surgery when the lights went out. Only two other deaths in New York City were attributed directly to the blackout: one man suffered a heart attack from climbing ten flights of stairs, and a second fell down a stairway and struck his head. Injuries, of course, were much more common: at the emergency ward of Bellevue along, 145 patients were treated for blackout injuries—broken arms or legs from falls, car accident victims, and some heart cases. Police, firemen, and volunteers rushed dry ice to the city's hospitals to keep stored blood from spoiling, whereas a distress call from St. Vincent's brought forth thirty volunteers from a Greenwhich Village coffee house to hand-pump iron lungs.

Although New York offered perhaps the most spectacular, and in view of its well-deserved reputation for ruthless competition, the most unexpected examples of mutual aid, the same pattern was repeated everywhere throughout the blacked-out area. It was solidarity, ingenuity, lack of hysteria, consideration, etc., and little or no government. In Toronto, Ontario, businessmen directed traffic, and in the process unsnarled the city's all-time record traffic jam. Among other things all the street-cars and trolley buses had stopped dead. In Albany, New York, teenagers with transistor radios went from house to house advising residents to turn off electric appliances. In Burlington, Vermont, 200 people hurried with flashlights to the local hospital in answer to a radio plea which later turned out to be a prank. In Springfield, Vermont, a barber finished trimming a customer's hair by the headlights a motorist aimed in his front window. All over the stricken territory civilians patrolled areas, directed traffic, and maintained order. Included among all these civilian volunteers would have to be the contingent of Boston gendarmes who rushed out the Policemen's Ball dressed in tuxedos. Devoid of badge, uniform and gun these were on identical footing with the students from Boston University who also pitched in.

Incident after incident offered irrefutable proof that society can function without the implicit threats of force and violence which constitute the state. There was probably more freedom from law, however temporary, in that blacked-out 80,000-mile area than there has been at any time since it was originally stolen from murdered and/or defrauded Indians. And it yielded compelling evidence of anarchist theories. As Kropotkin once stated: "We are not afraid to say 'Do what you will, act as you will' because we are persuaded that the great majority of mankind, in proportion to their degree of enlightenment, and the completeness with which they free themselves from existing fetters, will behave and act always in a direction useful to society."

Such then might be the blackout's confirmation of Kropotkin. What reinforcement does it offer Bakunin? Actually a good deal, but I'll cite only one case—a frequently distorted quotation which Max Nettlau once described as "a clarion call for revolution in the widest sense." Written in 1842, some twenty years before Bakunin became an anarchist, in fact before he could even be considered a conscious revolutionary, it appeared at the conclusion of an article entitled "Reaction in Germany," under the pseudonym Jules Elysard: "The urge to destroy is a creative urge." Bakunin's detractors, both in and out of the anarchist movement, invariably swoop down like vultures on that line. However Bakuninists might suffer less dismay (and, let's face it, embarrassment) if they viewed it in context with a heartwarming article which appeared in the Financial Section of the *New York Post* the day after the blackout: "Without power, Computers Died and Wall Street Stopped."

On the other hand, if the blackout provided all sorts of verification for decentralists, anarchists, Kropotniks and Bakuninists, what comfort did it offer to pacifists? The answer is damn little. As both James Wechsler (*New York Post*) and Brad Lyttle (*Peace News*) pointed out, the same sort of unfathomable but infallible electronic technology which blacked out thirty million of us temporarily is exactly what we're relying on to prevent an accidental World War III blacking out three billion of us permanently!

Small solace to me is the fact that the whole god-damned Pentagon will come down as local fall-out: my urge to destroy is not quite that creative. What with the hot line conked out, and the blithe "asurance" from the First Regional Army Air Defence Commander that despite the blackout "all of the Army's missile sites on the Eastern Coasts are operative," it was obviously a case of genocide continued as usual. Bring on the Dark Ages!

The final object lesson the blackout? The predictable, virtually automatic, responses of various members of society when confronted by crisis: soldiers fall back on their weapons; clergymen fall back on their prayers; doctors fall back on their antibiotics; bureaucrats fall back on their desks; and politicians fall back on their asses. But people fall back on one another, and in that fact must remain all the hopes, however minimal, for the survival of the human race.

14.

A New Consciousness and Its Polemics

John O'Connor

A dilemma which is often written about and discussed, and presents itself to every type of social revolutionary, is: Whether, to improve the quality of life, you attempt to change the social structure and wait for public awareness to adapt to the new context. Or do you produce polemics aimed at bringing about the change of consciousness first, so that it will come into conflict with and destroy the old order of society?

Overwhelmingly, I think, it's this last course of action which is being tried by those involved in revolutionary social propaganda at the moment. The counter-culture and underground (and the rest of the political left is following them in this) are stressing self exploration, with its ecstasies and insights, through art, drugs, sex and music, which is seen as the preliminary to a time when a "new consciousness" has tasted so much freedom that it will demand the overthrow of a repressive social order.

Improved living standards and increased leisure have given us the social revolutionary who has lost faith in better housing and nutrition, and has turned his attentions to what he sees as the deeper psychological and emotional sickness of a society that has been able to achieve these first essentials. Inevitably though, he has brough the same style of bullying exhortation to meet this new situation that once proved so suitable in demanding higher wages from intransigent employers. The polemicist who might have been hammering away trying to rouse the workers to revolt, in a less favourable economic context, now attacks their emotional and sexual conditioning with the enthusiasm and disregard for complexity which would almost certainly be required in the drastic reorganization of industry. Since it's one thing to tamper with somebody's delicate feelings concerning a factory or two that they own, perhaps even to the extent of burning them to the ground, and another altogether to advise somebody, for political reasons, to take a mind-changing drug or tell him with whom he should be going to bed and what, for the sake of the peace movement or the greater social good, he ought to be doing when he gets there, it's a shift of balance in this kind of rhetoric which has important implications in itself, regardless of whether it is being used by an establishment or anti-establishment figure at this time.

If a king or czar and his family, or a prime minister and his cabinet, are shot to remove the head of a social order which has been oppressing the main body of a people, it might be unfair to the individuals involved but it is likely to be politically necessary.

If, on the other hand, the politician turns his attention to the consciousness of the main body itself, and if he happens to discover that the Rule of Reason is tyrannizing the Western consciousness, repressing the palpitating mass of emotions and individual intuitions underneath, we can't expect a revolt against the tyrant Linear Logic to end in a nice fair situation in which it is allowed to live quietly among the reinstated mob of disparate emotions. Once moving inexorably in its chosen direction against the announced oppressor, the centuries of injustice which have been perpetuated in the Western mind, can only be revenged for him when it ends in a destruction of the tyrant.

This is a characteristic of the active political consciousness and it has its important uses. Since I'm subject to attacks of crusading zeal myself, I've also discovered its drawbacks. The most enjoyable aspect of the rhetorical drive is its singularity of direction and manipulation of bias. It can't be used to reveal truth however, which has more to do with the balance itself. On the social and material level, truth isn't too important: a little injustice is what the tyrant has coming to him. But if, as has happened, polemics is used to uphold various partisan stances along the spectrum of mental and emotional attitudes, it can only help to fragment a public consciousness which should contain all these elements. Guillotining a few landowners and bourgeois might come to seem a very insignificant event, if in our case the freakout philosopher, the militant artist, the millionaire musician, the anti-rational American academic and the acid salesman or metaphysician, succeed in decapitating the consciousness of a whole people.

Ecstasies and Insights

If people are horribly repressed then a little exhortation to an all-inclusive sexual, political and mystical experience — with revolution seen as the orgasm of society and experience of the divine presence as copulation with god — might be quite a good thing. But a time could come (and it already has come among those most exposed to this rhetoric) when the bias of the New Consciousness has pushed so far in one direction that people are as tremulously and determinedly ecstatic as they were once scrupulously and determinedly repressed. Whether this would be an improvement on the condition, whether it would be more revolutionary or just noisier, is best found out by looking in at its birth in the Melting Pot of consciousness. If what we find has little to do with the inert body of the larger social context, we can rely on the mechanisms of fashion, politics and capitalism to spread it evenly sooner or later.

I take it for granted, unfortunately, that peoples' feelings can be reorientated by means of propaganda. If there happened to be a country which had a large number of obsolete but demanding patriots on its hands, would it be possible, depending upon that country's economic development and the extent of its imperialistic ambitions, to turn it all upside down until it had a large number of shameless masturbators and just a few furtive patriots? It would be difficult to prove even if we could find an example of this phenomena, because the actors in such a drama would all believe that they had chosen what they wanted to be regardless of economic development.

If anybody wanted to point out that free people would be neither flagwavers or cockwavers, or join together to make films of themselves involved in either activity, then he should leave polemics alone. The practical issues, the choice having been presented to us, to make love or to make war, people are going to want to leap around a little bit whatever their individual choice, and polemics is concerned with the realities as they present themselves.

Gnomes, Hobbits and Little Furry Animals

A characteristic of acid fairyland that revolutionaries find encouraging is a noticeable sensitivity to any form of authority among its inhabitants. Policemen loom onto the horizon like malignant alien beings and even a ticket collector can assume the proportions of a formidable barrier to freedom. I started to look for the Exit in an art gallery at the height of a trip one time, calmly enough at first, but the shuddering impression passed through me that I had circled the same impassive attendant five times and that if I passed him again, he must (and here the voice becomes conspiratorial) notice . . . something . . . ODD!

He didn't of course, but it's an incident that illustrates the fact that the sensitivity to every form of authority, the whole place swarming with police spies and the group paranoia which this feeling can induce, is because of an increased vulnerability to anything that could rate as a jarring incident. I imagine, and some value acid for this insight, that it reproduces the extreme sensitivity of a child at the stage when park-keepers, schoolmasters and parents are mysteriously in league with each other.

This will definitely involve a revolt against externally imposed authority, but is a long way from the revolutionary awareness which deliberately hardens itself to tackle that authority. Acid awareness can become a squeamishness, a rancid sensitivity, to which anything as harsh as an idea or project, needs must learn a great deal of pussyfooting and dissembling (sotto voce) if it isn't to tread on some horribly swollen susceptibility and cause a sudden scurrying for cover. The acid metaphysician or freakout specialist can point out that this vulnerability is a temporary state best passed among comfortably undemanding fellow freaks, and that a knowledge of brutalizing authority so gained can then be used to oppose its existence. This can happen, but I've known others who have been broken by the experience and turned into trembly furry people whom I only see now on their rare and talkative week-end holidays from the madhouse. It isn't acid itself which has brought this about. It is an overwhelming awareness of the unpleasantness of their condition, perhaps the human condition, which hasn't surrounded itself with any of the means of support before stepping into this awareness.

Some say that they would like to enter acid reality completely and not step out and begin to use it. In the communes I've been to, or in one of the large houses I usually end up in, full of the people called "heads" I suppose, one of the most striking characteristics which seems as yet inseparable from an awareness of arbitrary human authority in the world, is what might be called a Revolt against the Obvious. The intolerable authority of a clock which indicates an unfavourable hour or a statement that contains an ominous linear truth, are equally the enemies of people seeking the unique and personal view of existence. Bakunin's statement in which he told us that he would only bow to the authority of men "when it is imposed upon me by my own reason", has a peculiarly reactionary tone to it in this context. Why, when every book that has ever been written or any possible thought that man can think, is already contained within oneself, bother to take into account any of these intrusive external realities?

A Groovy New Model Citizen

The utilitarian and functional stuff of life is going to be in very short supply in the near future, and if people aren't able to find the meaning of existence in self exploration and various forms of play activity, there will be no place for them. By no means all people will be dissatisfied with this arrangement and we ought to ask ourselves, what temperament, perhaps better adapted to the offered possibilities, might welcome a replacement of the grey utilitarian modes of being with opportunities and outlets for multi-coloured self display. Would we find such a person enthusiastically in the forefront of revolutionary social propaganda at the moment? In keeping with the shifted bias of polemics, he would be stressing the need for a change of consciousness and an internal revolution. (Politics proper wouldn't appeal to him in any case.) His hope that when the troglodyte worker and his enslaved woman have become benign brothers and sisters, there would be a revolution against government, might be a cover for what are essentially subjective views on the ideal mode of existence, but is probably quite genuine in its way.

Fun City or the Pleasure Dome would have no place for the functioning capacity of man, only the gratifications of self display and the wonders of sheer Being would be left to him. The person who is producing propaganda towards this end at the moment however, does have a function in our society, which helps to conceal even from himself the true nature of the world he is helping into existence. The skirmishings with authority, the company of people who are more freaky or original than the mass of humanity, even calling a few people strights or pigs I suppose, help to intensify a life which would become noticeably limp if it was allowed to sink gratefully into its espoused ideal. Guevara isn't really a suitable person to compare with our own polemicists, but he too was geared to the utilitarian outlets for his energies, and whether or not he helped to bring it into existence, he couldn't have lived in a society which didn't offer him similar opportunity to express himself.

The social propagandist, often a rich one, who is creating the microcosmic Pleasure Dome, puts forward the theory that when this ideal engulfs the whole of society, to which end he spreads his message, and people have become undemanding and playful fun-lovers and destroyed the last vestiges of the authoritarian elements in the mind, then the outer embodiment of these impulses, the state machine, will disappear. If you doubted whether this would happen in real life, he might say that when everybody had turned into the recommended groovy citizen there wouldn't be anybody left to run the state machine. If you were still taking deep breaths and shuffling your feet round, you might here the final argument.

In any case, he can add, government wouldn't be able to allow people to be like this, so that the more we spread the new consciousness, the sooner there will be an explosion against a repressive social order.

These are the three arguments which can be used to support a change in consciousness in theory. Allowing that the brothers and sisters, who are the subject of revolutionary polemics that with this end in view, had a sincere dislike of control over their lives, they would be unlikely to do much about it. The human qualities being urged onto them by this propaganda, might create a nice person who didn't want to control others himself, but he would be very vulnerable to the manipulations of those who did want power over others. The state might one day need as many groovy citizens as can be indoctrinated into being satisfied with the pleasures of just existing, drinking in a beautiful universe in an Eternal Present unhampered by the exigencies of the utilitarian. (The howls of boredom would come too late to change anything.) Whether a government would be able to provide an air or a country worth breathing in, is a point of conflict which has forced many to believe that they are revolutionaries opposed to the "idea" of state control, rather than the means of control which are used and the environment which is created at this stage in the development of capitalism.

It Doesn't Grow on Trees!

Ortega y Gasset suggested that the urban landscape has assumed the aspect of a natural environment to the man who was born into it and in accord with the instinct which makes him oppose real nature, he has turned against the concrete jungle and is trying to destroy it. This seems a better explanation for the perversity that will jeopardize its own existence so as to demonstrate its freedom, than either Dostoevsky or Poe offered for the same phenomena. (Although Dostoevsky did think that man might one day be forced to choose madness as the only freedom left to him.)

The deliberate disruption of consciousness that is being attempted, probably has its origin in a similarly hopeless and very unrevolutionary urge to freedom. An art which resurrects the random and arbitrary elements in life and says that "it means whatever your own unique self would have it mean"; is using a familiar piece of political flattery, except that for the individual artist it is probably a last ditch attempt to gain an audience among people who don't want anybody else's trip to be laid on them.

It must have been an achievement once to grasp order out of the surrounding chaos, and those who managed it had something to be pleased about. Now that universal education and an automated environment seem to be imposing linear thoughts and linear acts upon us, it becomes a point of pride to escape again into chaos and to regain the personal and to reclaim freedom in that way.

The Academic Freak

A struggling race of people living under the conditions which the Negro experienced in the southern states of America, has enough of flux and chance in life itself, and creates a tightly patterned and "together" art and the lithe and tenacious mentality that goes with it. Disruption of consciousness is only conceivable to a people so cocooned in affluence that it never makes contact with the implications of its theories. An individual example of somebody in a different type of cocoon is Andre Breton whose authoritarian personality (arguing over the precise way minds should be blown!) ensured that he didn't come into naked contact with his own theories. Some of his younger followers who did, later went crazy or shot themselves.

The anti-rational academic hasn't allowed his personal rebellion to run its full course. He doesn't live among people who are spontaneously irrational. (Or better still, attempted to explain the all-inclusive perception to them in a suitably linear manner.) If somebody earns their living in a university and doesn't mix with the counter-culture people at whom his theories are aimed, he might dream of the rebellion which involves dumping a steaming turd into the administration's examination files, or taking off one's clothes in the campus garden. He wouldn't be in a position to do either of these things, and would be more likely to provide the theoretical arguments and philosophical justification for those who have less to lose. He would be much better at expressing this supporting rationale than the few who will actually carry out the acts that illustrate it. But if he did drop out of society, as he might recommend, particularly the stiffling environment which could engender such theories, he would enter a much cooler reality in which he would discover them evaporating into thin air and the contradictions between Nature and Order, Spontaneity and Repression, resolving themselves into something a bit better.

If You Can't Be Original, Be Arbitrary

Almost any anarchist will join in with an attack on the elitism and preciousness of fine art, attempting to substitute some form of decentralised experience for the uncritical worship of anything. He can't help being depressed though, after the first euphoria when the dusty hundred-year-old classic is thrown away (now, at last, people will think for themselves!), as five-year-old classics and the Golden Age of the Sixties are resurrected in their place with as much snobbishness and exclusive worship as annoyed him so much about the last herd of true believers. It calls for a change of ground. History has been abolished, a sigh of relief and temporary euphoria, now we are getting the hangups of the Eternal Present forced upon us.

When the disruption of consciousness, by means of drugs and the random element in art, is used as a political "message", it has appeared in response to the inert mind of the larger public. The polémicist can justify his use of the irrational by pointing out that a state machine which depends on linear control and a rigid logic, can be sabotaged by the inconsequential, the silly laugh. What happens though, apart from a few courtroom or mass media confrontations, is that the only people who pay any attention to this doctrine are large numbers of the intelligent young, who sometimes come to believe in the recommended mode of thinking. Instead of using it as a sound tactic with a snide deliberation (the game's rigged, don't play it, etc.) they take it onto themselves as their own possession, establishment, and turn into a walking "tactic" . . . a silly laugh. But at least it is their own creation! One man's irrationality is never the same as another's, which makes the communally binding objective truth seem insipid by comparison.

Alongside this reversion to the irrational elements in the mind is a willingness to accept as progress every rational modification that helps control the naturally random and arbitrary in the external environment. Contraception is a rational measure which gives people more choice, more chance of self-determination. (If that's what they want.) It could also be said to remove another element of chance and destiny from their lives, forcing them to submit to other risks and arbitrary destinies. A progressively chaotic mind, and an art and music that reflect it, might be the price we pay for a progressively determined existence which can only find novelty in a self-induced madness. It means that the unity of the internal structure of society and the complex fauna and flora of rational authority among the individuals who bind it together, is under attack not only from the politically neutral forces which are at play in our society, but by a counter-culture which has made itself the avant-garde of these forces. A new consciousness it is, but it's helping along the disintegration of the only structure which an anarchist could point to and say: This is the alternative to an externally-imposed unity.

World in a Grain of Rice

Huxley's description of a first experience with the hallucogenic, mescalin, is misleading to a consideration of the mental attitude which forms from the continued use of any hallucogenic. Acid is an intensity experience which forces a person to the Overwhelming Question which, as Eliot knew, usually finds its answer in sex. The reason why so many different kinds of dogmatists recommend others to take it, is because they think (as we all do) that the same heightened awareness which attached them to their own beliefs, must repeat itself in another at the same point of intensity. Soldiers fall around laughing when they realise the silliness of being a soldier in a place where there is no fighting. Put them into combat under acid, however, and their heightened awareness will reveal to them the importance of fighting with even greater intensity than before. The acid itself is quite neutral, it only brings to a head and forces into a direction, any element of internal or external necessity which is uppermost at the time. This is why, in our own country, it can produce the strange phenomena of "turning on" somebody to making money or gaining control — the predatory Bread Head or Power Freak, for instance. As it has been well recorded though, most people when their "direction" is intensified, find that they want to communicate and make contact with others through loving and working with them. This tells us something about people and our own social context, but not about the effects of acid.

The key to the acid experience is the condition Naked Need, an openness to the flux which cries out for an answer: for peace, for revolution, for Jeanne Moreau, for god or the end to vivisection, for love or universal nakedness, or for anything and anybody else that might help at the time. Much raving polemics originate from these desperate fluctuations, demanding an all-inclusive revolution. If you take acid often enough, approaching this crossroads of Naked Need and asking the Overwhelming Question, instead of plunging into one of the escapes which offer themselves, it can become a very painful experience. This is the psychological bridge between acid and the use of barbiturates or heroin to remove the rawness of acid reality. Many people who started taking acid several years ago have returned to alcohol for the same reason, although at one time one of the novel forms of puritanism which acid produced, was the somewhat pious rejection of this drug. Vegetarianism and yoga, whatever good sense they represent, are two other forms of puritanism which I think result from the Good Resolutions which sometimes answer the Overwhelming Question.

Acid has nothing to do with revolution in the ordinary sense, though sometimes the desperation of Naked Need makes people aware that SOMETHING must be done, and this usually involves social change. It gives no answers concerning what can be done, given the available material and the human predicament, and is likely to end up banging its polemics against the latter. The underground's first attachment to Buddhism represents a delight in the flux, still mesmerised by a grain of rice or a chair, the infinite variability and complexity of it all. Its recent interest in Christianity (with its personal saviour) indicates an increasing horror at the emptiness of the void, which Buddhism to some extent is able to accept.

The State of Grace

The popularity of the word "grace" in underground writings, it has appeared quite suddenly, could mean an important change has taken place in the attitude and approach to acid among the people who still take it. Since grace is the opposite to fantasy and illusion in the Christian theology, and is supposed to be the reward you will be given for refusing to submit to the latter, an interest in this concept would indicate that people are resisting the acid experience as it takes hold of them.

Resist acid while under its influence, perhaps by trying to get together something decidedly linear, and it can create waves of pain accompanied by a trilling noise in the ears. The regularity of this trill which is almost electrical, is the origin, I'd guess, of rumors that we have been bugged by aliens from outer space. It's a sound which has also been used in some progressive music which gives me the odder notion that certain kinds of art are being produced to give pain to a complacent society rather than pleasure to a struggling one. This would seem to tie up a disruption of consciousness being used politically to attack the cocoon of affluence.

As the acid wears off, the waves of pain subside into a sense of relief, a blessed release — a state of pseudo-grace. This was well enough illustrated by the closing scences of Disney's *Fantasia* when the night of torment on the Black Mountain switches to the cool mistiness as the procession moves towards the churchyard. For most, a walk at dawn after a "trip" will induce the same experience.

The same mechanism was at work on a larger scale as the Dadaists moved into Surrealism, but it didn't reach the final stages. The Dadaists suspended themselves over the void, refusing hope or belief until, unable to hold out any longer, they accepted the rich reward of fantasy which is offered at this point. The Surrealists then had to attach themselves to Communism instead of to one of the more supple forms of anarchism that would seem to be the corollary of their own theories. Potential commisars and their grim procedural methods had become the natural complement of a fantastic world view which could only find balance by attaching itself to its opposite. Similarly, the more parts of the counter-culture move into hobbit-land (the commune movement is very much this scene), the greater its dependence on an external authority which embodies the more stridently practical components of the mind that the search for gentleness and peace recoils from. To some extent, ignoring the ritual coursings against authority, the distance of government makes it a more acceptable form of control to this attitude, than what might turn out to be the never ending strictures of real opposition.

Unutterable Revelations

Most people never reach the Overwhelming Question — just as well probably. The ones who do from each generation pass on a message which seeps through to all layers of that generation. If the message is bad, only a few are destroyed or destroy themselves, the rest absorb the message but remain protected from its full impact. What happens in the Melting Pot then is of more importance than the ebb and flow of the larger tidal phenomena: it is the source both of the gravitational pull which allows us to observe these movements, reflecting down to us the answers it has received to its askings.

Some of the most adventurously creative of the young have become obsolete to society. This, in spite of the fact that the middle ground of opportunity which capitalism has to offer them, has expanded beyond precedent. Perhaps society grows from its roots upwards, but it dies from the head downwards and if those who want to meet fate head on can no longer contribute to the social good, or attach themselves to a credible revolutionary alternative, they will explode into extremes in search of absolutes. Dean's unutterable revelations, even if we believe they existed, had no point of contact with life, and could only end up running round the streets "starving hysterical naked", as Ginsberg noted. A lot of people have been broken already, I think. They still have their tolerance of others and dislike authority, yes. But these can add up to a benign listlessness which is farther away from practical revolt that the attitude that tackles each barrier as it gets in the way and doesn't look too far ahead. Perhaps acid removes too many of the seven veils at one time, revealing layer on layer of secret repressions and oppressions — a view of infinity and complexity, a contact with the absolutes — which can cause a horrified recoil from the laborious effort of destroying the first of those barriers.

The "discovery" that words don't mean anything, and the reiteration of this fact (which is incontestable anyway) is an aspect of the contact with absolutes that leads to a rejection of a conscious compromise with one of the useless tools we use to create civilization. (A colossal compromise in itself.) Acid can tempt into a belief that you can solve the meaning of existence to the exclusion of everything else. Usually in the form of a piece of paper, for me: I catch sight of it out of the corner of an eye. It is trying to avoid me, so I chase it down the spiral it moves in and corner it, and grab it. Then I surface, holding it tight. I don't hurry to read it, because I like the feeling that I'll soon discover what it's all about. Unfortunately my pieces of paper usually turn up things like: when the dogs in Golders Green learn to ride bicycles, it will mark the regeneration of the human race. Others, who have had a similar experience, have discovered that the only answer is Violence, that they are Christ or Hitler, or that nothing exists, or that love makes the world go round, and BELIEVED it.

Decline in Decadence

When the European consciousness began to find itself released from its burden of social purpose, the first sweet langors and pleasures of this condition soon turned into shrieks of boredom and paralysis (in individual terms, possibly Wilde to Artaud is a good enough outline). Now that we have a mass movement of seekers after ecstasy and insight, all of them obsolete to the greater social purpose as it exists, we see people at every different stage, from ravings about cosmic consciousness and its spasms of belief through to the detached listlessness which has lost any handhold in the present. Also a new phenomena has appeared. People now want the drugs and orgies and the social approval, which leads to the philistine pleading for acceptance that would have horrified the individual debauchees and seekers of the turn of the century who still had the cheek and spirit to say: Yes, we are as bad as you say. Wicked even, damn you — but you can keep your social purpose.

Instead of being enjoyed for their own sakes, hash, acid and various sexual activities are the subject of reports and surveys trying to prove how socially beneficial they are. Instead of being pleased with his unique nosethumb at nature and society, the homosexual wants to be considered as good and normal a contributor to mankind as any other good and normal contributor, competing with other individualities for the privilege of having the most socially beneficial outlook, in a jargon that would have had Wilde at the smelling salts. Everybody wants in on the social approval racket, and there has probably never been such a fear of individuality as there is today. If this kind of justificatory polemics was aimed at friends, it would discover that the acceptance already existed and there was no need to appeal to a general public. As one of the Blake followers might tell us: only that which is self-delighting is complete and innocent in itself and that when drug use of copulation advertise themselves for social approval, another element, which is perhaps the desire for influence or self-display, has taken the place of the desire to indulge for its own sweet sake. There is still as much puritanism about offending current morality as there was in an age of more obvious moral totalitarianism. There is a hidden aggressiveness in much pornography (see *SUCK* magazine) which mirrors the threat of social ostracism that the old morality tracts wielded for their own purposes. Either way it's a power scene, and the new one is as oppressive and ludicrous as the last one.

> The ability to engage unashamedly in desired sexual behaviour, experiencing therefrom whatever pleasure her individual sexuality, without irrational repression, inclines her to, is certainly one criterion of a woman's inner liberation. Women feel baffled by the apparent need to assert something so obvious to them as the fact that this does not preclude the occurrence of healthy, individually varying disinclinations to sexual activity, and that immunity from psychological coercion that enables a woman to respect her disinclinations is also a criterion, no less categorical *(Anarchy* 1, p. 17).

I didn't change a word of that unfortunately. (It's getting too much for me now, and when I risk coming to my own conclusions I'll go.) I gather that a loophole is being added to his charter, that if at some time the individual doesn't feel like doing it, then she must feel assured that there isn't necessarily anything unradically wrong with her. But there is still the wish to advise and to control, that we find in any moralist.

The majority of counter-culture rebels find themselves in conflict with a jarringly repressive society which can't, at this stage in its development, give them the ease they are seeking. When somebody talks about sex being "as natural and pleasurable a function as eating", they are talking of a utopia in which every requirement of the body, including those at present ignored by a hypocritical society, will be duly served up. Compared to the striving for material affluence among the other classes, this represents the most advanced and revolutionary demand for bourgeois case that has ever been made. Somebody slumped against the wall muttering about Love, Revolution and Beauty, soon becomes a rival in funniness to the old drunkard who amazes everybody by getting to his feet and giving a speech on God, Queen and Country. Stay around a little longer and you find that the appeal to duty and fraternity is a prelude to asking for a loan of two shillings. When this is still new to you, and you are prepared to listen and nod a great deal, you're probably quite happy to come forward with the required amount. But when you've heard enough of them, the confessions of madmen and freaks and the drunkard's life story, begin to sound remarkably similar. The only surprise left then is the discovery that the sociologists and polemicists, the academics and journalists, who have no wish to move from the profitable novelty of diagnosis into the boredom of prognosis, are still nodding and listening, and more important to us, basing their hopes for a changing society on pipe dreams floating out of the underground, when all that was required of them, is to arrange greater ease of access to the particular dope, which in this case isn't alcohol, that engendered them. It's a revolution we can hope soon gets what it wants.

15.

Some Secular Myths

Jack Robinson

One of the prevailing beliefs of the twentieth century, despite the horrors of two world wars and the horrors of the intervals of "peace," is the belief in "progress." The conviction that mankind was moving steadily forward with the aid of science and education to a world of peace, democracy, and leisure. This was to be accomplished by the spread of education, therefore of literacy, hence of reason.

The history of the twentieth century, indeed the history of mankind shows very different forces operating. Great historical movements, mainly wars, have been motivated by forces far removed from sweet reason. The three threads which form the pattern of war and power-politics are nationalism, patriotism and militarism. Taken in isolation each of them have factors which cannot be denigrated. Love for a particular region and its people, loyalty and solidarity with a group, cultivation of courage, all of these are virtues (not unflawed) but taken together they lead only to the grave. With the welcome decline in organized religion, the misty concepts of patriotism, nationalism and militarism, took its place with the miracles of nationalism, the mystery of patriotism and the authority of militarism with its icons of banners and its robes of a priesthood of the death-cult. When, with increasing totalitarianism fostered by communism out of nationalism, the leader figure arose, the apotheosis of the god-king cult, we know the shocking results for humanity. Even now in times of national despair comes the call for a leader "above all parties."

The secondary factor in "progress" and the only one which can be physically witnessed is that of science and technology. The capacity of scientists for prostitution turned out to be unlimited. The so-called pinnacle of scientific achievement of the twentieth century was the splitting of the atom and its use in the atom-bomb. This would have never come about except for the willingness of scientists to work for a project that had no other aim but death and destruction. Recent voyaging in space and to the moon owes its conception to the military genius of Adolf Hitler's "revenge" rockets invented by his willing slave Werner von Braun. Von Braun proved no less a willing slave to the Americans when they wished to launch spy-satellites.

Herzen pointed out the increased power given to the state by technology and wrote of "Genghis Khan with telegraphs." Technology is not merely something which can be taken over lock, stock and barrel by the free society. Much of it would never have been invented, mass production for example, but for the rapacious needs of capitalism and the death-producing devices of militarism.

The conviction of the scientists that they are the rational and practical men of the world lead them to rationalize the idiocies of life into scientific systems and to accept as "practical" the totalitarian systems which have been established themselves. They will cheerfully officiate at the conditioning of mankind for whatever lunacy is prevalent. Social adjustment to the madhouse is their norm.

It was said in the House of Lords when one of the Education Bills was passed in the 1880s "now we must educate our masters." The growth of the popular newspaper ("edited by office boys for office boys") effectively took over this task and the mass media, reinforced by television, have continued it with the resultant propaganda-fed public, conditioned into a consumer-mass. The "soft-sell" of the salesman transferred itself to politics and the cult of pesonality is marketed like soap powder or cigarettes. Thus "education" negated democracy. Illiteracy at least once preserved one from the idiocies of the popular press.

One of the grand dreams with which man was forced to accept the industrial revolution (and, even now, the computerized society or the cybernetic system) is that of increased leisure. This proved to be an illusion, or the grim reality of unemployment. The vicious rat-race of the consumer society leads to overtime and the working wife, all to pay for labor-saving devices. Whatever wisps of leisure are left after the time-consuming journey home are all too frequently filled with mechanized leisure. Television slays its millions nightly. Man has become a vicarious consumer of other people's activities. His living is still done in the dreams of gambling and astrology. Life is so predictable that only chance can give him a thrill, and the dangerous narcotics for the body or for the mind offer escape. Winning the pools is still an idea of heaven for a materialist age.

The dream of democracy, given a foretaste in the French Revolution, led to a bloody Thermidor and the rise of Napoleon with the accompanying military conscription in the name of equality and fraternity — not to mention liberty. The sham of parlimentary democracy was followed by the sham of revolutions which put another ruling class into power. The idealism utilized by the Russian Revolution was shamelessly betrayed in the *real-politik* of Lenin, Trotsky and Stalin followed by the pragmatic conventionality of Khrushchev, Brezhnev and Co.

Drugged by propaganda, mankind takes refuge in political apathy, but even there Big Brother reaches down and interferes with the idiot existence which is the lot of the average man. He is taxed, conscripted, and hounded by authority. His homelessness is ignored, his lack of employment is made an economic device, his home or livelihood are snatched away for some fool scheme by the State. All the time the State, whatever the labels of the parties, grows more and more powerful and less and less rational. Baffled by this impotence, mankind seeks for scapegoats and picks on those nearest at hand be they Jews, Negroes, immigrants or hippies.

The secularism bred in man by the gross betrayals of the church and the destruction by science and education of the stupid mythology have led to strange cults flourishing with millennial promises, more satisfying fantasies or dubious pseudo-scientific premises. Such cults as Jehovah's Witnesses, the flying-saucer watchers, Scientology, witchcraft, and followers of J.R.R. Tolkein are all symptoms of a sick society.

It may be thought that this catalogue of man's irrationality and lack of real progress is a death-knell for anarchism. This is not so. The false choice put before man is that he is such a creature of original sin that he needs government. The false choice put upon the anarchists by some of their best friends (and worst enemies) is that man is of such unoriginal goodness that he does not need government. If man is so awful as some claim he is not to be trusted to govern, if he is as good as some claim he does not need government. The truth is he is neither, human nature is a recipe not an ingredient.

The modern state is designed to enhance the most deplorable aspects of humanity. Man's irrational impulses are used scientifically by those who wish to use him. His rational strivings are balked by the monster State. Man can evolve but all his steps in evolution are revolutionary and are challenges to the established order which is for stabilization and ultimate death.

The problems of mankind — war, poverty and freedom — are soluble. War can be solved by states for their own protection — the *pax Romana* for example. Poverty can be solved by states with welfare schemes. both of these are necessary for the preservation of the State. Freedom can only be achieved by the individual in co-operation with other individuals. States will not grant this since it menaces their own survival.

16.

A Religious View of Anarchism

Neville Fowler

I will call myself a "religious" anarchist at the risk of evoking the usual misconceptions associated with that term. I certainly am not an individualist in the sense that some other comrades have recently used the word; rather I believe that the idea of community is an important as the idea of freedom in the practical implications of anarchism.

My journey towards anarchism was complex, gradual, in the end climactic, yet overall it was a logical progression. As a young Christian pacifist with vaguely socialistic ideas and a natural sympathy for the underdog, I was thrust suddenly in the harsh reality of a colonialist setup. The resulting revelation of capitalism in its crudest, most blatant and aggressive form, kindled my smouldering indignation, in a way which I may never have experienced in my native English environment where the workings of the system are so concealed and overlaid by the blanket of culture and tradition, and its exploitive effects both masked and cushioned by the materials rewards of generations of working class struggle.

Against such anger, my pacifist conscience labored and died. Marx I felt was surely right, that "force is the midwife of every old society pregnant with the new," force meaning violence, of course. For who could imagine the holders of wealth and power relinquishing it voluntarily, persuaded so to do by Christian principles? How might justice be restored to all God's children, if not by force of arms? And so, an atheist Marxist I became, accepting the necessity for violence, however regretfully, and hence the irrelevance, indeed the total inconsistency, of belief in a God of love and a prophet Jesus who accepted suffering willingly in preference to imposing it on his opponents.

Putting above all things the priority of establishing "socialist justice," morality and ethics are soon re-orientated away from an abstract God or "good," which one is persuaded is but the subjective result of social conditioning. Any inconvenient idea can be labelled "bourgeois" and thus dispensed with. Everything must be re-valued on its usefulness to the cause, the supreme and justifying any means. And so I accepted the necessity for violent revolution, wars of national liberation, the dictatorship of the proletariat, and not least the centralized State, the consolidation of Workers' Power, which would eventually "wither-away."

Disillusioned

I have now been disillusioned with all this, but more positively I have been recaptured by God. The Hound of Heaven caught up with me, and I am quite convinced that there *is* an absolute focus of spiritual values, there is a cosmic reality and an eternal purpose which man can glimpse and his heart respond to. Because I believe in God and trust that the purpose is real, valid and good, I believe also in the equality of all human kind and respect the right of all creatures to life and freedom. My enmity towards all which enslaves or exploits is if anything more intense and certainly less selective. Never again can ends justify the means. Ends and means must cohere, for as Martin Luther King says, "Means represent the ideal in making and the end in process. If a free, just society is our aim, freedom and justice shall dictate our methods of working for it. No person should be physically coerced to achieve it. The real revolution is total and begins with ourselves. We have first to live our principles so far as we possibly can. To my mind nothing is more pathetic than the wealthy socialist financier, unless it is the violent peacemaker. Man must commit himself to live as Jesus taught and lived with an insight one can only describe as divine; yet an insight which may be shared by all who seek it at its source. In summary the way is this: to live and let live, treating others as we would like them to treat us, loving one another, forgiving one another, not judging, not punishing, not seeking restitution of loss, theft or damages, but centering always upon the greater needs of others rather than on our own desires. And to do all this, not at some future time when a different order of society prevails, but to do it now." For he knew, as anarchists know, that society does not improve simply as a result of talk alone, and even less as a result of the political transfer of power from one group to another, or one class to another. It changes when we, the people, individuals, decide to live differently, and to do it now. The more closely we adhere to this ideal, the less shall we depend on the institutions of the State. We shall need no laws, prisons, judges or police, for never shall we be willing to see a person deprived of his liberty or self-respect, still less of his life, on account of his offenses against either our persons or property.

How to be Free

As men take back the responsibility for running their own lives, the pillars of authority will crumble. I believe that this is happening even now as a result of the massive awakening of the desire for personal involvement and participation on the part of people, especially young people, all over the world. Every small victory in this battle is a direct blow against authoritarianism, a weakening of the centralized power structure and a forward step in the march towards true freedom and equality which is the only genuine democracy and the true destiny of mankind. Only when that age dawns will the necessary conditions exist for the full flowering of the human spirit. Man's soul needs freedom as his lungs need air. It is though a quality hard to identify. Material freedom has been enjoyed by a privileged few throughout history, usually at the expense of others. Spiritual freedom has been realized frequently by those under physical bondage. A man cannot be truly free is he is ignorant, and however wealthy he may be he cannot be though of as free if he is a victim of his own irrational prejudices. And there is a sense in which none of us is truly free until all men are, both spiritually and physically, such is the inter-related nature of life. I would go further and say that men are not free so long as they depend on the barbaric enslavement of other creatures for their food or pleasure.

Let me hasten to add that freedom does not guarantee automatic perfection. Free man is not to be equated with super-man, whom I do not believe in. Man probably always will have weaknesses and make mistakes, but anarchism, and only anarchism, can ensure that individual faults remain individual, to be accepted and forgiven by the community, and not transmuted through the distorting lens of power politics into the horrific forms of nuclear war and bacterial plague.

Freedom Valued

Now I must take issue with those trends at the present time which devalue freedom by interpreting it as meaning license for unrestricted pleasure seeking and personal gratification without reference to the needs of others and especially the wider needs of the community. To me this appears but an attempt to use anarchism as a philosophical basis, almost a justification, for a personal attitude which is basically selfish and self-centered; an attitude which, far from being revolutionary, is only too prevalent under the existing materialistic authoritarian pattern of life. Indeed, such an outlook is most aptly seen as a fruit of authoritarianism rather than any positive part of anarchism. How can intelligent people really see things that way? We are all part of society whether we like the fact or not. We are inter-dependent. There are many millions of people in the world and we must live together somehow. What each of us does affects our neighbor and like ripples from a stone thrown into a pool, our influence extends out into the wider world. It is foolish then to talk of freedom outside of the context of social responsibility, or love of our neighbor. The fact is, if we are to dispense with externally imposed codes of behavior, it must be because we have begun to outgrow the need for them, because we are conscious of that inner guidance which I call God, and others may call conscience, and because we are upholders of a way of love which makes all laws irrelevant. Freedom to me is thus inseparable from love. Indeed, I think it is the regimentation of authoritarianism, in religious as well as in secular affairs, which destroys man's innate capacity to respond positively to the goodness in his own soul, and rots his faculties of spiritual awareness.

In conclusion, anarchists would do well to remember that there are two lies. In exposing the one we should not allow ourselves to be deceived by the other. In the words of W.H. Auden,

> All I have is a voice
> To undo the folded lie,
> The romantic lie in the brain
> Of the sensual man-in-the-street
> And the lie of Authority
> Whose buildings grope the sky;
> There is no such thing as the State
> And no one exists alone;
> Hunger allows no choice
> To the citizen or the police;
> We must love one another or die.

17.
Man — the Creator and Destroyer

Justin

Catch — Man — The Creator and Destroyer POLLUTION IS IN THE AIR. It is also very much in the soil, in the rivers and in the sea. In this World Conservation Year, the world has suddenly become aware of the extent to which Man, the greedy predator, is fouling his own invironment.

No other species on earth betrays such sustained determination to wreak its environment as does Homo Sapiens. Compared with him, the Gadarene swine and the lemmings are far-sighted visionaries, leaving the environment for future generations rather than destroy it. But not Man, made in the image of God, Lord of Creation and possessed of a soul and a higher intelligence. The trouble with Man, well, one trouble with Man, is that he has developed his intelligence at the expense of his soul. He has left his soul to God and concentrated on the business of using his intelligence for his own self-betterment. Unfortunately he did not listen to those who told him that God does not exist and so the soul became nobody's responsibility and the organizations which clever man set up to liaise with the non-existent God became power institutions for the stamping out of natural love, the inculcation of guilt and the disintegration of human society.

They succeeded admirably. What we have today is a world full of hate, riddled with guilt and morality, where human society cannot really be said to exist. A plundered world dominated by the greedy and the clever. A soulless world.

Too Many of Us!

But not an antiseptic, soulless world. Although the hospitals in which most of us in the "developed" countries are born are no doubt as clean as human agency can make them, once we are outside in the "real" world, we are on our own, breathing air poisoned by the petrol engine, eating food poisoned by pesticides, at the mercy of machines and useful only as long as we do as we are told.

And on top of that — there are too damn many of us. Of all the agents of pollution that threaten our environment — carbon monoxide from cars, chemical waste from factories, radioactive fallout from bombs, the filth disposed of by the military and its poison factories and just plain garbage — over and above all these, Man himself is the greatest pollutant of all.

For modern man sets out to be a consumer, not a producer. Especially in the industrialized countries, a higher proportion of people find occupations which pay well but are completely non-productive, enabling them to buy and consume the products of poorer people. Mechanization in the basic production and distribution industries mean that fewer workers produce more ("productivity deals" making redundancy acceptable if coupled with higher pay for those who remain, help this tendency) so that the ambitious workers find themselves moving towards "white collar" jobs which make them consumers but not producers.

The vicious circle starts to rotate and the contradictions of "Progress" multiply. As the "standard of living" goes up, the "quality of life" goes down. The more car-owners there are, the less space there is for each car; the more motorways are built, the more houses are pulled down to make room for them and the more land goes out of production for food. So more food has to be produced by factory methods that everybody says they don't like, and the greater the shortage of houses. So more tower blocks are built concentrating more people in a smaller area, putting a greater strain on public transport so that more people buy their own cars. The compensations for living in tower blocks lie only in the convenience offered by electrical gadgets, so the demand goes up for more refrigerators, electric fires, television sets, washing machines, telephones, record-players, air-conditioners, etc., etc., backed up by detergents and convenience foods packed in indestructible (and damn nearly unopenable) plastic containers bringing their own disposal problems.

It Can't Be Contained

As life in the cities becomes more and more unsatisfying and unreal and intolerable, more people try to move out — thereby creating another demand for better communications leading to the building of more motorways, knocking down more houses and putting more land out of agricultural production.

This process, born out of demands for more of everything, could perhaps — perhaps — be contained if population were static. But it isn't. The population of the world will double itself in the next forty years. Look out of your window and try to visualise everything doubled up. Twice the people means twice the number of houses, twice the schools, twice the hospitals, twice the prisons and borstals, twice the motorways, twice the cars on them, twice the power stations and pylons, twice the aeroplanes in the sky stacking up to come into twice the airports . . . in fact all this is underestimating the situation grossly, since in forty years' time, the expectations of everyone born will be much higher than now, so that twice the number of people will mean much more than twice the demand for goods and services.

In Britain alone, today, there is a daily surplus of births over deaths of 800. Even allowing for the fact that 50,000 more people emigrate from Britain than immigrate into it, every year there are about 250,000 more trying to find living space in this little island. This means that we have to provide facilities equal to a new city the size of Bristol every year, over and above improvements in housing, roads, schools, etc., for the existing population.

Progress Will Get Them!

In the poorer countries, plagued by Catholicism or other religious ignorance, the rate of growth is higher and the consequent problem more menacing — except for the fact that their expectations are so much lower that their demands are not nearly so high. But progress will get them too, and peasant economies will grow into industrial economies and then more and more of what are now primary producers will become consumers just like us. And in capitalist terms — why shouldn't they?

There is only one way in which capitalism can get humanity out of this mess and that is by war. By so reducing populations, by so poisoning the planet, by so destroying property, that what is laughingly called "civilization" must start all over again — this is the way the power game will go. It will even leave the opportunity for authority, in some form or another, to continue. There is certainly no other way out for capitalism, since capitalism depends upon continual growth and expansion. The continual development of markets; the continual stimulation of demand, the continual growth of population as both consumer market and workforce. Behind capitalism, in any form, lies the State, equally interested in the maintenance of populations which serve it. The authoritarian path, therefore, leads to the virtual extinction of the human race.

What is the anarchist answer to this? Social revolution, as ever? Oh yes! Destruction of the State and abolition of the money and profit systems? Certainly, and the sooner the better! Distribution of the world's wealth on equalitarian lines, so that the gap between the poor and rich nations no longer exists? By all means!

In the past, anarchists were in the forefront of the birth control movement for reasons of personal liberty and women's emancipation. (Women's Liberation movements of today — please not!) Among others, Emma Goldman in America, and many comrades in Italy and other Catholic countries, have suffered prosecution and persecution for demanding contraceptive knowledge to be made freely available. Then, it was for personal freedom. Now, it seems, it must be for the very survival of the human race. Ironically, for the human race to survive, it must be cut down its own fertility.

This may not seem a very exciting campaign to launch nowadays, but a little thought of what is implied in an all-out campaign for sexual freedom, with free contraception on the National Health (!), abortion on demand (which would fall away with adequate contraception knowledge, anyway), leading inevitably to the end of the authoritarian family and marriage and in fact the complete breakdown of the moralistic nuclear family, with women achieving equality with men. Then, when they get it, they will discover that equality as wage-slaves is not good enough and the real economic revolution will be on!

In the meantime, anarchists have got to do a lot of homework. While it is true that smashing the bourgeoisie will help to end the pollution of our planet, simply shouting "Smash the Bourgeoisie" in an empty city street on a Sunday afternoon doesn't add much to our chances. How are we going to stop the State making nerve gas and then dumping it in the ocean? How are we going to defeat the military-industrial complex? How are we going to make the revolution? How are we going to save the world?

18

Education and the Democratic Myth

George Cairncross

A democratic system is that form of system which is governed by the rule of the majority. The Democratic way, is that way by which the majority, through the exercise of the electoral vote at a secret ballot, select the form of government, which they as a majority, wish to rule the society in which they live. However, in this society, there will exist a minority of groupings and individuals who, although not in agreement with the majority, nevertheless have to abide by the decisions of the government empowered by the majority vote, any protest they may like to make, is on the whole ineffectual. If an individual wishes to make some form of protest, there exist established channels open to him. This however, is not protesting, but merely conforming to the prescribed order of things. This is the Democratic way, the minority living under the rule of the majority decision. John Stuart Mill, the Victorian Economist and Philosopher, once wrote: "The majority is a majority of individuals, and that for the majority to suppress the opinions of the minority is to challenge the very foundations upon which majority rule itself is ultimately based." This is the chief crack in the structure of Democracy, the individual can be and often is suppressed. The only remedy open to the minority groupings, is that at another election to hope for a change in the majority vote, so that another government can replace the one with which they are not satisfied. Thus another majority vote establishes another ruling power, but there will again remain the minority. Can a Democracy be converted into a more Libertarian form of society in which the individual rather than a majority or a minority be catered for? Again John Stuart Mill wrote: "that if the State ensured that each individual within that State was happy, then that State would be automatically happy."

Behind the Democracy lies the all-powerful, ever pervasive shadow of the State; and by the State I mean the Government, the Established Church, the Police Forces, the Armed Forces and the Educational System. Society, where the electorate stems from, lives within the auspices of the State. the ultimate authority in the Democracy lies with the State. An electoral change only implies the transfer of power from one body politic to another, the State Apparatus remains to a varying degree intact, and it is with the State that the ultimate decisions concerning the running of society remains.

We have seen that the Head of a State is decided by electoral majority vote. The State by reason of its very existence and the fact that the educational system is State controlled, decides the policy as regards the running of the educational system of the country. A child is faced with two major environments, the home and the school. At home, the child is subject to the values and pressures fo his family, who in turn are subject to the values and pressures of society as a whole. At school, the child is subject to the values and standards of the State educational system, his teachers and school peers, eventually he in turn becomes a parent and perpetuates the same standards and values, which on the whole parallel those of society, to his children. In the long run, the State to survive, has to rule a society that accepts the authority of that State. The only way the State can ensure that this will happen, is by perpetuating a society that is conditioned to believe in the State and not in the existence of the sovereign individual, cooperating freely with other sovereign individuals. Martin Buber has said: "Freedom is a condition of education." The school system therefore has to be geared to producing a society which will accept without question this premise, and this plays a great part in the machinery of conformity. Thus it becomes apparent that the educational system cannot be geared to producing self-thinking individuals but has to be geared to the producing of indoctrinated persons who will accept that the Democratic way is the best form of society and government. G. H. Bantock says: "Education can only be understood when we know for what society and for what social position the pupils are being educated. Education does not mould men in the abstract but in and for a given society."

Ours is a competitive society. The majority accept this situation and act out their desires for self-improvement in this atmosphere. Surely it is not irrelevant that the whole system of schooling is one in which success is rewarded and failure punished. Not only this, but the success of one person is the failure of another—the failure and humiliation of having failed in front of the whole class. Success at school becomes equated with successful examination results, a philosophy which carries over into most homes just as success in society is equated with reaching a position of high financial reward in the hierarchy of one's own chosen field of work. An authoritarian system must by necessity encourage a hierarchy and not only that, but an hierarchy that it can trust. Those who conform to the standards and values laid down by the conditioning and indoctrination of their particular social groupings in society, and through the successful attainment of qualifications eventually reach a recognizable position within the structure of society; a position which could be threatened by any signs of Libertarianistic individuals challenging the social structure. The individual has to be curbed either by seduction to the accepted norm, and if this fails, then by repression. Anti-social behavior cannot be tolerated and eventually the individual who refuses to accept the values of the society in which he exists, is then met with the full force of the law (or sometimes more subtly by social stigmatisation or ostracism). The law, which is enacted by society for the good of the people in that society, whether or not they have desired it, on the principle that a democratic government acts for the majority.

The same attitudes apply to a child in school. The education system reflects the values and standards of society and the child is expected to conform to the system within the school. A pupil hierarchy is often established by the appointment of prefects, house or team captains, etc., combined with such methods as team points or a star system for good work or behavior. Children who show any signs of rebellion are considered trouble makers and are effectively punished in one way or another. Thus, just as in adult society, the individual has to appear to go along with society if he is to have any sort of a peaceful existence, and if not, then he must be prepared to take the full brunt of society's displeasure, so must the child in the school. Short of revolution, education is the only way that a society can be changed from within. Adults, as much as children, have to be educated to the idea of a new society for the old one to be superseded. A society that considers itself and its values to be responsible and just, is not likely of its own volition, to countenance a change in its structure through the educational system. As Mill said: "The majority, being satisfied with the ways of mankind as they now are (for it is they who make them what they are), cannot comprehend why those ways should not be good enough for everybody." It is only the minority individuals within a society who will desire any great change in that society, and as it is not in society's interest to encourage the individual in his aspirations, then the individual must ultimately suffer through the educational process in a Democratic system, which believes in the rule of the majority over the minority.

19.

The Machinery of Conformity

Antony Fleming

In the conflict of anarchist aims with the existing social structure it is clearly of vital importance to be fully aware of the tools at the disposal of the State in inducing conformity, and to attempt to work out positive alternatives.

I propose to discuss two central means of bringing about conformity. The first is upbringing, the second the activity of the State towards the adult nonconformist. The child has to cope with two environments—home and school. Both these, as we shall see, are remarkably potent forces for conditioning conformist behavior patterns. No doubt anarchists are aware of this anyway, but I think it is crucial that we recognize the full depth and extent of it.

In adulthood, the State copes with deviation in two ways—by sending the offender to prison, or giving him psychiatric treatment. Again it is obvious that this is so, but again I feel we must recognize just how important it is.

Childhood

The parents provide love, in particular the mother. She provides too frustration. At one time she allows the child to feed: at another time she denies him this possibility. The child reacts, reasonably enough, by loving her in the first case and hating her in the second. As he grows older, however, he must adapt to these conflicts. At the same time, he is totally dependent for the satisfaction of his needs on his mother. He must conform: if he does not he is threatened by the withdrawal of the very thing he depends on.

Clearly it is not difficult for the parent to exploit this dependence on her. Progressively she introduces patterns of behavior that represent conformity to what she wishes for the child and of it. It starts with training it to defecate in the appropriate place: it ends with indoctrinating it with the attitudes of the parents. Sarte remarked: "Long before our birth, even before we are conceived, our parents have decided who we will be." (Foreword to *The Traitor,* by Andre Gorz.) But the attitudes of the parent may contradict with those of the society in which they live. And let us remember that however we try not to impose our attitudes on the child, we give them away by our approval or otherwise of their behavior.

It is well worth noting in all this that the most successful method of conditioning to our society is love—at least to the more "liberal-minded" sections of our society. But at the same time a certain frustration probably helps to produce the more successful businessman. He is less concerned for his fellow man, more with getting what he wants. The petted child though is the same: having got everything from his parents, he intends to get it from society.

Society however produces various child-rearing techniques. These the parent will tend to adhere to. In a society where the middle-classes, at least, have a variety of techniques to choose from, generally running in fashions—as much for the progressive parent, so-called, as for anyone else.

It is more revealing to study the child-rearing techniques of more static societies, as they stand out clearer. But we should not assume from this that our techniques don't produce conformity: the rapid changes in technique are equalled by changes in technological methods and every other aspect of our culture, if not the basic system of competition—though even this is converting from .the direct struggle of the nineteenth century to competition within an increasingly bureaucratic system of management that is likely to become more so as time goes on and at the same time increasingly state-controlled or private monopolist (see, e.g., Paul Cardan: *Modern Capitalism and Revolution*).

Erikson in *Childhood and Society* provides a good deal of information on two particular examples of the relationship between child-rearing techniques and the demands of the societal structure. It is worth summarizing part of it—the part on the Yurok people. The newborn baby is not breast-fed for ten days: it is then generous and frequent, but it is terminated at the sixth month, the time of teething. The Yuroks' sweets are salty foods, while pregnant the mother does heavy work, with the general aim of preventing the child from resting against the spine! A taboo on sex until the child can creep vigourously ensures the parents do their best to bring this about. Even during the breast-feeding period, a number of devices are used to prevent the child from feeling too comfortable during this activity.

The supernatural providers arrange that the Yurok salmon fisherman be successful. "The Yurok attitude towards the supernatural providers is a lifelong fervent 'please' which seems to be reinforced by a residue of infant nostalgia for the mother from whom he has been disengaged so forcefully."

The child was taught to slow down his eating, to carry out the whole process rather laboriously, and at the same time to think of getting rich—to concentrate on money and salmon. But he must also be convinced that he means the salmon no harm, and it is said that the fish only leaves its scales, which then turn into salmon on the nets—surely a throwback to the deprivation of the breast when the desire to bite arose, and thus guilt feelings for having wished harm, one might suggest. "All wishful thinking," says Erikson, "was put in the service of economic pursuits." He adds: "Later, the energy of genital day-dreams is also harnessed to the same economic endeavour. In the 'sweat house' the older boy will learn the dual feat of thinking of money and not thinking of women." Apparently in fact the wife is paid for: the status of the wife and her children is determined by the price the would-be husband offers her father for her. Deviant behavior among the Yurok is explained solely in terms of the father having made a worthy girl pregnant prematurely—before he could pay for her, or simply married her on a down-payment, and being unable to pay off the instalments. Thus money is even necessary to marry.

The association between the frustration of oral satisfaction and the wish for money and salmon is, as we have seen, made clear. The removal of the breast at the time of biting, reinforced by the general atmosphere of frustration, at the time and later, the whole system of making the child feel uncomfortable, frustrated and thus anxious, is directed into economic gain energy. And thus the Yurok are a money-fixated tribe. But the anxiety has also the effect of making life a long plea—especially the anxiety-invoking situation surrounding oral satisfaction at the breast.

It has been said that "conformist individuals in abnormal cultures, such as the Yurok or the Dobuan, are in fact abnormal in an absolute sense, even though they find complete acceptance within their own culture." (Andrew Crowcroft: *The Psychotic.*)

But as Laing in particular brings out very clearly, our own culture does not qualify as the ideal-type. "We are bemused and crazed creatures, strangers to our true selves, to one another, and to the spiritual and material world—mad, even from an ideal standpoint we can glimpse but not adopt. We are born into a world where alienation awaits us. We are potentially men, but in an alienated state, and this state is not simply a natural system. . . .What is to be done? We who are still half alive in the often fibrillating heartland of a senescent capitalism—can we do more than reflect the decay around and within us?" (*Politics of Experience.*) A point that is accepted by anarchists anyway, so hardly needs stressing.

School is also a crucial means in the process of turning the child into an obedient conformist. This is done, not only by such methods as Citizenship Classes and Religious Instruction. Far more relevant and effective is the indoctrination by the very method in which the teaching is carried out.

Ours is a competitive society. Ninety per cent accept this situation and act out their desires for self-improvement in this atmosphere. Surely it is not irrelevant that the whole system of schooling is one in which success is rewarded and failure punished. Not only this, but the success of one person is the failure of another—the failure, and the humiliation of having failed in front of the whole class. This latter technique is especially effective where the teacher is popular. The more traditional technique of a public punishment for failure served to frighten people into conformity—with the result that they were a much more aggressive type, taking out their sufferings on those who stood in their way.

But we are discussing the modern, and much more effective techniques. For in the traditional method there was the inherent danger that resentment would be transferred from the master to the ruling class. In the modern method this danger is dealt with. The children feel solidarity with the teacher against the failure. The shame is therefore far greater. J. Henry describes a concrete example of this technique for linking competitive success with praise and failure with shame.

A teacher invited a pupil to reduce 12/16 to the lowest terms. He had trouble with it. She ignored the other pupils howling to supply the answer and concentrated on him, telling him to "think", although he was probably mentally paralyzed. Finally she turned to the rest of the class, asked the question, and selected one of the children to supply it. Henry comments: "Boris's failure made it possible for Peggy to succeed; his misery is the occasion for her rejoicing. . . .Such experiences force every man reared in our culture, over and over again, night in, night out, even at the pinnacle of success, to dream not of success, but of failure." (*Culture Against Man.*) One could point out that Peggy's success would make a dream of this: the two dreams seem to me likely to co-exist. Admittedly Henry is describing an American School, but there seems at least a chance that, as time goes on, we may adopt this kind of technique.

Henry also observes another phenomenon in education. The teacher did not ask who had the answer to the next question, but who would like to provide it. "A skilled teacher sets up many situations in such a way that a negative attitude can only be construed as treason." Thus the shame is added to by the sense that in failure one has betrayed the group: and how many children want to feel an outcast?

Perhaps, though, the method of the future will be that now present in some primary schools and secondary moderns—the permitting of the child to tackle the subjects it wants at the rate it can cope with. This does seem possible, perhaps more so than the method discussed by Henry. It has one setback—that it is less compatible with society, apparently.

But it is necessary to ask whether in fact this is so. For it does seem unlikely that such a system would develop if it were incompatible with society. In the most modern schools, the teacher, as I understand it, is just there to help. The child decides what it is interested in, and works on this basis, seeking advice from the teacher from time to time, but also using books and other sources of information.

Society can only accept this as a total system if the end is seen as contributing to a career, or to spare-time compensatory activities. Thus the poet and writer of mediocre standard, or better than average, who is not good enough to make the market, has a means of fulfilling himself in his spare time. His leisure horizons are widened. And the gradually shrinking time spent at the factory will thus be less unbearable. The budding scientist is likely to be far better at his job in the end if he has been allowed to work it all out for himself, with just advice and information—he is likely to be a better scientist if his profession springs out of an inner "vocation."

But these free development tedchniques are at present confined to primary schools and secondary moderns. In the latter, the assumption is anyway that the children are of average intelligence or below. It may well be that we will get the same techniques in bottom streams in comprehensives, but for the higher levels it seems reasonable to expect a firmer direction being provided by the teacher—a job to aim at being selected and worked towards, particular standards to be reached to get into University.

It does seem possible, on the other hand, to see psychological techniques being introduced more and more, and the use of these to achieve the desired effect (desired by society) even in a supposedly free-development situation. Even now it is obvious that the child is largely reliant on the teacher for advice, and especially in the early stages for information and recommended books. It is in these early stages that the basis for development is laid. Clearly the choice of books and the type of advice and information will be strongly affected by the personality of the teacher and teachers are not a noticeable revolutionary section of society!

Robert Jay Lifton records a faculty seminar discussion following his having given a talk on the relationship of education to thought reform and ideological totalism. One professor declared that there was no difference, that at this college they did brainwash the children. Another declared that "We do not care what the girls believe when they graduate. Our main concern is that they learn something from their college experience," but questioned more closely it emerged that she did care what her students believed and what they would become.

A third professor concluded a solution: "Perhaps we can avoid this by holding our beliefs with a certain amount of tension . . . with an attitude that 'I believe in this, but recognize that there can be other beliefs in opposition to it.' In this way we can subject any belief which we hold to the tension and pressure of its own limitations and of other alternative beliefs." Lifton comments that this third professor "grasped the necessity for both commitment and flexibility." *(Thought Reform and Psychology of Totalism.)*

But the skilled teacher has succeeded in persuading the child to accept him as someone to be looked up to, like a parent. Therefore the child is more likely to accept his views. The skilled teacher will be able to maintain her authority through the troubled years of adolescence, but being prepared to talk out dissident views.

And it seems not unreasonable to expect that teachers' training colleges will, in providing techniques, evolve those most likely to induce conformity. The very act of becoming a teacher, indeed, implies a sense of responsibility to the community (whatever the psychological basis for this sentiment), which can be reinforced, and dissident views negated. The teachers would be encouraged to look forward, but within the context of the existing structure—thus any idealistic tendencies would be turned up the blind alleyway of reformism.

Another point that is is important to remember is that adolescent revolt is only a passing phase: we can be sure those who operate the education machine are aware of this. Even in revolt the teenager often continues to hold the same views: but those who move on to the plane of ideological rebellion (a small minority, unfortunately, especially in this country) will move back to earlier conditioned patterns of behavior and thought. The adult nonconformist will continue to be something of a rare being. In this connection a recent *Daily Mail* survey of teenage opinion is interesting: it gave surprisingly high figures for the percentage of those who stood by outdated prejudices. Even among the teenagers, a referendum would, apparently, bring back hanging and make life uncomfortable for residents of other pigments.

Even if the next generation are going to be more liberal, this doesn't mean much for us—it is only faintly comforting to think that the social services will be improved. Indeed, this is likely to happen—care from the cradle to the grave, with legislation constantly being introduced, as it is now in the motoring sphere, to reduce loss of life, regardless of the cost to what liberty there is left.

Laing supplies a very relevant comment to round off the discussion of both home child-rearing and educational techniques. "Children do not give up their innate imagination, curiosity, dreaminess easily. You have to love them to get them to do that. Love is the path through permissiveness to discipline: and through discipline, only too often, to betrayal of self."

And thus we conclude with the adolescent entering adulthood, his conformist patterns of behavior reasserting themselves. But what happens if for various reasons the conditioning fails? It may be that the family environment has contradicted the societal, or that pressures within the family have made a conformist reaction impossible and provoked radical and lifelong revolt or escape from reality, as certainly happens in many cases. We call such family environments abnormal—but some at least are too normal to be compatible with societal structure, if most are bizarre to a degree, as Laing has shown present in the genesis of schizophrenia (cf. *Divided Self: Sanity, Madness and the Family*, Vol. 1), not forgetting of course that it seems feasible that the schizophrenic experience involves a certain amount of truth apart from the projections and dissociations.

Thought Reform

We have seen how, under certain circumstances, cultural conditioning can break down. Our particular form of society recognizes two types of deviant—the mentally ill, and the criminal. Up till recently it has regarded them as separate groups. Now increasingly the more liberal at least are taking up the cry that criminality too is a sign of mental disorder. Instead of punishment, therefore, the prisoner must be helped to become a productive member of society. He must be rehabilitated. His attitudes must be revised to a position compatible with the society in which he lives. So the prisons follow the lead of the mental hospitals in attempting to fit our failures to become acceptable and responsible citizens.

The libertarian must be quite clear on his attitude to this. He has no common ground with the liberal. Our basis is totally opposed to theirs. They say society is sane, even if it needs humanizing a little: we say, as the Marxists do, that society is of its nature dehumanizing and degrading. The liberal sees modern techniques in rehabilitation as an advance: we must see them as, in the hands of society, lethal. Never before has the State been able to use so much knowledge of man to bring about his conformity. It is increasingly recognizing this: the deviant must be helped, not by punishment, which reinforces inner alienation, but by the psychological manipulation of our very being—to twist us so we are no longer alienated from society. We cease to be human beings in the process but the liberals, seeing welfare capitalism as the epitome of freedom, are blind. They are so wrapped up in their middle-class cotton wool they do not realize they are caricatures of the whole man they idealize yet know nothing about.

Thought reform is a euphemism for "brainwashing". But ours is an open society, protests the liberal. We do not brainwash people. We only coerce them to prevent them hurting themselves or others. How blind can you get. You are free to do as you like as long as you conform, as long as you remain within acceptable limits. Step out of them and we will incarcerate you. Mind you, we will persuade you to change your mind. We would not use physical violence as they did in China. We will just lock you up in a cell and feed you drugs and electric shocks to block what is inside you and allow our carefully conditioned patterns of conformist behavior to reassert themselves.

What if I do not conform then, the outcast replies. We'll just do the whole thing all over again. We do not care how petty your revolt. If you persist in it, we will make you suffer—at the same time of course we're glad to say we'll try and show you the Light, the Way of Truth and Honesty. The way of truth for the liberal—and so we die.

Or we eke out our lives incarcerated, like the recidivist who stole a total of £178 over a long period, and has spent twenty-six years of his forty-eight in Her Majesty's Prisons (cf. Tony Parker: *The Unknown Citizen*).

Psychiatric Treatment

Psychiatry defines three types of mental illness—neuroses, psychoses, and psychopathy. In the first of these, the patient accepts that he is ill and wishes to be cured. He has accepted the validity of his cultural conditioning and wishes to have those experiences and patterns of behavior felt as incompatible with "normality" corrected. In the second, the patient was withdrawn into an inner world, which includes personified projections of those parts of himself he cannot face, and perhaps some valid experiences as we have mentioned before. Unlike the neurotic, the psychotic is convinced that his mode-of-experience is valid and that of the culture invalid. The psychopath, too, does not recognize his mode-of-experience as abnormal. Society defines him as someone suffering from persistant mental disorder resulting in abnormally aggressive or seriously irresponsible behavior, requiring medical care and training.

Psychiatry has a number of approaches to the deviant, of whom the neurotic is the easiest to cure, except if obsessional. However, this type of illness, obsessive neurosis, is in fact usually a symptom of some underlying, deeper problem, such as depression or latent schizophrenia.

The first of these is drugs. The effect is to chemically counteract the deviant behavior patterns, thus allowing the culturally conditioned patterns to reassert themselves. This is brought out especially in schizophrenia, where after a long time they can produce apparent "normality", but the removal of the drug brings about a rapid return to the former state of mind. In depression, in less fundamental deviations generally, the drug seems often to get the person over that particular bout, as part of a medical program.

The second is electro-convulsive therapy—electric shock treatment. We know very little about the effects of this, but it was found that dream-starved rats could be relieved by electric shocks: they showed less need to catch up on REM (i.e. dream) sleep than those that were not given shocks. One could hypothesize that, since dreams are our unconscious problem-solving technique (c.f. J.A. Hadfield: *Dreams and Nightmares*), the psychosis is, as is the neurosis, solved.

However, an experience with one psychotic patient suggests an alternative. He had, up till his first ECT, insisted that he must play for real, that he was not going to act any more (backing up Laing's environmentalist explanation of schizophrenia). After the first ECT he said he had fooling us for too long and would go on doing so. He also, having up to then begged for a shock so that he could break through "the sex-barrier" when told that he was getting a second ECT said he did not want that kind of shock.

It is possible, on this basis, to tentatively suggest that in fact the sheer power of the ECT-induced dreaming was unbearable, in normal life he would have dreamed about it much slower, and drove him to return to his earlier false self-true self split, to protect himself from this overpowering annihilation. The schizophrenic's basic problem is a sense of insecurity of being. The power of such an experience as ECT, which would overwhelm him, clearly could propel him into such a reaction.

Either through the solving of the problem in dream, or a return to pseudo-sanity, the culturally conditioned patterns of behavior would be restored—which after all is the object of treatment.

Occupational and industrial therapy are another standby in psychiatric treatment. These, like habit-training with geriatric patients, are ways of easing the patient back into work—a combination of group pressure and psychological satisfaction. Occupational therapy allows for rather more creativeness than industrial, but even so it is rather limited in the scope it provides. The general aim is to help the patient to concentrate, and indeed to get them back into the general habit of work. The psychological needs of companionship, security, stimulus and even very occasionally, when advice is asked, of independence, are satisfied, and thus the deviant is drawn into the net. If his cure is long term, he may then be moved to industrial therapy.

This is nothing more or less than the factory brought to hospital. The person is of course helped to adapt to it and so on, but the whole purpose is to get him so that he can go out of the hospital, if not on to the labor market, at least into a sheltered workshop, where he is making his contribution to the perpetuation of the system, and helping the capitalist to keep up his rate of profit. Or, in the terminology of the System, so that he can make a useful contribution to society.

In fact, both these forms of therapy have the objective of making the patient ready to work. The former, as we have noted, also stimulates concentration—not always a requisite of factory work but perhaps one the System would like to see in it. Concentration is of course important in such things as keeping yourself smart, and in fact generally fitting into the culture, if you are inclined to lapse.

Finally, we have the various types of analysis, and group psychotherapy. We will deal first with group psychotherapy.

This is a method of "resocializing" the patient by providing the use of group pressure as well as the satisfaction of psychological needs. As in occupational and industrial therapy, the ability of the group to provide or withhold psychological satisfaction is a potent force for coercion into conformity. The patient is able to talk out his problems in communication with the others and assist them to work out theirs. Both by the advice of the psychotherapist and by the fact that it is something all the participants, or most of them, share, it is culturally conformist patterns of experience and behavior that are worked towards. Group psychotherapy is in fact probably the closet thing we have to thought-reform brainwashing. For the lonely psychotic, the person who does not regard the culture as valid, is subjected to tremendous group pressure. And the very fear of the psychotic is that he will be overwhelmed and engulfed by other people, and the total loss of identity in the overwhelming of self by the other. A high-pressured group psychotherapy could, if kept up consistently, drive the psychotic into superficial conformity. And society only requires that we conform: it is not worried about what goes on inside us provided it does not influence our relationship to reality.

Analysis, whether direct, or with the aid of drugs or hypnosis, is aimed at discovering the primary causes of the "disorder." It works on the principle that every symptom has a traumatic origin, which is correct, but ignores the fact that the cultural conformist pattern of behavior is equally abnormal—since analysis takes conformism as the ideal. It also, by its nature, treats the person as a collection of parts, rather than a whole. This must be so, because to liberate the whole person from inhibition and repression is to make him human, and thus incompatible with a dehumanized society. The analyst can only release what is incompatible with society. Modern psychoanalysis sees a place for the superego—yet the sole function of the superego is to inhibit our natural instincts.

And, as we believe, a person is only fully human if he is free to seek his own fulfilment unrestricted and unconditioned—and that in a free environment with such inner freedom he will not indulge in a complete free-for-all.

Prison Techniques

The main technique throughout the prison service is of course the traditional one, emphasizing punishment. We have recently added to this the shock treatment of the Detention Center, a spreading phenomenon aimed at shaking the deviant so much he will cower in terrified conformity, and the terror will last long enough for the cultural conditioning to reassert itself in the depths of the person, instead of just on the surface.

Group psychotherapy has also appeared, in particular, in "special prisons." The violence of the aggressive psychopath criminal is stimulated by the sense of imprisonment, the desire to escape, and directed into tremendous group pressures to conformity, as each feels that his way out is to pretend conformity, and in interacting, inauthentic psychological violence on each other to which is added the unavoidability of the situation. For the psychopath is prepared to use any means to achieve his aims and each affects the other possibly more than superficially.

In its crushing of his positive emotional being his family situation has made him the ultimate caricature of the capitalist ideal—it has shown in him all that goes to make up the successful businessman, the successful politician, that society prefers to close its eyes to. But it cannot face its ideal gone too far. It must tone him down, make him less extreme, his crude self-interest less apparent, his lack of concern for others less obvious. And in the meantime it must mark him out as horribly evil, even if his evil is a product of his sickness.

People always turn most violently on those who epitomize their own being, the being that they cannot face. So it is with capitalism. But with capitalism the horror that it cannot face is the very ground of its being—not some repressed and contradicted element.

As time goes on we can see the invasion of the prison service by psychiatric techniques, in spite of the rearguard struggle of the upholders of free will and morality. The crude system of punishment is a failure: it works with a few, but compared to the increasing possibilities of psychological manipulation it is archaic. The System simply says the criminal is sick. Perhaps it does not even realize that its methods are manipulation, or will not face it. It is just the product of the social environment, and as such it meets its needs, irrelevant of who produces it. The Chinese Communists too regard thought reform as a purging of abnormal behavior patterns.

We see in thought reform the increasing use of psychological knowledge to achieve conformity. The purpose of this manipulation is to negate the nonconformist, deviant patterns of behavior, even modes of experience, though this is a joy in store still a little in the future on the whole, and to allow the conditioned, conformist patterns of behavior to assert ourselves. For it is vital to remember that thought reform already has these patterns of behavior instilled in the deviant: it simply has to activate them. They need reinforcing as well, but the groundwork has already been carried out. It only needs to be elaborated on.

Anarchist Solutions

We have seen, then the effectiveness of cultural conditioning. It is therefore clearly insufficient to simply usher in a free society, because it will simply revert back to cultural conformity. We do not introduce freedom simply by providing a free environment: we must also set ourselves free psychologically. We must set out to decondition ourselves, so that the natural man that now lies suffocated by an accumulation of indoctrination can be released.

And we must remember the problem of our conditioning especially in dealing with ways of bringing up our children.

But a contradiction arises here. We must at the same time create a free environment and liberate ourselves. The process must in fact be an interacting evolution. To liberate ourselves before we have a free society is to face ourselves with the impossible task of working within a coercive structure—that is the quickest way to a mental breakdown. What is necessary is to establish a libertarian environment as far as we can, and then work towards setting ourselves free, at the same time with the environment evolving to this change in situation.

But this requires that everyone wants to be free, whereas most are successfully conditioned. How do we break out of this?

Surely it requires, in fact, the establishment of libertarian environments within the coercive society, started by people wishing to be free, evolving situations relative to their own evolving humanization, presenting an alternative to existing society. I, at least, can see no other way.

The most essential basis, then, is the will to be free, and to accept that, conditioned as we are to a coercive, stratified society, we have only a faint inkling of what it means to be fully free and human. To be prepared to accept that the community we form in the beginning may appear free to us, but it is only so in terms of our largely culturally conditioned being. And thus, as I have said, to evolve inner and outer freedom in the interaction of one with the other.

In our study of cultural coercion, we dealt first with the techniques of child indoctrination, and secondly with thought reform on its various levels. In our study of anarchist solutions it is clearly necessary to reverse the scheme, since it is adults with the will to freedom that one expects to set up these potentially free communities.

As has been made clear, the evolution of freedom is an interaction of increasing psychological freedom with increasing environmental freedom. But since the outer reality is moulded, ideally, to the inner image, the start must be with psychological freedom. The expression of this growth in the environment will influence the inner evolution by showing certain lines of development valid and others, at that stage, invalid.

Such a libertory process demands extensive involvement of the identity and the personality with the group, a source of potential pain as well as satisfaction. And yet it demands that a person only becomes involved to the extent he chooses, because this is the essence of a libertarian outlook. But this is a conflict that will resolve itself, as the person unwilling to involve himself at depth finds the depth-relationships of the ideas as to what sort of being liberated man, and therefore rehumanized man, is likely to be. This, as has been said, is because our ideas of what freedom means and will produce are expressions of our largely conditioned personalities.

Nevertheless, on the basis of anthropology, it is possible to put out various ideas. Are we going to have far greater communalization, or are we going to see Stirnerite self-sufficiency? Is the Marxist picture of sexual communism or the alternative of the family going to occur? Will factories be operated on a system of workers' management? The anarchist has never been very specific about his utopia, and when he has differences of opinion have been obvious. Because in expressing his utopia he is expressing his largely culturally conditioned being. It is interesting, even helpful, to have some idea of which we will go: but the fact remains it is very largely guesswork.

20

Towards Workers' Control

P. Turner

Anarchists must recognize the usefulness and the importance of the workers' movement, must favor its development, and make it one of the levers for their actions, doing all they can so that it, in conjunction with all existing progressive force, will culminate in a social revolution which leads to the suppression of classes and to complete freedom, equality, peace and solidarity among all human beings. But it would be a great and fatal illusion to believe, as many do, that the workers' movement can and must on its own, by its very nature, lead to such a revolution. On the contrary, all movements founded on material and immediate interests (and a mass working-class movement cannot be founded on anything else), if the ferment, the drive and the unremitting efforts of men of ideas struggling and making sacrifices for an ideal future are lacking, tend to adopt themselves to circumstances, foster a conservative spirit, and the fear of change in those who manage to improve conditions, and often end up by creating new privileged classes and serving to support and consolidate the system which one would want to destroy.[1]

The above was written by Malatesta in October 1927 and refers to the situation existing in Italy at that time. However its description and analysis are applicable to this country in present-day circumstances.

It is certainly true that the present role of trade unions has created a privileged class of bureaucrats whose functions are to serve and consolidate the present economic system. Any change in this system will have to have the support of those who are at present organized within these unions. It is not a case of changing the leadership of the trade unions to one of men who believe in revolutionary action, but rather one of changing the outlook of the members.

At certain periods in the history of the trade union movement, some unions have adopted a revolutionary approach to their problems. In Britain during the years 1910-1922, railwaymen, miners and engineers formally adopted resolutions which either demanded a share in the control of their industry or the complete take-over under workers' control. These periods may be the exception rather than the rule but they nevertheless indicate the desire of workers, in certain situations, for revolutionary change.

Nationalization, No Answer

Many of the dreams for workers' control, like those put forward in the "Miners' Next Step"[2] for the taking over and running of the industry, have ended in disillusionment under nationalization. Instead of giving the control of an industry to the workers who are employed in it, nationalization has made these industries larger, more rigid and more remote. Far from investing the ownership with the community, it has strengthened the State. Nationalization is a political concept which has given the State industrial power and this, coupled with social and political power, gives the State enormous authority over all aspects of our lives. The idea that nationalization was a step towards eventual workers' control has proved not only wrong but disastrous. Those industries that have been nationalized have also been those in decline and the resulting program has meant that huge numbers of workers were made redendant. Rather than giving workers more control, nationalization has made management more remote, more powerful and therefore more able to resist the demands made on them by the workers.

Man's desire for control over his own life runs very deep among his basic instincts. Nobody will admit that he or she enjoys being pushed around. Certain freedoms have been won and not given and these are more less taken for granted. We have the freedom to change our political masters, we can express and generally propagate our ideas, but in present-day society industrial power is the most important thing. We spend nearly one-third of our lives at work creating wealth and power for a minority of employers and the State. During this time we have little or no say in the way the work is to be organized and carried out. We are hardly ever consulted or given any responsibility over the jobs we perform. When there is no work we are sacked and when there is an abundance we are expected to give up our leisure and work overtime. In return we receive a wage packet to enable us to procure the necessities to feed, clothe and shelter us and our families.

Little or No Say

The paradox is that those who actually produce the goods, distribute them and provide the necessary social services for the community have little or no say on how this is done, while those who cream off the wealth from the productive work have control over the work processes. Productive workers are the most important section of the community. Many workers perform useful jobs, such as bus conductors, but without the drivers and the mechanics to service the vehicles, the bus service would be non-existent. The position is that some of the most important workers who perform vital jobs are amongst the lowest paid in the country.

As producers and distributors of goods, workers are obviously in a strong position, but the average workers does not appreciate this. Most men are quite content with their present position as receivers of orders, but many also have a desire to gain some control over matters which affect them at work. Trade unions are organizations of such a collective desire for control and regulation of conditions, but some mistake this job organization for workers' control. "Workers' control exists wherever trade union practice, shop stewards' sanctions and collective power constrain employers." (*Participation and Control*—Ken Coates and Tony Topham.) No one would deny that this control at job level is a desirable thing but it is not workers' control. However such job organization has achieved a high degree of control which fosters responsibility and initiative.

Reg Wright describing a form of job organization which operated in Coventry writes, "The gang system sets men's minds free from many worries and enables them to concentrate completely on the job. It provides a natural frame of security, it gives confidence, shares money equally, uses all degrees of skill without distinction and enables jobs to be allocated to the man or woman best suited to them, the allocation frequently being made by the workers themselves. Change of jobs to avoid monotony is an easy matter. The 'gaffer' is abolished and foremen are now technicians called in to advise, or to act in a breakdown or other emergency."[3] Such a system of control in a mass product conveyor belt factory is obviously advantageous to workers, but it nevertheless remains a work method which only alleviates the inhuman and humdrum drudgery of modern car factories. The gang system ended when Standards found themselves in financial trouble and were absorbed into the lorry empire of Leylands.

Control of the Unions?

Workers' control is a .term being used today to describe so many different situations and Ken Coates and Tony Topham would no doubt apply it to the gang system. But this was not workers' control but only a very good way of making a tedious job worthwhile. Some other advocates of workers' control stress that control of the unions as a first step is imperative. One such group or rather a potential political party is the *International Socialists*. Their aims have varied over the years from "public ownership under full workers' control"[4] to "workers" power-democratic collective control of the working class over industry and society through a state of workers' councils and workers' control of production.[5] Both the prominence of "public ownership" and, later, "a state of workers councils" does presuppose some form of state or state machinery. This acceptance of the state is also linked with the idea of a political party. One of their editorials stated: "The urgent need is to develop a credible socialist alternative to the Tories and Labour. The International Socialists are committed to building such an alternative party." Their final advice was to "Keep the Tories Out. Vote Labour and prepare to Fight."[6]

This advice is basically the same as that proffered by the other fifty-six varieties of Trotskyist groups. It calls for support for a party which, if it were in power, would in fact become a new ruling class and would create new privileges for itself and subject the workers to the same basic alienation which is an integral part of capitalist production. Any form of State control of industry must inevitably mean that decisions which affect workers will be made by others who are not directly affected.

Russian Example

Malatesta, writing of the State, said that "should it survive, it would continually tend to reconstruct, *under one form or another* [my italics], a privileged and oppressing class."[7] There have been many examples to bear this out. Just such a situation arose at Kronstadt, fifty years ago, as well as during the preceding revolution of 1917. Emma Goldman had the following to say about these important events:

> The process of alienating the Russian masses from the Revolution had begun almost immediately after Lenin and his Party had ascended to power. Crass discrimination in rations and housing, suppression of every political right, continued persecution and arrests early became the order of the day. True, the purges undertaken at that time did not include party members, although

Communists also helped to fill the prisons and concentration camps. A case in point is the first Labour Opposition whose rank and file were quickly eliminated and their leaders, Shlapnikov sent to the Caucasus for "a rest" and Alexandra Kollontay placed under house arrest. But all the other political opponents, among them Mensheviki, Social Revolutionists, Anarchists, many of the Liberal intelligentsia and workers as well as peasants, were given short shrift in the cellars of the Cheka, or exiled to slow death in the distant parts of Russia or Siberia. In other words, Stalin has not originated the theory or methods that have crushed the Russian Revolution or forged new chains for the Russian people.

I admit, the dictatorship under Stalin's rule has become monstrous. That does not, however, lessen the guilt of Leon Trotsky as one of the actors in the revolutionary drama of which Kronstadt was one of the bloodiest scenes.[8]

A Worse Subjection

Certainly the Communist totalitarian state has provided a lesson and has proved the anarchist case against the capture of state power for revolutionary aims. This has given workers new and more powerful industrial masters. The Communist state has taken over more and more functions of society together with economic power. This means that the State not only controls the economy by various means such as outlawing strikes but because it has become the political and economic master, it condemns workers to a worse subjection than its counterparts in the West by the very fact that the means to improve conditions of work are denied by law. The State in Communist countries has become all powerful and embracing. It decides on the distribution of raw materials, the type and distribution of goods, investments and the appointments of managers of factories. In a "workers' state" all is decided upon from above.

The Communist Party makes no pretense of allowing workers' control. Bert Ramelson, Industrial Organizer for the Communist Party, had this to say:

> While management have the responsibility to ensure safety and provide welfare, training and educational facilities, their enforcement and supervision is done by workers' elected representatives and committees. Thus, because of the absence of a fundamental clash of interest between workers and management in a socialist state there is a tremendous expansion of industrial democracy. Nevertheless it would be wrong to assume that all differences between management and workers disappear or that

'workers' control' or 'self management' exists or is theoretically possible, that is if by these phrases, is meant control over all aspects of production, e.g. including what to produce, pricing, investment, etc.

Management, even under socialism, will tend to show greater concern for output and unit costs and, at times, this could very well encroach on the workers' rights and interests [my italics]. That is why trade unions are essential in socialist society and why basically their major function remains the same as in a capitalist society—the safeguarding of the workers' interests and upholding them against all comers—including management and state.[9]

Anarchists would claim that a fundamental clash of interests still remains in a Communist state for a worker's position remains virtually the same, as Bert Ramelson has admitted in the sentence emphasised. He lays great stress on the role of trade unions to defend workers' interests and yet it is these same organizations which are thoroughly integrated into the state machine. They are no longer independent and free organizations but a part of the totalitarian system and because of this Soviet workers are worse off than their Western counterparts. Revolts by workers in Communist states reinforce the anarchists' contention that a fundamental difference divides the workers and the state. The official trade unions have not taken the workers' side in these conflicts and in such situations the workers have created their own organizations against the system that has ruled and dominated them.

Hungary, Poland and France

In revolutionary situations organizations of workers' and peasants' councils, representing the interests and aspirations of the working class have emerged. Such occurences are not peculiar to the distant past for Hungary, Poland and France have been recent examples. In all these countries the power of the state and the government was overwhelmed by the opposition of the people. Workers' and peasants' councils were organized and the official trade unions and the party officials were ignored. The committees formed at the places of work were linked with similar committees in other factories, while these in turn were linked with other industries on both a district and national basis. This sort of organization, federated throughout the country, has often grown up very quickly, while the production of essential goods and the distribution of foodstuffs has continued.

During the Hungarian uprising in 1956 the *Observer* (25.11.56) commented:

A fantastic aspect of the situation is that although the general strike is in being and there is no centrally organized industry, the workers are nevertheless taking it upon themselves to keep essential services going for purposes which they themselves determine and support. Workers' councils in industrial districts have undertaken the distribution of essential goods and food to the population, in order to keep them alive. The coal miners are making daily allocations of just sufficient coal to keep the power stations going and supply the hospitals in Budapest and other large towns. Railwaymen organize trains to go to approved destinations for approved purposes. It is self-help in a setting of Anarchy.

The opposition to the Hungarian Communist State and the Soviet invaders was not just a negative one of strike action but took a revolutionary initiative in creating a basis for a new free society. There are many examples of this where workers and peasants find that the hold of the state over society has loosened. There is an almost natural inclination to seize this initiative and take over the means of production. For those who work on the land this is made easier by the fact that all the necessary requirements are at hand and workers have only to continue planting and harvesting after the landowners or bureaucrats have fled. Industry, on the other hand, has to rely on raw materials and factories to enable these to be turned into the finished product. When the State's power is weakened it has just had to accept the situation but when the authorities feel strong enough they legalize the situation. The State did this in Russia in 1917 and Spain in 1936. This legislation did not make workers' control and also succeeded in preventing any in existence from developing and spreading.

Where the factories and work places have been taken over, the workers have shown initiative and continued to produce, improvising to offset the lack of parts and materials. They have shown that they can run and control industry, even during the most difficult times. The failure to maintain this control and to consolidate the social revolution has not been a failure of an idea but rather because of the overall strength of opposition from those who eventually came to power and took over the state.

Ripe for Workers' Control

In this country, workers' control is once again being discussed. It has been described as an idea "looking for a movement,"[10] and "an idea on the wing."[11] That idea is vitally needed today when workers throughout industrial societies are facing inflation and increasing unemployment. The time was never so ripe for looking beyond the sterile reforms of the social democrats, turning away from political action and the equally useless support for one trade union leader or another.

An increasing number of strikes reflect that workers are no longer satisfied to be just wage slaves. Many strikes are protests against the alien conditions under which a worker performs his job for he is considered to be just a mere cog in an enlarging wheel. The strikes are taking on a non-monetary nature as workers are seeking a larger say in their conditions and greater control of their work places. Just such a movement for workers' control grew up in this country between 1910-1922.[12] This movement was particularly strong among engineers and committees were formed in Sheffield, on the Clyde and in London. It not only had an industrial base but also extended to other matters affecting the working class. Although the committees were part of the engineer's union, they worked and organized on an unofficial basis. They not only sought greater control over their conditions at work but they also advocated the overthrow of the capitalist wage system. They declared their faith in revolution and workers' control of production and distribution.

A movement like this, built on the shop floor, is needed today and can grow from the organizations of shop stewards which exist throughout industry. The increasing number of stewards is a sign of the desire to organize and control some aspect of work conditions. It is a revolt against being continually told what to do by those in authority. It expresses a determination not to be dictated to about the way a job should be done and the conditions under which it should be performed. Organizations at this level are the main weapon in the struggle against the employers for it is the unofficial strike that is hurting and damaging them the most. The trade unions have a far too big stake in the present system of capitalist exploitation for their leaders to ever want to overthrow it. This can and will be done by the active participation of the working class.

Chances Today

What are the chances of such a movement developing out of the existing shop stewards' organizations? Unfortunately many stewards are members of political parties and see industrial action taking second place to political action and the capture of the State. Indeed it was this change of attitude after the First World War and the Bolshevik seizure of power that led shop stewards away from industrial action and workers' control and along the political path.

However there are certain parallels between the second decade of this century and today that give the idea of workers' control a chance of getting off the ground. The emphasis is moving away from the political representatives in Parliament towards industrial action. Workers are realizing that they can only defend the conditions by their own efforts. Wage increases over and above the rates set by national union agreements are gained by unofficial action and the center of activity for trade union affairs is fast becoming the place of work. In recent years the number of stoppages reported has risen from 1,220 in 1961 to 2,350 in 1968 with further increases in the last two years. They include industries where unions have not called out members on official strike since 1926 and unions like the National Union of Railwaymen who have only had one official strike of one day, on October 3, 1962, since that year.

Obviously this shift towards direct action has meant an increased number of shop stewards. They are the direct representatives of the men on the shop floor, delegated to carry out a job of work. They can be and are recalled if they do not fulfill that function. The Donovan Report estimated that there were 175,000 shop stewards in Britain and from the increasing number of strikes, it appears that more of them are taking an active and positive part.

There has also been a general disillusionment with all political parties who profess to support the aspirations of the working class. They particularly felt the effects of the Wilson Government's incomes policy on their living standards. We are now reaching a similar situation where increased wages are being swallowed up by higher retail prices and rents. At present there seems to be no end to inflation and the outlawing of unofficial strikes, together with the cuts in social services, will further depress living standards. The increase in the number of unemployed could cause further disillusionment with political parties and governments in general who have failed to solve the present economic recession.

We are still being told that the strike weapon is outmoded. Trade union leaders like Jack Peel of the National Union of Dyers, Bleachers and Textile Workers, have attacked strike action for political ends. He said that the battle against the Industrial Relations Bill "will be won by using our heads and getting public opinion behind us, winning the next election and repealing the Act." Despite these leaders, workers are turning to industrial action rather than relying on the politicians of the Labour Party or seeking out the aid of other political parties. Because of this the workers will become more aware of their strength and look beyond the present-day struggles towards workers' control.

Control, from the Bottom Upwards

In common with the rest of society, industry is at present organized from the top down. Workers' control is a revolutionary principle which would give workers the responsibility for the organization and control of their industries from the bottom upwards. In the past they have proved their ability to take such a step and make a success of it and that they do not need the State, the employers and governments. When these forces are weak workers naturally turn to workers' control. It is a desire for responsibility and control over their lives.

Obviously such a revolutionary desire for change would be opposed by the authorities and the government would take action on behalf of the employers to protect their ruling position in society. This would mean the use of troops and the full force of the State being turned against a revolutionary movement for workers' control, for such a movement would mean an end to the power of the employers and their profits and privileges. It would mean an end to the wage system. The production of goods and the growing of food for needs would be the way of life, with the decisions regarding this being taken by people at their place of work or in their communities.

The capitalist society treats people as mere units of production. It creates shortages and wastage, pollutes our earth and makes wars. Anarchists want an end to this insane society. Instead we want workers to have dignity at work with industry being run and controlled by the people at their work places for the benefit and welfare of the community.

NOTES

1. *Malatesta, Life and Ideas,* by V. Richards, pp.113-114.
2. "Miners' Next Step." A pamphlet written by the South Wales miners in 1912.
3. *Anarchy 2,* "Workers' Control," p.50.
4. *Labour Worker,* June, 1967.
5. *Socialist Worker,* June 13, 1970.
6. *Ibid.*
7. *Anarchy,* by Errico Malatesta, p.22. Freedom Press.
8. *Trotsky Protests Too Much,* by Emma Goldman, p.3.
9. *The Debate on Workers' Control,* pp.14-15. Institute for Workers' Control.
10. *Anarchy 2,* 'Workers' Control', April, 1961.
11. *Anarchy 80,* 'Workers' Control', October, 1967.
12. See *The Shop Stewards Movement and Workers' Control 1910-1922,* by Branko Pribicevic.

21

From: Manifesto for a Nonviolent Revolution

George Lakey

The New Society

Just as many present problems are inter-related, creating a vicious circle leading to general collapse of civilization, so our vision of a new society involves a number of inter-related features which cannot be considered piecemeal if they are to hold their full promise. Without going so far as to blueprint the new institutions, we nevertheless want to suggest the direction of our thinking, confident that years of continued dialogue among people's movements will produce the creative vision needed.

The new society requires ways of living in harmony with the Earth, a just economic order, institutions for democratic participation in political life, a just world order, egalitarian cultures, and nonviolent styles of conflict.

Harmony with the Earth

The industrialized nations should develop their economies to use energy and materials in a way which can be sustained over centuries rather than for only a couple generations. This does not mean taking as our model the

European Middle Ages; it is impossible to turn back the clock. It means using the knowledge gained in many parts of the world over many centuries to develop means of production and distribution which are ecologically sound.

Scientists and engineers should develop designs for long-lasting products which can be easily repaired and, finally recycled. While some complex technology, like kidney machines, will be justifiable, the norm will be simple or small-scale technology. Bicycles, for example, would be the normal private transportation instead of cars, with free and rapid mass transport the normal means of going any distance.

The break-up of large cities into villages and towns seems essential for conservation and recylcing of resources. Cities are enormously wasteful from an ecological point of view; in towns less energy and material is needed per capita and waste, including human waste, is more easily recycled. The added advantages of reduction of noise and relative crowdedness, and easy access to farms and wooded areas are substantial. We believe that these changes would ease the habits of consumereism and egoism which have taken root in industrial society. In community the satisfactions of interpersonal relations and the sheer visibility of ecological processes will promote self-discipline; people will more likely see their links with each other and with nature rather than seeing their Selves pitted against others.

The human value which can be fully expressed in an ecologicallly sound new society is the value of *being,* as contrasted with the value of *having.* The arts can flourish, sport can again be broadly participative, education can develop a variety of means of sharing knowledge, skills, wisdom.

A vegetarian diet may be ecologically imperative, since protein is more efficiently produced on the planet level than higher on the food chain through meat.

A decentralizing economy will enable people to see more readily the impossible pressure on available food supply which continued population growth produces, even assuming the vegetarian diet as a norm. One group of experts estimates the optimal population of Britain, for example, as thirty million people (in contrast to the present fifty-six million). That is, the British environment has a carrying capacity which will provide food and other necessities at a decent standard for that many people. The additional population is getting its food from countries which will themselves have greater and greater need for it. Unless the British insist on unfair appropriation of food from other countries, using military and other means, they must reduce their population.

For quite a long period, therefore, the new society may maintain a social norm of one child per couple. Of course an alternative might be that some couples could have as many children as they pleased while others should surrender the opportunity entirely, but that would violate the value of equality. The desire many people feel for a family with many children might be met by voluntary extended families, or intentional communities. Communal living might become the norm in any case, since consumption of energy and space is less per capita in extended families than in nuclear families.

The highly industrialized societies, then, can become ecologically viable only through drastic changes in their institutions. The plans for redevelopment will vary from place to place and we can only be suggestive here. It should be clear, however, that the materialistic ethos which is so prevalent in the industrialized world must die, to be replaced by institutions which genuinely reflect respect for persons and for the Earth.

The peasant peoples of the agricultural countries have, in some ways, an easier task. Traditions of community, of extended family, of living in harmony with nature are stronger; urbanization is only in process; many resources have not yet been taken away to Europe or Japan or America and used up. The People's Republic of China has shown that it is possible to increase the standard of living of the poor without breakneck industrialization and urbanization. In the Arusha Declaration President Nyerere of Tanzania proclaimed the priority of agricultural and village development over heavy industry, of reliance on the work of the people over reliance on money.

Many decades ago Gandhi and some of his associates saw the dangers of industrialization at the expense of the villages and the dignity of the worker. Gandhi rejected "factory civilization" because of the exploitation and war which it involved rather than for explicit ecological reasons, yet his intuition is confirmed by new understanding of ecology. Technology would be simpler rather than elaborate, labor-intensive rather than the kind which throws people out of work, and village-based rather than city-based.

Lacking modern ecological understanding, Gandhi failed to see that limiting deaths through more food, better sanitation, etc., necessarily implies limiting births on a finite Earth. In this respect China, by devloping a social value on late marriages, has accepted the challenge.

In the new society we envision, mineral resources will be controlled by the region in which they are, rather than by distant metropolitan powers, and will be extracted carefully with minimum environmental destruction. The rural-to-urban migration should be reversed and development focused on the decentralized economic patterns which are conducive to recycling and saving of energy.

Some centralization is, of course, necessary, as with utilities and communications. Some complex technology will be essential. The burden of proof, however, needs to shift from those who argue for simplicity to those who argue for elaborateness; the primary task of engineers needs to be the development of technology which facilitates respect for persons and for the Earth.

A Just Economic Order

An economic system can do a great deal to help or to hinder the growth of full, loving human beings. In many ways the present capitalist economic system stresses the opposite of human values: it demands that people take a "me-first" attitude, competing fiercely to achieve their own individual security, even at the expense of others.

We believe a just economic order will stress cooperation, not competition; relative equality of income, no wide disparity; democratic self-management, not dictatorial management by others; self-reliance and initiative, not dependence on bureaucracies.

The conglomerates and multi-national corporations must be dismantled and their pieces put under people's ownership and control. The Yugoslav experience with workers' councils suggest to us that a system could be devised in which the basic ownership of industry resides in the people as a whole, but in which particular enterprises are managed by the workers who are involved in them on a day-to-day basis.

In Yugoslavian self-management all the workers of a particular enterprise vote directly by secret ballot to elect worker candidates to a one-year term on the Workers' Council, which is the supreme management body of the enterprise. This body in turn elects a Management Board, which, within the framework of Workers' Council policy and legislative enactments, determines all issues of policy. It hires and fires a managing director of the enterprise, decides what to produce and how, what wage levels are set, where to purchase raw material and equipment, how to reinvest earnings, etc.

This basic approach is applied in Yugoslavia to theater companies, universities, hospitals — organizations of many kinds. It may be the best form in situations where substantial size and complex division of labor cannot be avoided.

Cooperatives should play a major role in the economy of the new society. By their principle of one-person, one-vote, and the opportunities for participation and initiative, they can add richly to the productive life of humanity. Consumers' cooperatives can provide a check against the possibility of producers' cooperatives and enterprises seeking an unjust price for their products. The cooperatives are non-profit and created to serve specific needs of the people who take advantage of their services, returning any excess earnings to the very people whose purchases supplied the funds in the first place.

Much of the housing in the new society could be constructed by housing cooperatives and could be owned cooperatively, thus taking tenants out from under the thumb of the private profit-oriented landlord, and also giving people the power of democratic decision-making over how their living conditions will be arranged.

A small sector might exist for individual enterprises employing no more than a few people such as small farmers, craftsmen, shopkeepers. Even though this sector might be more inclined to carry forward the individualistic, competitive, private profit orientation of the capitalist economic system, its size would be so small that it would have relatively little negative impact on the system as a whole. Since it would exist within the general economy of social and cooperative ownership, it might tend to adopt the more positive values of the new society. We see a need for this sector for the diversity and flexibility it would add ot the toal system.

The organization of agricultural production is likely to be most influenced by the traditions of the various countries. Certainly the imposition of state farms, bringing the characteristic alienation of factories to the countryside, is no answer. In many countries there might best be a mixture of cooperatives and small private farms, the private farmers using cooperative arrangements for marketing, credit, and large machinery.

We propose, then, three basic sectors in the new economic sytem: a large sector of cooperatives, a large sector of socially owned but decentralized and self-managed enterprises, and a small sector of individually owned shops and so on.

We reject the view that work is merely a question of productive efficiency, to be regarded as a regrettable necessity which takes time away from genuine living. We must either humanize work, or it will dehumanize the rest of our lives, as it does now when clerks and factory workers alternate from routinized labor to nearly as routinized consumption of entertainment. Here again the ecological imperatives coincide with the dream of an end to alienation: the imperative of durability and non-waste coincides with craftsmanship, the imperative of *being* (rather than having) coincides with self-management and cooperative decision-making, the imperative of hard work coincides with the self-reliance and initiative of small-scale production units.

The ecological dimension also reinforces the requirement for truly human work that people be in charge of technology, rather than (as presently) the other way around. The Soviet Union and Eastern European countries clearly need to change as drastically as the capitalist countries in this, and in other respects.

The economy of the new society should be one in which children can grow up without fear of hunger or poverty, men and women can live in dignity and self-respect, and the elderly can live out their final years in security without fear of destitution. The wealth created by the work of the people can be distributed through universal services and through income. Services such as public transport, medical care, education, and cultural events might be free to all. A minimum income for persons unable to work will be matched by a maximum permissible income. The incomes ratio should be low, for example one to four, in order to promote equality. No one should be able to extract from the economy an income which gives him or her vastly superior powre and privilege. No one should recieve an income based on the exploitation of the labor of others. Income should come from wages and salaries, rebates from cooperatives, and social security transfer payments. Through taxation of inheritance and other assets wide disparities of wealth could be avoided.

Democratic Participation in Political Life

Politics in a large industrialized society approximates a cinema, in which many individuals react to the film but little to each other. In the large liberal state the political parties seek to engineer support through images and slogans which avoid the basic issues. Candidates "sell themselves" to a market of consumers, rather than engage in genuine dialogue with a group of citizens.

It can hardly be anything else in a large social order dominated by high mobility, mass communications, centralization, swollen cities — what has been called "mass society." The essence of participative democracy, discussion among peers on the great issues of the day, is eclipsed by one-way communication via the press and television. Mass society can only result in the politics of manipulation.

We reject the bureaucratic centralist model of the Soviet Union as well, in which the power of government officials continues unchecked by democratic participation despite Lenin's statement that the state should begin to wither away immediately. The call in the *Communist Manifesto* to centralize and create industrial armies completely overlooked the rigidities of bureaucratic power which would thereby be created. Government by the workers can only mean government *over* the workers in such a model.

Decision-making in the new society should be rooted in the face-to-face discussions of the citizenry, starting on the neighborhood level. As many decisions as possible should be made on the local level; economic decentralization should be matched by political decentralization.

Education, that is, the transmission of culture and work skills, should be largely community-based. Peace-keeping, including the definition of what is breach of the peace, should in general be locally determined within a general consensus of human rights. Health and welfare should also be locally determined. The ecological impact of production and distribution should be strongly influenced by local communities.

The actual structures of decision-making will of course vary according to tradition and local ingenuity. In the council structure, for example, a group small enough for face-to-face discussions selects one of their number to represent them in a council for a larger area, in which the same is done for a still larger area. The council model has the advantage of close connection to the grass roots, yet can be extended upward for coordinating tasks involving larger areas.

An ecological imperative reinforces our belief in the desirability of a decentralized, communitarian society. The long period in which the industrialized societies change their exploitative relation to the Earth will be a period of difficulty and will require great restraint. The habits of materialism and environmental destruction have gone deep. New norms will have to be established and enforced. This could be done by state mechanisms and the police, but such external controls could not be as effective as the self-discipline of the people. This self-discipline could emerge through full participation in decision-making and persuasion by public opinion, except that exactly that participation and persuasion are less likely the larger the political unit. In the heterogeneous, centralized societies of most industrialized countries the restraints of the ecologically viable, stable society will seem like coersion, like arbitrary restructions issued by a distant and unsympathetic government.

We believe that large nation-states should be dissolved into a variety of coordinating structures on local, regional, and transnational levels. The tendency for nation-states to gather more power to themselves should be reversed; the only justification for coordination of resources and decision on a larger level should be that it cannot be adequately done on a local level, due to the nature of the problem. If the local level could in theory handle the problem but lacks the knowledge or the will, it should be offered the knowledge by others in the broader society and pressured to develop the will by other communities. A weak community will only become weaker if it has its work done for it by others.

But some human needs cannot be reduced to the local level. Regional planning will be necessary for development of some resources in a sound way; regional arbitration of ecological disputes (say between an upstream community and a downstream community) will be necessary. Depending on the function, then, some structures will include many local communities, coordinating their democratic discussions into a larger pattern.

A Just World Order

Nearly everyone agrees that world community is needed, but we have difficulty agreeing on what that phrase would mean. Many decentralists expect that world community will emerge by splitting the existing large nation-states into small ones and moving power back to local communities. They see the trend toward larger and larger political units over the past several centuries to be fundamentally anti-democratic and subversive of human values.

Advocates of world government, on the other hand, rejoice in the trend toward larger political units and find the problem in the stalling of the process at the point of today's national rivalries. They consider the arms races and hot wars inevitable without international organization and urge that a world government be created to end the violence.

The decentralists rightly complain that large nations-states are incompetent for many decisions they make because the decisions should fit the community and communities differ among themselves. But as the world government people correctly see, there is a community of interests which is as large as humankind, and some decisions need to fit that community. What to do with the riches of the seabeds, how to relate to space, how to cope with pollution, how to distribute wealth to the poor: these are humankind-sized solutions.

The decentralists are, however, quite right to attack the tendency toward centralization and bigness which makes the individual a cog in a machine he or she cannot even comprehend. If a citizen has little access to his or her government, what chance is there to be heard in a world government? Or, to put it more realistically (since the average citizen has never had much to say about government action): if large social movements have difficulty gaining change from the government of 200 million people, what chance will it have in getting a hearing in a government of three billion people?

An advocate of world government would want to put the question more precisely. What effect can a movement have now in preventing a nuclear war, which might occur tomorrow or next week or next year? The lack of a world government means that the greatest decision of all—survival—is in the hands of no one, but will get made in the face-down and struggles of a nuclear jungle. What could be more undemocratic than that? If the majority of the world's people decide they prefer survival and choose the instrumentality of government to get it, it would be a step toward self-determination. And if a world parliament, democratically-elected, made decisions about that which is now simply the result of cut-throat competition, the general public interest would gain.

The question of enforcement of decisions remains an awkward one, however. A government is, by definition, an agency which monopolizes the legitimate use of violence. Will a world government have more troops than anyone else? If it makes a decision contrary to the interests of a large number of people there may be civil war. Wars are not ended by setting up a world authority and calling the battles "civil conflict."

We do advocate the development of transnational institutions but realize that they become legitimate only in a world changing rapidly toward a condition where the hungry are fed, the empires dismantled, and the generals retired. We realize, too, that a revolutionary movement for justice will get farther if it has a program for counter-institutions which can supplant the older order.

Our central concept for democratic world institutions is *people's enforcement*. Through the techniques of nonviolent struggle the people can themselves enforce the law on those occasions when the selfish interests seek to evade it.

Let us imagine that a World Seabed Commission, after months of study finds that a certain miners cooperative is extracting minerals in a way which runs against the best long-term interests of humankind. It directs the cooperative to stop the work, but the group, which has become corrupt and has underworld connections, refuses. The Commission then publicizes the issue and the voluntary associations around the world which have a special interest in conservation, put pressure on the cooperative. The pressure might mount to a direct action campaign on behalf of the Commission's decision.

The Commission might itself have a weak case or be wrong; the test would be whether the voluntary associations would mobilize for a campaign, and whether, in the course of the struggle, new facts came to light which revealed that the miners were right after all. Compromises would be possible, as well as new solutions to the conflict which no one would have thought of in the beginning.

The commission is the kind of structure which might meet the insights of both world government and decentralist advocates. Commissions would be organized by function: for the seabeds, space, air pollution, world trade, currency, and so on. Each commission would have a comprehensive view of our planet, would have a staff of experts, would be composed of respected and public-spirited women and men, and could make humankind-sized decisions for humankind-sized problems. Commissions would not lend themselves to tyranny because their major means of enforcement of decisions, where decisions are resisted, would be the people's willingness to struggle. Their composition would give them great legitimacy, however, and people struggling on behalf of their considered decisions would be quite different from the usual ad hoc campaigns.

The commissions would deal only with global problems; they would not try to solve problems which could be handled on a more local level. World and local perspectives would, on the other hand, occasionally clash. The commissions' mandates are supreme, but could not be forced on a determined local opposition. Since the commissions have different functions, a locality which is at loggerheads with one commission may be the most ardent supporter of another commission; these cross-cutting conflicts would help to stabilize the system and prevent civil war. War, in any case, would be very unlikely because the commission has no troops and many localities will have converted to nonviolent means of conflict resolution.

Other forms of transnational organization may also be needed, especially for setting priorities among functions and development. Imaginative use of cable television, for example, might make possible world-wide debates of pressing matters which could then be decided by electronic referendum.

An end to neo-colonialism, made possible by the dissolution of corporations and large nation-states, and the growth of common vision for planet Earth will provide a more promising context for democratic world institutions than we can now imagine.

An Egalitarian Society

In the new society goods and opportunities will be distributed more equally, and this will deprive racism and sexism of their material support. Participatory democracy will facilitate the full engagement of women and racial minorities in social life. A culture which stresses the value of each personality will undermine the stereotyping of race and sex. Sexual expression of affection will have a place among men and among women.

In the new society we do not expect that everyone will have the same status. Every society has values: athletic prowess is approved, killing is disapproved, hard work is approved, cheating is disapproved, and so on. Individuals differ in their achievement of positive values, and naturally rank each other in that way. A status heirarchy emerges unavoidably.

What an egalitarian society *can* do is develop structures which reduce unfair advantage to some in attaining those prized values, and which decentralizes power to prevent the persons with highest status from attaining overweening influence.

Education will play a role in helping people see their abilities in the context of the basic worth of every person. The capitalist ethos which has led to competitive individualism must be replaced by a communitarian ethos which encourages individuality without selfishness. Education, by enabling a person to experience the variety of human work and means of creation, relates the person's inner self to the evolution of the community.

People in the new society will probably value intelligence very highly, because of the complexity of maximizing freedom in a world which will by then have more people and fewer resources. To avoid elitism it will be necessary to be very clear: the work of experts is to develop sets of alternatives for the people's decision, not to make those decisions themselves.

A society characterized by equality and community cannot be created only by institutional structures. The spirit of cooperation must be very strong force, reflected in every area and exemplified especially by the cultural movements which will continue to push society toward higher goals of human achievement.

A Nonviolent Society

Conflict is inevitable and a natural part of life. People who no longer care about anything enough to fight for it are, in a sense, already dead.

In the new society people will be engaged in many conflicts. They will usually struggle, however, without raising the question of each other's continued existence. They will, even though angry, use means which encourage the emergency of solutions which include them all.

The changed values of the new society should support this development: physical fighting will not be linked to maleness and there may even be a general value of gentleness which will influence conflict styles.

But value change is not enough. The people need a technique, a set of methods which can be used in situations of conflict even when one side of the conflict uses violence to achieve its ends. We believe that technique has already been found although it needs further development. It has been called civil resistance, satyagraha, positive action. Puerto Ricans have recently coined the term "pacific militancy" to describe its combination of very strong action with an inherent peaceableness. Some of the methods include strikes, boycotts, occupations, civil disobedience, marches, fasts, sit-ins, tax refusal, parallel institutions.

This technique can be learned. Education can play a strong role, offering specific training in the tactics of pacific militancy as well as more general understanding of its history and dynamics. Just as a violent society equips many of its members with the skills of the gun, etc., so a nonviolent society develops the skills of nonviolent conflict resolution.

One major large-scale use of the technique has been described in the section on transnational institutions; just decisions by commissions will be enforced, when necessary, by pacific militancy. Another important use is for peace-keeping when conflicts spill over into violence; third parties with nonviolent skills can return the conflict to forms which encourage the emergence of truth. The Shanti Sena (Peace Army) of India has experimented with these methods.

Civil resistance can also be used to defend a community or region against exploitation or domination by another region or by a would-be dictator. Even though most of the planet may have made the transition to a new society, there may remain nations which manage to hold out against the winds of change. These might try to exploit neighboring societies which have eliminated militarism and transarmed to civilian defense.

Some hints of the potential of noncooperation and other nonviolent means for resisting invasion can be found in history. The German government used a policy of massive noncooperation in the Ruhr to oppose French and Belgian invasion there in 1923. The Germans refused to mine coal, to make steel, even to serve food or operate the trains for the occupation, and received harsh reprisals from the frustrated invaders. The French were forced by the German resistance to accept a re-scheduling of reparation payments and to give up hopes of annexing the Ruhr. The Germans paid a price for this in human and material terms, but nothing like the price of resistance on a similar scale with weapons.

The German resistance occurred without preparation or a sophisticated sense of strategy, of course. The *concept* of civilian defense did not yet exist. This and other cases suggest the potential power which can be used in the new society to replace the destructive effects of violent defense.

Interdependence of Our Vision

Frequently a single one of these proposals is put forward as the key to solving the world's problems. We believe, following from our analysis, that the situation is too complex to be remedied that way.

Some say that developing a socialist economy is the key, neglecting the ecological destruction and neocolonial relations maintained by the Soviet Union which has abandoned capitalism.

Some say that national independence is the key, failing to see the independent states which oppress their people, and the changing conditions which prevent anything but *inter*dependence in the world.

Some emphasize nonviolent struggle as the key, failing to realize that a means without an end can easily result in reformism and little modification of the status quo.

Some say that international institutions are the key, neglecting the likelihood that these will be oppressive unless they are founded on justice community, and participation.

We believe that our struggle must be waged on more than one front. Single-answer solutions are as inadequate as single-cause explanations. We realize that our vision, integrated though it tries to be, is also incomplete. Even if we considered it perfect it would be nothing to impose. We put it forward as part of humanity's dialogue on its own future.

PART VI.

ANARCHISM AS CRITIQUE
AND POSSIBILITY

"The urge to destroy is also a creative urge," proclaimed Mikhail Bakunin more than a century ago. The reciprocal relationship between radical attack upon a tyrannical status quo and radical affirmation of a brighter future marks anarchist writing. Though there have been many social upheavals called revolutions in our century, none has satisfied the minimal anarchist definition. The Bolshevik and Chinese revolutions resulted in stronger, more centralized organs of control than their corrupt predecessors. Anarchists, at first hopeful, have been severely disillusioned by the "progress" of revolution in the east and west. But they continue to indict authority and dream of a stateless freedom which shall dawn tomorrow.

In recent decades a distinct historical period seemed to be coming to an end. The limits of bourgeois democracy, one can fairly state, were growing obvious in the 1960s and early 1970s. Antistate radicals, given hope by the uprising of young people, by resistance to symbols of oppression such as the draft, and encouraged by the spreading public recognition of government's moral and political turpitude, produced (once again) a series of critiques and proposals. What seemed to be needed, above all, was a break from the past coupled with a reasonable mechanism for movement to a better future.

A group of Philadelphia Quakers, in 1972, produced a serious, limited, and rational program for the new society. "Revolution: A Quaker Prescription for a Sick Society" displays both a sense of emergency about the present and optimism about genuine social change in the direction of freedom and equality. It is a balanced work presenting, for example, arguments for and against political participation in electoral systems. It is typical of anarchist writing, for it emphasizes the need to live the revolution *before* it is made.

An essay by Murray Bookchin, from his influential book *Post-Scarcity Anarchism,* combines the critical with the utopian. In urging the unity of revolutionary process and goal, it centers upon the issue of power or, rather, the dismantling of the forms and forces of authority. Bookchin, writing in 1971, displays the hope of many anarchists for the spread of a new consciousness which can lead to the new society.

An anarchist revolution, I have emphasized, has never been made. And, perhaps, it never can. But it in no way demeans the antistate radicals to note that their criticism may be more significant than their aspirations. Bakunin used to say that to get to the possible, one must imagine the impossible. A signal contribution of anarchist defiance has been a willingness to question *all* the revered institutions of the present order.

One of the best such critiques is Howard Zinn's "The Conspiracy of Law." In a clear, sustained and logical fashion, Zinn shows that the so-called "rule of law" and the systems of legislation, enforcement, and required obedience to law have a single, concentrated foundation: to maintain inequality and perpetuate social injustice. His penetration of the myths of legalism results in what Zinn calls a "proper disrespect" for law itself.

22

From: Revolution: A Quaker Prescription for a Sick Society

Sue Carroll, George Lakey,

William Moyer and Richard Taylor

Reform or Revolution?
Revolutionary Reform: The Movement in a "Pre-Transition" Society

We are now living in a socio-economic-political system which needs to be fundamentally changed. We hope, in the future, to live in a society which is much more supportive of human dignity, world community, and ecological harmony. To move from the present system to a new one involves a "transition" to socio-economic-political institutions which are radically different from those of the present system. Therefore, we are living now in what may be termed a "pre-transition society."

Resistance to Change

But will there be a transition at all? Certainly not, if no effective power is generated to challenge the present system and to build a new one. The present arrangement of institutions, while disadvantaging many millions of human beings here and abroad, does convey vast wealth and power to the privileged few. We do not believe that these privileged persons are necessarily more evil than anyone else. We do believe that they are trapped by a system which undercuts their ability to act according to values such as love, shared power and world community, which forces them, in fact, to act in a way directly contrary to such values. They are expected to continue to maximize their privilege. And one of the lessons of history is that wealth, power, and privilege will be defended by those who benefit from them. Although concessions can be made, there will certainly be strong resistance to any attempt to radically reduce such wealth and power.

Another source of resistance to transition is rationalizations for the status quo ("our free enterprise is the best in the world," "people who foment radical change are communists," etc.) which have convinced many of those who do not share in the system's wealth and power that, nevertheless, the present system is a desirable one. Those who believe in the desirability of the present system and who do not envisage a better one, can be expected to stand by the resistance to change. So also can the many who, while not sharing in the *vast* wealth, have been brought to a degree of relative comfort and affluence within the system, and who fear that major change will harm them.

Given this resistance, then, the "pre-transition" phrase is a time in which significant preparatory work needs to be done if there is to be a transition at all.

Lines of Action in the Pre-Transition Stage

We have already described several aspects of this preparatory work, e.g., conscientization and mass education, organization-building, nonviolent direct action, the development of nonviolent revolutionary groups, radical caucuses, training centers, and counter-institutions. We have said very little so far, however, about the targets of this preparatory work in the *existing* politcal and economic system. Should we simply ignore present political and economic institutions? Or are there specific political and economic changes which the movement should advocate in the pre-transition period?

Some advocates of social change believe that it is futile, perhaps even harmful, to work for such changes. They fear that any partial steps forward within the present framework will simply reinforce it and make it more durable. They worry that the movement will become so caught up in "reformism" that it will forget its real mandate of bringing about change toward a new society.

We agree that the main focus of action must be on the development of the movement itself and the building of a new society within the shell of the old. This is consistent with our Quaker-Christian insight that we can begin to live the Kingdom now, by being open to its Spirit and conforming our individual and common lives to its principles. Thus our stress on education, organization-building, and the development of counter-institutions.

But we cannot agree that amelioration and limited change in the present political economy is always worthless. For one thing, there are specific changes which, while limited in scope, would do much to relieve human suffering and ease the burden of fear which hangs over so many millions of people. For example, we support all efforts to change the practices and policies of the American government and business so that they will eliminate the hunger and malnutrition which afflict some ten million destitute Americans, even though the changes required to bring everyone an adequate diet would not necessarily be revolutionary. Our concern is that human life be more full, loving and joyful, and it would be cynical indeed to sacrifice real present betterment of life in hopes that the continued suffering of the hungry will inspire revolutionary fervor.

Revolutionary Reforms

Also, we agree with the French theoretician Andre Gorz that it is possible to work for revolutionary reforms i.e., "reforms which advance toward a radical transformation of society."[1] That is, there are changes in the present political economy which while not immediately ushering in the new society in toto, nevertheless advance us toward its actualization. Such "non-reformist reforms" bring about a more fundamental change. Although it is not always possible to distinguish in advance between a reformist and a revolutionary reform, the following criteria (there may be others) suggest themselves:

1. *Decentralization:* A revolutionary reform nearly always involves decentralization of decision-making power, the extension of popular control; and on the other hand restriction of the power of the centralized state or private profit-oriented capital.
2. *New society:* A revolutionary reform creates and/or strengthens post-revolutionary institutions, mirroring in the present society an aspect of the new, post-transitional society.
3. *People's control:* A non-reformist reform brings about a shift (or assumption) of control over resources to the people.
4. *Movement resources:* Revolutionary reforms release resources to the social change movement, thereby building its strength.
5. *Establishment resources:* A revolutionary reform erodes the resources of the establishment, giving it less access to power, privilege and wealth.
6. *Action:* A revolutionary reform comes about "where the action is" in terms of people's interests, and demands.

Perhaps some examples will illustrate how these criteria may be used to choose an action. Take, for example, the present tenants' rights movement, led nationally by the Washington-based National Tenants' Organization (NTO) and supported locally by innumerable tenants' councils, rent-strike groups, tenants' unions, etc., across the country. A major goal of NTO is that tenants, in both public and private housing, have real control over the decisions affecting them in their housing situations. Let us assume that the achievement of their goal requires a vast extension of cooperative, tenant-controlled housing throughout the private housing market, and the establishment of a high degree of tenant control in public housing, planning management, and budget allocation.

Because of the nation-wide interest and involvement of many people in the movement, it meets the citerion (#6) of being "where the action is." Should cooperative ownership and tenant control become widespread, landlords, housing speculators, real estate men, and public housing authorities (whose board of directors are usually drawn from the local power structure) would find their power and control over wealth (criterion #5) considerably reduced. Control over this decision-making power and these resources would shift in a major way to millions of tenants and tenants' organizations in cities and towns across the country (#3 and #1). To the extent that NTO and like organizations at the local level participate in the process of demanding changes, and then implementing and controlling them, resources will also shift to the social change movement (#4). Since our vision of a better economic system includes a situation in which "practically all housing could be constructed by housing cooperatives and could be owned cooperatively", a decisive move toward coops in this field would also meet the criterion (#2) of foreshadowing an aspect of the post-transition society here in the present.

In evaluating the success of a particular campaign, Nonviolent Revolutionary Groups might use four additional criteria:

1. The extent to which a proposed revolutionary reform was actually achieved.
2. The extent to which participants' radical consciousness was increased.
3. The extent to which mechanisms of transformation to the new society (e.g., more NRG's, parallel institutions, radical caucuses, etc.) were enhanced.
4. The extent to which the social change group was strengthened in its own internal democracy.

Transition to a New Political Economy

It is extremely difficult to try to peer into the murky future and to speculate about how a completely different society might come into being. Here is an area in which judgment, prophecy, utopianism, unanticipated historical events, and human fallibility are inextricably mixed. How much easier it would be to content ourselves with the years immediately ahead, to see ourselves as confronting immediate injustices and struggling for short-range humanizing reforms, forgetting about visions of a possible future with a radically different political and economic system.

Yet we are committed to the view that the present political economy must be replaced by a better one. Therefore, we must ask ourselves, not just how the present system can be *reformed,* but how its replacement can come about.

Lack of Clarity about a Political-Electoral Role

But, as can be seen from our scenario, we are not clear about the role of the political factor in the movement for revolutionary change—political in the sense of an organized movement that works to mobilize a majority behind its program in order to elect candidates for public office.

This issue is put in its sharpest form by the question: Mustn't there be organized, at some point, a mass-based, democratically-controlled *new party,* a revolutionary party which will advocate an American form of humanistic socialism, run candidates for national office, and try to gain control of the government?

We feel strongly that advocates of radical change should not try to form a political party now or in the immediate future. The task of the years immediately ahead is to do a great deal of organizing and educational work to develop a strong, nonviolent people's movement committed to fundamental change in America's political economy. We also feel that, if a party is ever formed, it should be intimately related to the nonviolent people's movement. We are not talking about *either* a party *or* a people's organization, but about a people's movement with a political wing.

Thus, we feel relatively clear about timing and about the form of a party, *if there should be a party at all.* But this latter point is one of the important matters that we have not been able to resolve. Would it be valuable for the people's movement to have a political wing, and should it engage in electoral campaigns?

Arguments for a Political-Electoral Approach

1. We are intrigued by countries such as Chile, Finland, and Sweden, and by Canadian provinces like Manitoba, in which socialist-oriented governments have gained power by nonviolent, electoral, and/or parliamentary means and have been able to use the leverage of governmental office to bring about far-reaching changes. Although the economies of these areas are still basically capitalistic, the economic sector has been humanized to a high degree and the governing parties are pressing for full-scale socialism. These historical examples suggest that the electoral route can be an important lever in working for fundamental change.

2.   An electoral approach is basically democratic. Rather than relying on coups or other elitist forms of change, it requires education of the public and winning a majority to your side. Also, as Engels pointed out,[2] electoral politics enable you to (1) count your supporters, (2) judge the strength of your opponents, (3) get in touch with the masses and do educational work, and (4) have opportunities for debate with other parties in public view, and put your opponents on the defensive.

3.   Once government power is achieved, the legal and administrative structure of government can be used to bring about and to sustain fundamental change, e.g., the setting up of the comprehensive system to guarantee income, work, health care, etc., which are part of the new society's vision. While unusual, it is not unknown for central government (e.g., Yugoslavia) to implement decentralized power, which we also see as crucial to the new society. A movement-type party could run on a platform calling for both decentralization and transnationalization of many of the functions and powers of central government.

4.   In one sense, a party and electoral approach is inevitable. That is, if a nonviolent people's movement begins really to gain mass adherence, there will be a political response in the form of candidates who will run on platforms embodying people's new consciousness. So, we might argue, there will be a political-electoral response anyway; why not take advantage of it and try to influence it in the right direction?

Arguments against a Political-Electoral Approach

1.   Practically the whole thrust of liberal and socialist thought during the past century has focused on strengthening the nation-state as a way of moving forward. But we have grave reservations about the nation-state, particularly a state which encompasses 200 million people. Its vast power makes it almost inevitable that is will use up far more than its share of world resources and that it will be tempted to military adventurism. Perhaps the goal of a nonviolent people's movement should be the *dismantling* of the American Goliath, rather than taking it over. Yet the goal of the electoral process is the achievement of control over the nation-state. Would such control be an advantage, or an albatross around the movement's neck?

2.   The party-electoral route facilitates control at the center. It tends to validate and sanction central bureaucracies of government and party. Yet the challenge of the kind of social change we have been describing is to build *people's* power, rather than make people subservient to power centers far removed from their daily lives. The issue shouldn't be posed as "taking power," but as "redistributing power." The goal is not to elect a

benevolent vanguard who run the central government for the benefit of the people, but the return of power to the people.

3.   Leaders of a people's movement should be validated, not in partisan debate, but in leadership in the streets; not for their skill in parliamentary games, but for their ability to lead significant mass struggle. People need to learn the skills of mass nonviolent action, and electoral action will divert their energies from this important task.

4.   Politics inevitably involves compromise. Politicians are brokers of power, and it is extremely difficult for the people to know what is happening in the inner councils of power. A mass nonviolent movement cannot occur behind closed doors. Its nature is mass struggle in the open, where the people can see what is going on. Revolutions are betrayed, not by the masses, but by their leaders.

5.   Even if candidates running on a people's platform were elected to Congress, they would find that they have very little power, since so much real decision-making in the country now emanates from the Pentagon, the White House, and the corporate hierarchy. Yet, in order to get elected, candidates would need to promise that they can deliver meaningful changes—when they fail to do so, demoralization sets in. The choice seems to be between strong radical candidates who don't compromise and don't get elected, or candidates who *are* elected but find that they don't have any real power.

In the movement-party-electrol route to change, we envisage a revolutionary party, controlled and supported by a nonviolent people's movement, which wins elections and eventually gains a majority in Congress and control of the presidency. Using education and legislation, its sets about the transformation of the political and economic system, creating public corporations, setting up cooperatives and worker-controlled enterprises, passing a maximum income and assets law, organizing a comprehensive planning system, dismantling the military forces, setting up a universal social and medical services, working out equitable relationships with the Third World, transnationalizing some functions formerly filled by federal government, and so on. When it meets resistance from entrenched wealth, privilege, and power, it cooperates with the people's movement, using nonviolent protest,noncooperation, and intervention to support its initiatives. If faced by an attempted coup d'etat, it uses the same kind of noncooperation that was so effective in preventing the 1920 coup of Wolfgang Kapp in German. (Kapp was established in power by a group of military officers, but was faced immediately with a complete general strike, including even the civil service. this was so effective that the erstwhile head of government found himself wandering up and down the corridors of power looking in vain for a secretary to type his proclamations. Despite his efforts to repress the resistance by shooting unarmed demonstrators, Kapp found himself without the means of governing and fled to Sweden.)[3]

In the *non-electoral, people's movement route,* the transition comes about after the establishment finds itself unable to make any more concessions. An active and well-organized people's movement has engaged in widespread demonstrations, mass boycotts, and strikes, all aimed at protesting existing inequalities and demanding radical change to a new kind of economic and political order. At first, the government and corporate system is able to make concessions in the shape of reforms, but eventually every "outpost" of reform is taken and the "fortress" is reached—the establishment realizes that it cannot give further changes without radical reduction in its privileges and power.

Discredited and confronted on every hand by protesting groups, it tries to defend its privilege, but finds that even the formerly reliable police and military can no longer be counted upon because of movement fraternization and nonviolent tactics, and that repression discredits the government still further. Eventually, the government and business establishment find themselves powerless to prevent radical caucuses and workers' cadres from taking over existing factories and institutions, or to stop NRG's from occupying and controlling the organizations of local and national life. Local NRG's parallel institutions, and radical caucuses elect representatives to regional "Congresses of Free Americans", to which more and more citizens pay their taxes and which become, in effect, the functioning government. The old, delegitimized structure of government and corporations collapses and is replaced by new structures which grow directly out of people's institutions. The regional Congresses institute much the same kind of eco-democratic socialist system described in the movement-party-electoral route, and then cooperate with revolutionary movements in other countries in creating transnational institutions.

The Need for Further Discussion

The kind of revolution that we are advocating—with its nonviolent methodology, its particular view of a desired future, its emphasis on the ecological imperative, its democratic participation—has never before been achieved. Therefore, although we can learn from history, there are no existing historical models to tell us the best direction when we come to the transition state. For this reason, we look forward to intense dialog among ourselves and with others who believe in a living revolution to come to greater clarity concerning the best route to follow.

But there is no need to delay action until such a dialogue is far advanced. We can begin *now* in the task of conscientization and organization building, and can begin *now* to "live the revolution" in our own individual lives.

LIVING THE REVOLUTION

We have written a great deal about the vision of a better society and the need to generate a powerful movement in the direction of that vision. Yet there is a danger of becoming too fascinated with the goal, the vision, the ends of our action. The danger is to rationalize and justify inhuman acts in the present in order to build a more humane situation in the future, "after the Revolution." But the fact is that we cannot be sure that our ends will be attained, whereas we *can* be sure that the means we use are humane in themselves, and to that extent be sure that our action is contributing to the forces of humanity in the world.

We are convinced that the American political economy must be profoundly transformed. We want to build a new society whose institutions will be structured to do all that institutions *can* do to encourage the development of full, loving persons. But we are clear that such a new society will not be *produced* unless the "agents of social change" are doing all they can to become full, loving persons *themselves.* And that kind of new society won't be sustained unless it is thoroughly "infiltrated" by people whoe commitment is to such values as love, justice, community, cooperation, simplicity, world equality, shared power, mutual well-being, and harmony of humanity with nature. We believe, with Gandhi, that "if we have no love for our neighbors, no change, however revolutionary, can do us any good." Institutions and structures can do much to enhance human dignity, or to crush it, to enable love to find expression, or to subvert it, but no system can *automatically* assure that humans will behave toward one another in a spirit of brotherhood and sisterhood and justice. Ultimately, such behavior depends upon a choice made deep within each person, and we would be unfaithful to our vision if we did not say something about the kinds of choices we believe individuals must make if a real revolutions for life is to come about.

Getting Our Heads Together

For a person truly interested in fundamental change, there is no substitute for careful thought and study. No one can do our thinking for us. All of us must become involved in the most searching kind of study until we can begin to answer the basic questions of social change: "How do *you* analyze what's wrong with the present in the present system?" "What's *your* vision of a better society?" "What's *your* strategy for moving toward that better society?"

Life Style

The six percent of the earth's population found in the United States presently uses up about forty percent of the world's resources. Thus burning up of resources not only reflects a tremendously unjust distribution of wealth, but also threatens human survival because of its damage to the eco-system. We have an opportunity to begin to right this balance in the way *we* live. We can adopt much simpler life styles. We can find ways to recycle goods, to have less elaborate clothes, cheaper food and transport, to overcome thé tyranny of egocentric accumulation. We can experiment with shared, simple life styles, living in community with others and learning from each other how to transcend over-individualism and over-accumulation. (For those of us who are Quakers, it is fascinating to wee how the traditional Friends' testimonies on simplicity and brother and sisterhood are found consistent with the ecological imperative.)

Inner Life-Consciousness

The revolutionary changes we foresee will not be brought about without crisis, struggle and pain. Our lives are bound to be interrupted, whether by periods in prison or by other incursions. Because of our confrontation with evil, injustice and lovelessness, there will be a constant temptation to let our love grow cold. There will be times of disagreement and tension with friends and comrades, and it will be tempting to engage in egocentric struggle with those closest to us.

Because each of us has been reared in a social order deeply pervaded by the accumulated results of individual and corporate materialism, exploitation, and irresponsible self-seeking, each of us adds a share to the existing over-abundance of evil.

We need to discover depths within ourselves upon which we can draw for inner peace, a sense of self-respect, the capacity to give and receive love. We need to use any means necessary (e.g., mediation, reading, prayer, group worship, counseling) to personally live at the deeper levels, to grow in the ability to express and to receive love, to find inner security and strength, to develop the capacity for courage, and to otherwise transcend our all-too-human proclivities to egocentric assertion on the one hand, and irresponsible apathy on the other.

Everything, Peguy says, begins with mysticism and ends in politics. Prayer, meditation, and other means of individual transformation are among the most concrete, super practical means we can use to overcome prejudice, hatred, exploitation, and lovelessness—i.e., our own! They provide one of the sure-fire places where we have an opportunity every day to turn evil into good and to begin building a revolution which makes love more possible.

Relationships and Emotion

It should go without saying that anyone trying to build a new society should do everything possible to free himself or herself or any traces of racism, sexism, or class snobbery. Recognizing how easy it is to develop antagonisms against those closest to us in the movement, we can find ways to be reconciling, forgiving, affirming the good in others, not being authoritarian or domineering. We can draw on the resources of sensitivity training, group dynamics, encounter groups, etc., to find new ways to creatively express our anger, to be freed up to be more open, more able to express love by touching as well as by words. We can learn by singing, nature, and the enjoyment of relationships to be more relaxed emotionally and to celebrate the simple joy of being alive.

Alternative Institutions

One practical way to "live the revolution" and to affirm new values and institutions immediately is to support those groups and structures which now exist and which mirror, however imperfectly, the values of the new society, e.g., shopping through a food co-op, sending children to a cooperative school, worshipping in an underground church, participating in a radical caucus.

Non-exploitation

Although we cannot divorce ourselves entirely from the present system, we should try to free ourselves as much as possible from its exploitative aspects, particularly in terms of giving up or re-channeling into movement support the unearned income which comes from the ownership of stocks, bonds, or real estate or which flows from inheritance. And we can refuse war taxes, giving the amounts saved to organizations and movements which are trying to build a new society in which militarism will be an anachronism.

These are some of the qualities which we would hope to see growing in ourselves and in those with whom we work in the movement. The Quaker leader, Rufus Jones, expressed this view very well in a talk at the Friends World Conference in 1937, when he said:

The social order must be profoundly transformed and adjusted to the demands of justice and fairness for all men. But whatever happens to the social and economic order, the quality of spirit of those who compose the social structure will always be the essential matter . . . Even now, in a world far from being rightly fashioned, we can help toward the reorganization of it by a faithful and consistent practice of simplicity of life, sincerity of heart, brotherliness of spirit toward all men.

NOTES

1. Andre Gorz, *Strategy for Labor* (Boston: Beacon Press, 1968), pp.6 ff.
2. "Introduction to the Class Struggle in France, 1848-50."
3. George Lakey, *Strategy for A Living Revolution.* (unpublished, mimeographed manuscript), pp.63-64.

23.

From:
Post-Scarcity Anarchism

Murray Bookchin

Preconditions and Possibilities

All the successful revolutions of the past have been particularistic revolutions of minority classes seeking to assert their specific interests over those of society as a whole. The great bourgeois revolutions of modern times offered an ideology of sweeping political reconstitution, but in reality they merely certified the social dominance of the bourgeoisie, giving formal political expression to the economic ascendancy of capital. The lofty notions of the "nation," the "free citizen," of equality before the law, concealed the mundane reality of the centralized state, the atomized isolated man, the dominance of bourgeois interest. Despite their sweeping ideological claims, the particularistic revolutions replaced the rule of one class by another, one system of exploitation by another, one system of toil by another, and one system of psychological repression by another.

What is unique about our era is that the particularistic revolution has now been subsumed by the possibility of the generalized revolution —complete and totalistic. Bourgeois society, if it achieved nothing else, revolutionized the means of production on a scale unprecedented in history. This technological revolution, culminating in cybernation, has created the objective, quantitative basis for a world without class rule, exploitation toil or material want. The means now exist for the development of the rounded man, the total man, freed of guilt and the workings of authoritarian modes of training, and given over to desire and the sensuous apprehension of the marvelous. It is now possible to conceive of man's future experience in terms of a coherent process in which the bifurcations of thought and activity, mind and sensuousness, discipline and spontaneity, individuality and community, man and nature, town and country, education and life, work and play are all resolved, harmonized, and organically wedded in a qualitatively new realm of freedom. Just as the particularized revolution produced a particularized, bifurcated society, so the generalized revolution can produce and organically unified, many-sided community. The great wound opened by propertied society in the form of the "social question" can now be healed.

That freedom must be conceived of in human terms, not in animal terms — in terms of life, not of survival — is clear enough. Men do not remove their ties of bondage and become fully human merely by divesting themselves of social domination and obtaining freedom in its *abstract* form. They must also be free *concretely:* free from material want, from toil, from the burden of devoting the greater part of their time, indeed, the greater part of their lives, to the struggle with necessity. To have seen these material preconditions for human freedom, to have emphasized that freedom presupposes free time and the material abundance for abolishing free time as a social privilege, is the contribution of Karl Marx to modern revolutionary theory.

By the same token, the *preconditions* for freedom must not be mistaken for the *conditions* of freedom. The *possibility* of liberation does not constitute its *reality*. Along with its positive aspects, technological advance has a distinctly negative, socially regressive side. If it is true that technological progress enlarges the historical potentiality for freedom, it is also true that the bourgeois control of technology reinforces the established organization of society and everyday life. Technology and the resources of abundance furnish capitalism with the means for assimilating large sections of society to the established system of hierarchy and authority. They provide the system with the weaponry, the detecting devices and the propaganda media for the threat as well as the reality of massive repression. By their centralistic nature, the resources of abundance reinforce the monopolistic, centralistic and bureaucratic tendencies in the political apparatus. In short, they furnish the state with historically unprecedented means for manipulating and mobilizing the entire environment of life — and perpetuating hierarchy, exploitation and unfreedom.

It must be emphasized, however, that this manipulation and mobilization of the environment is extremely problematical and laden with crises. Far from leading to pacification (one can hardly speak, here, of harmonization), the attempt of bourgeois society to control and exploit its environment, natural as well as social, has devastating consequences. Volumes have been written on the pollution of the atmosphere and waterways, on the destruction of tree cover and soil, and on toxic materials in foods and liquids. Even more threatening in their final results are the pollution and destruction of the very ecology required for a complex organism like man. The concentration of radioactive wastes in living things is a menace to the health and genetic endowment of nearly all species. Worldwide contamination by pesticides that inhibit oxygen production in plankton or by the near-toxic level of lead from gasoline exhaust are examples of an enduring pollution that threatens the biological integrity of all advanced life forms — including man.

No less alarming is the fact that we must drastically revise our traditional notions of what constitutes environmental pollutant. A few decades ago it would have been absured to describe carbon dioxide and heat as pollutants in the customary sense of the term. Yet both may well rank among the most serious sources of future ecological imbalance and may pose major threats to the viability of the planet. As a result of industrial and domestic combusion activities, the quantity of carbon dioxide in the atmosphere has increased by roughly twenty-five percent in the past one hundred years, and may well double by the end of the century. The famous "greenhouse effect" which the increasing quantity of the gas is expected to produce has been widely discussed in the media; eventually, it is supposed, the gas will inhibit the dissipation of the world's heat into space, causing a rise in overall temperatures which will melt the polar ice caps and result in the inundation of vast coastal areas. Thermal pollution, the result mainly of warm water discharged by nuclear and conventional power plants, has had disastrous effects on the ecology of lakes, rivers and estuaries. Increases in water temperature not only damage the physiological and reproductive activities of the fish, they also promote the great blooms of algae that have become such formidable problems in waterways.

Ecologically, bourgeois exploitation and manipulation are undermining the very capacity of the earth to sustain advanced forms of life. The crisis is being heightened by massive increases in air and water pollution; by a mounting accumulation of nondegradable wastes, lead residues, pesticide résidues and toxic additives in food; by the expansion of cities into vast urban belts; by increasing stresses due to congestion, noise and mass living; and by the wanton scarring of the earth as a result of mining operations, lumbering, and real estate speculation. As a result, the earth has been despoiled in a few decades on a scale that is unprecedented in the entire history of human habitation of the planet.

Socially, bourgeois exploitation and manipulation have brought everyday life to the most excruciating point of facuity and boredom. As society has been converted into a factory and a marketplace, the very rationale of life has been reduced to production for its own sake — and consumption for its own sake.

The Redemptive Dialectic

Is there a redemptive dialectic that can guide the social development in the direction of an anarchic society where people will attain full control over their daily lives? Or does the social dialectric come to an end with capitalism, its possibilities sealed off by the use of a highly advanced technology for repressive and co-optative purposes?

We must learn here from the limits of Marxism, a project which, understandably in a period of material scarcity, anchored the social dialectic and the contradictions of capitalism in the economic realm. Marx, it has been emphasized, examined the *preconditions* for liberation, not the *conditions* of liberation. The Marxian critique is rooted in the past, in the era of material want and relatively limited technological development. Even its humanistic theory of alienation turns primarily on the issue of work and man's alienation from the product of his labor. Today, however, capitalism is a parasite on the future, a vampire that survives on the technology and resources of freedom. The industrial capitalism of Marx's time organized its commodity relations around a prevailing system of material abundance. A century ago, scarcity had to be endured; today, it has to be enforced — hence the importance of the state in the present era. It is not that modern capitalism has resolved its contradictions and annulled the social dialectic, but rather that the social dialectic and the contradictions of capitalism have been expanded from the economic to the hierarchical realms of society, from the abstract "historic" domain to the concrete minutiae of everyday experience, from the arena of survival to the arena of life.

The dialectic of bureaucratic state capitalism originates in the contradiction between the repressive character of commodity society and the enormous potential freedom opened by technological advance. This contradiction also opposes the exploitative organization of society to the natural world — a world that includes not only the natural environment, but also man's "nature" — his Eros-derived impulses. The contradiction between the exploitative organization of society and the natural environment is beyond co-optation: the atmosphere, the waterways, the soil and the ecology required for human survival are not redeemable by reforms, concessions, or modifications of strategic policy. There is no technology that can reproduce atmospheric oxygen in sufficient quantities to sustain life on this planet. There is no substitute for the hydrological systems of the earth. There is no technique for removing massive environmental pollution by radioactive isotopes, pesticides, lead and petroleum wastes. Nor is there the faintest evidence that bourgeois society will relent at any time in the foreseeable future in its disruption of vital ecolotgical processes, in its exploitation of natural resources, and its use of the atmosphere and waterways as dumping areas for wastes, or in its cancerous mode of urbanization and land abuse.

Even more immediate is the contradiction between the exploitative organization of society and man's Eros-derived impuses — a contradiction that manifests itself as the banalization and improverishment of experience in a bureaucratically manipulated, impersonal mass society. The Eros-derived impulses in man can be repressed and sublimated, but they can never be eliminated. They are renewed with every birth of a human being and with every generation of youth. It is not surprising today that the young, more than any economic class or stratum, articulate the life-impulses in humanity's nature — the urgings of desire, sensuousness, and the lure of the marvelous. Thus, the biological matrix, from which hierarchical society emerged ages ago, reappears at a new level with the era that marks the end of hierarchy, only now this matrix is saturated with social phenomena. Short of manipulating humanity's germ plasm, the life-impulses can be annulled only with the annihilation of man himself.

The contradictions within bureaucratic state capitalism permeate all the hierarchical forms developed and overdeveloped by bourgeois society. The hierarchical forms which nurtured propertied society for ages and promoted its development — the state, city, centralized economy, bureaucracy, patriarchal family, and marketplace — have reached their historic limits. They have exhausted their social functions as modes of stabilization. It is not a question of whether these hierarchical forms were ever "progressive" in the Marxian sense of the term. As Raoul Vaneigem has observed: "perhaps it isn't enough to say that hierarchical power has preserved humanity for thousands of years as alcohol preserves a fetus, by arresting either growth or decay." Today these forms constitute the target of all the revolutionary forces that are generated by modern capitalism, and whether one sees their outcome as nuclear catastrophe or ecological disaster *they now threaten the very survival of humanity.*

With the development of hierarchical forms into a threat to the very existence of humanity, the social dialectic, far from being annulled, acquires a new dimension. It poses the "social question" in an entirely new way. If man had to acquire the conditions of survival in order to live (as

Marx emphasized), now he must acquire the conditions of life in order to survive. By this inversion of the relationship between survival and life, revolution acquires a new sense of urgency. No longer are we faced with Marx's famous choice of socialism or barbarism; we are confronted with the more drastic alternatives of anarchism or annihilation. The problems of necessity and survival have become congruent with the problems of freedom and life. They cease to require any theoretical mediation, "transitional" stages, or centralized organizations to bridge the gap between the existing and the possible. The possible, in fact, is all that can exist. Hence, the problems of "transition," which occupied the Marxists for nearly a century, are eliminated not only by the advance of technology, but by the social dialectic itself. The problems of social reconstruction have been reduced to practical tasks that can be solved spontaneously by self-liberatory acts of society.

Revolution, in fact, acquires not only a new sense of urgency, but a new sense of promise. In the hippies' tribalism, in the drop-out lifestyles and free sexuality of millions of youth, in the spontaneous affinity groups of the anarchists, we find forms of affirmation that follow from acts of negation. With the inversion of the "social question" there is also a inversion of the social dialectic; a "yea" emerges automatically and simultaneously with a "nay."

The solutions take their point of departure from the problems. When the time has arrived in history that the state, the city, bureaucracy, the centralized economy, the patriarchal family and the marketplace have reached their historic limits, what is posed is no longer a change in form but the absolute negation of *all* hierarchical forms *as such*. The absolute negation of the state is anarchism — a situation in which men liberate not only "history," but all the immediate circumstances of their everyday lives. The absolute negation of the city is community — a community in which the social environment is decentralized into rounded, ecologically balanced communes. The absolute negation of bureaucracy is immediate as distinguished from mediated realtions — a situation in which representation is replaced by face-to-face relations in a general assembly of free individuals. The absolute negation of the centralized economy is regional ecotechnology — a situation in which the instruments of production are molded to the resources of an ecosystem. The absolute negation of the patriarchal family is liberated sexuality — in which all forms of sexual regulation are transcended by the spontaneous, untrammeled expression of eroticism among equals. The absolute negation of the marketplace is communism — in which collective abundance and cooperation transform labor into play and need into desire.

Spontaneity and Utopia

It is not accidental that at a point in history when hierarchical power and manipulation have reached their most threatening proportions, the very concepts of hierarchy, power and manipulation are being brought into question. The challenge to these concepts comes from a rediscovery of the importance of spontaneity — a rediscovery nourished by ecology, by a heightened conception of self-development, and by a new understanding of the revolutionary process in society.

What ecology has shown is that balance in nature is achieved by organic variation and complexity, not by homogeneity and simplification. For example, the more varied the flora and fauna of an ecosystem, the more stable the population of a potential pest. The more environmental diversity is diminished, the greater will the population of a potential pest fluctuate with the probability that it will get out of control. Left to itself, an ecosystem tends spontaneously toward organic differentiation, greater variety of flora and fauna, and diversity in the number of prey and predators. This does not mean that interference by man must be avoided. The need for a productive agriculture, itself a form of interference with nature, must always remain in the foreground of an ecological approach to food cultivation and forest management. No less important is the fact that man can often produce changes in an ecosystem that would vastly improve its ecological quality. But these efforts require insight and understanding, not the exercise of brute power and manipulation.

This concept of management, this new regard for the importance of spontaneity, has far-reaching applications for technology and community — indeed, for the social image of man in a liberated society. It challenges the capitalist ideal of agriculture as a factory operation, organized around immense, centrally controlled land-holdings, highly specialized forms of monoculture, the reduction of the terrain to a factory floor, the substitution of chemical for organic processes, the use of gang-labor, etc. If food cultivation is to be a mode of cooperation with nature rather than a contest between opponents, the agriculturist must become thoroughly familiar with the ecology of the land; he must acquire a new sensitivity to its needs and possibilities. This presupposes the reduction of agriculture to a human scale, the restoration of moderate-sized agricultural units, and the diversification of the agricultural situation; in short, it presupposes a decentralized, ecological system of food cultivation.

The same reasoning applies to pollution control. The development of giant factory complexes and the use of single- or dual-energy sources are responsible for atmospheric pollution. Only by developing smaller industrial units and diversifying energy sources by the extensive use of clean power (solar, wind and water power) will it be possible to reduce industrial pollution. The means for this radical technological change are now at hand. Technologists have developed miniaturized substitutes for large-scale industrial operation — small versatile machines and sophisticated methods for converting solar, wind and water energy into power usable in industry and the home. These substitutes are often more productive and less wasteful than the large-scale facilities that exist today.

The implications of small-scale agriculture and industry for a community are obvious: if humanity is to use the principles needed to manage an ecosystem, the basic communal unit of social life must itself become an ecosystem — an ecocommunity. It too must become diversified, balanced and well-rounded. By no means is this concept of community motivated exclusively by the need for a lasting balance between man and the natural world; it also accords with the utopian ideal of the rounded man, the individual whose sensibilities, range of experience and life-style are nourished by a wide range of stimuli, by a diversity of activities, and by a social scale that always remains within the comprehension of a single human being. Thus the means and conditions of survival become the means and conditions of life; need becomes desire and desire becomes need. The point is reached where the greatest social decomposition provides the source of the highest form of social integration, bringing the most pressing ecological necessities into a common focus with the highest utopian ideals.

If it is true, as Guy Debord observes, that "daily life is the measure of everything: of the fulfillment or rather the non-fulfillment of human relationships, of the use we make of our time," a question arises: Who are "we" whose daily lives are to be fulfilled? And how does the liberated self emerge that is capable of turning time into life, space into community, and human relationships into the marvelous?

The liberation of the self involves, above all, a social process. In a society that has shriveled the self into a commodity, into an object manufactured for exchange — there can be no fulfilled self. There can only be the beginnings of selfhood, the *emergence* of a self that seeks fulfillment — a self that is largely defined by the obstacles it must overcome to achieve realization. In a society whose belly is distended to the brusting point with revolution, whose chronic state is an unending series of labor pains, whose real condition is a mounting emergency, only one thought and act is relevant — giving birth. Any environment, private or social, that does not make this fact the center of human experience is a sham and diminishes whatever self remains to us after we have absorbed our daily poison of everyday life in bourgeois society.

It is plain that the goal of revolution today must be the liberation of daily life. Any revolution that fails to achieve this goal is counter-revolution.

Above all, it is *we* who have to be liberated, *our* daily lives, with all their moments, hours and days, and not universals like "History" and "Society." The self must always be *indentifiable* in the revolution, not overwhelmed by it. The self must always be *perceivable* in the revolutionary process, not submerged by it. There is no word that is more sinister in the "revolutionary" vocabulary than "masses." Revolutionary liberation must be a self-liberation that reaches social dimensions, not "mass liberation" or "class liberation" behind which lurks the rule of an elite, a hierarchy and a state. If a revolution fails to produce a new society by the self-activity and self-mobilization of revolutionaries, if it does not involve the forging of a self in the revolutionary process, the revolution will once again circumvent those whose lives are to be lived every day and leave daily life unaffected. Out of the revolution must emerge a self that takes full possession of daily life, not a daily life that once takes full possession of self. The most advanced form of class consciousness thus becomes self-consciousness — the concentration in daily life of the great liberating universal.

If for this reason alone, the revolutionary movement is profoundly concerned with lifestyle. It must try to *live* the revolution in all its totality, not only participate in it. It must be deeply concerned with the way the revolutionist lives, his relations with the surrounding environment, and his degree of self-emancipation. In seeking to change society, the revolutionist cannot avoid changes in himself that demand the reconquest of his own being. Like the movement in which he participates, the revolutionist must try to reflect the conditions of the society he is trying to achieve — at least to the degree that this is possible today.

The treacheries and failures of the past half century have made it axiomatic that there *can be no separation of the revolutionary process from the revolutionary goal.* A society whose fundamental aim is self-administration in all facets of life can be achieved only by self-activity. This implies a mode of administration that is always possessed by the self. The power of man over man can be destroyed only by the very process in which man acquires power over his own life and in which he not only "discovers" himself but, more meaningfully, in which he formulates his self-hood in all its social dimensions.

A libertarian society can be achieved only by a libertarian revolution. Freedom cannot be "delivered" to the individual as the "end-product" of a "revolution"; the assembly and community cannot be legislated or decreed into existence. A revolutionary group can seek, purposively and consciously, to promote the creation of these forms, but if assembly and community are not allowed to emerge organically, if their growth is not matured by the process of demassification, by self-activity and by self-realization, they will remain nothing but forms, like the soviets in post-revolutionary Russia. Assembly and community must arise within the revolutionary process; indeed, the revolutionary procees must *be* the formation of assembly and community, and also the destruction of power, property, hierarchy and exploitation.

Revolution as self-activity is not unique to our time. It is the paramount feature of all the great revolutions in modern history. It marked the *journées* of the *sans-culottes* in 1792 and 1793, the famous "Five Days" of February 1917 in Petrograd, the uprising of the Barcelona proletariat in 1936, the early days of the Hungarian Revolution in 1956, and the May-June events of Paris in 1968. Nearly every revolutionary uprising in the history of our time has been initiated spontaneously by the self-activity of "masses" — often in flat defiance of the hesitant policies advanced by the revolutionary organizations. Every one of these revolutions has been marked by extraordinary individuation, by a joyousness and solidarity that turned everyday life into a festival. This surreal dimension of the revolutionary process, with its explosion of deep-seated libidinal forces, grins irascibly through the pages of history like the face of a satyr on shimmering water. It is not without reason that the Bolshevik commissars smashed the wine bottles in the Winter Palace on the night of November 7, 1917.

The puritanism and work ethic of the traditional left stem from one of the most powerful forces opposing revolution today — the capacity of the bourgeois environment to infiltrate the revolutionary framework. The origins of this power lie in the commodity nature of man under capitalism, a quality that is almost automatically transferred to the organized group — and which the group, in turn, reinforces in its members. As the late Josef Weber emphasized, all organized groups "have the tendency to render themselves autonomous, i.e., to alienate themselves from their original aim and to become an end in themselves in the hands of those administering them." This phenomenon is as true of revolutionary organizations as it is of state and semi-state institutions, official parties and trade unions.

The problem of alienation can never be completely resolved apart from the revolutionary process itself, but it can be guarded against by an acute awareness that the problem exists, and partly solved by a voluntary but drastic remaking of the revolutionary and his group. This remaking can only begin when the revolutionary group recognizes that it is a catalyst in the revolutionary process, not a "vanguard." The revolutionary group must clearly see that its goal is not the seizure of power but the dissolution of power — indeed, it must see that the entire problem of power, of control from below and control from above, can be solved only if there is no above or below.

Above all, the revolutionary group must divest itself of the forms of power — statutes, hierarchies, property, prescribed opinions, fetishes, paraphernalia, official etiquette — and of the subtlest as well as the most obvious of bureaucratic and bourgeois traits that consciously and unconscously reinforce authority and hierarchy. The group must remain open to public scrutiny not only in its formulated decisions but also in their very formulation. It must be coherent in the profound sense that its theory is its practice and its practice its theory. It must do away with all commodity relations in its day-to-day existence and constitute itself along the decentralizing organizational principles of the very society it seeks to achieve — community, assembly, spontaneity. It must, in Josef Weber's superb words, be "marked always by simplicity and clarity, always thousands of unprepared people can enter and direct it, always it remains *transparent* to and controlled by all." Only then, when the revolutionary movement is congruent with the decentralized community it seeks to achieve, can it avoid becoming another elitist obstacle to the social development and dissolve into the revolution like surgical thread into a healing wound.

Prospect

The most important process going on in America today is the sweeping de-institutionalization of the bourgeois social structure. A basic, far-reaching disrespect and a profound disloyalty are developing toward the values, the forms, the aspirations and, above all, the institutions of the established order. On a scale unprecedented in American history, millions of people are shedding their commitment to the society in which they live. They no longer believe in its claims. They no longer respect its symbols. They no longer accept its goals, and, most significantly, they refuse almost intuitively to live by its institutional and social codes.

This growing refusal runs very deep. It extends from an opposition to war into a hatred of political manipulation in all its forms. Starting from a rejection of racism, it brings into question the very existence of hierarchical power as such. In its detestation of middle-class values and lifestyles it rapidly evolves into a rejection of the commodity system; from an irritation with environmental pollution, it passes into a rejection of the American city and modern urbanism. In short, it tends to transcend every particularistic critique of the society and to evolve into a generalized opposition to the bourgeois order on an every boradening scale.

In this respect, the period in which we live closely resembles the revolutionary Enlightenment that swept through France in the eighteenth century — a period that completely reworked French consciousness and prepared the conditions for the Great Revolution of 1789. Then as now, the old institutions were slowly pulverized by molecular action from below long before they were toppled by mass revolutionary action. This molecular movement creates an atmosphere of general lawlessness: a growing personal day-to-day disobedience, a tendency not to "go along" with the existing system, a seemingly "petty" but nevertheless critical attempt to circumvent restriction in every facet of daily life. The society, in effect, becomes disorderly, undisciplined, Dionysian — a condition that reveals itself most dramatically in an increasing rate of official crimes. A vast critique of the system devlops — the actual Enlightenment itself, two centuries ago, and the sweeping critique that exists today — which seeps downward and accelerates the molecular movement at the base. Be it an angry gesture, a "riot" or a conscious change in lifestyle, an ever-increasing number of people, who have no more of a commitment to an organized revolutionary movement than they have to society itself, begin spontaneously to engage in their own defiant propaganda of the deed.

In its concrete details, the disintegrating social process is nourished by many sources. The process develops with all the uneveness, indeed with all the contradictions, that mark every revolutionary trend. In eighteenth century France, radical ideology oscillated between a rigid scientism and a sloppy romanticism. Notions of freedom were anchored in a precise, logical ideal of self-control, and also a vague, instinctive norm of spontaneity. Rousseau stood at odds with d'Holbach, Diderot at odds with Voltaire, yet in retrospect we can see that one not only transcended but also presupposed the other in a *cumulative* development toward revolution.

The same uneven, contradictory and cumulative development exists today, and in many cases it follows a remarkably direct course. The "beat" movement created the most important breach in the solid, middle-class values of the 1950s, a breach that was widened enormously by the illegal-ities of pacifists, civil-right workers, draft resisters and longhairs. Moreover, the merely reactive response of rebellious American youth has produced invaluable forms of libertarian and utopian affirmation — the right to make love without restriction, the goal of community, the disavowal of money and commodities, the belief in mutual aid, and a new respect for spontaneity. Easy as it is for revolutionaries to criticize certain pitfalls within this orientation of personal and social values, the fact remains that it has played a preparatory role of decisive importance in forming the present atmosphere of indiscipline, spontaneity, radicalism and freedom.

A second parallel between the revolutionary Enlightenment and our own period is the emergence of the crowd, the so-called "mob," as a major vehicle of social protest. The typical institutionalized forms of public dissatisfaction — in our own day, they are orderly elections, demonstra-tion and mass meetings — tend to give way to direct action by crowds. This shift from predictable, highly organized protests within the institution-alized framework of the existing society to sporadic, spontaneous, near-insurrectionary assaults from outside (and even against) socially acceptable forms reflects a profound change in popular psychology. The "rioter" has begun to break, however partially and intuitively, with those deep-seated norms of behavior which traditionally weld the "masses" to the established order. He actively sheds the internalized structure of authority, the long-cultivated body of conditioned reflexes, and the pattern of submission sustained by guilt that tie one to the system even more effectively than any fear of police violence and juridical reprisal. Contrary to the views of social psychologists, who see in these modes of direct action the submission of the individual to a terrifying collective entity called "mob," the truth is that "riots" and crowd actions represent the first gropings of the mass toward individuation. The mass tends to become demassified in the sense that it begins to assert itself against the really massifying automatic responses produced by the bourgeois family, the school and the mass media. By the same token, crowd actions involve the rediscovery of the streets and the effort to liberate them. Ultimately, it is in the streets that power must be dissolved: for the streets, and the effort to liberate them. Ultimately, it is in the streets where daily life is endured, suffered and eroded, and where power is confronted and fought, must be turned into the domain where daily life is enjoyed, created and nourished. The rebellious crowd marked the beginning not only of a spontaneous transmutation of private into social revolt to the issues of everyday life.

Finally, as in the Enlightenment, we are seeing the emergence of an immense and ever-growing stratum of *déclassés*, a body of lumpenized individuals drawn from every stratum of society. The chronically indebted and socially insecure middle classes of our period compare loosely with the chronically insolvent and flighty nobility of prerevolutionary France. A vast flotsam of educated people emerged then as now, living at loose ends, without fixed careers or established social roots. At the bottom of both structures we find a large number of chronic poor — vagabonds, drifters, people with part-time jobs or no jobs at all, threatening, unruly *sans-culottes* — surviving on public aid and on the garbage thrown off by society, the poor of the Parisian slums, the blacks of the American ghettoes.

But here all the parallels end. The French Enlightenment belongs to a period of revolutionary transistion from feudalism to capitalism — both societies based on economic scarcity, class rule, exploitation, social hierarchy and state power. The day-to-day popular resistance which marked the eighteenth century and culminated in open revolution was soon disciplined by the newly emerging industrial order — as well as by naked force. The vast mass of *déclassés* and *sans-culottes* was largely absorbed into the factory system and tamed by industrial discipline. Formerly rootless intellectuals and footloose nobles found secure places in the economic, political, social and cultural hierarchy of the new bourgeois order. From a socially and culturally fluid condition, highly generalized in its structure and relations, society hardened again into rigid, particularized class and institutional forms — the classical Victorian era appeared not only in England but, to one degree or another, in all of Western Europe and America. Critique was consolidated into apologia, revolt into reform, *déclassés* into clearly defined classes and "mob" into political constituencies. "Riots" became the well-behaved processionals we call "demonstrations," and spontaneous direct action turned into electoral rituals.

Our own era is also a transitional one, but with a profound and new difference. In the last of their great insurrections, the *sans-culottes* of the French Revolution rose under the fiery cry: "Bread and the Constitution of '93!" The black *sans-culottes* of the American ghettoes rise under the slogan: "Black is beautiful!" Between these two slogans lies a development of unprecedented importance. The *déclassés* of the eighteenth century were formed during a slow transition from an agricultural to an industrial era; they were created out of a pause in the historical transition from one regime of toil to another. The demand for bread could have been heard at any time in the evolution of propertied society. The new *déclassés* of the twentieth century are being created as a result of the bankruptcy of all social forms based on toil. They are the end products of the process of properties society itself and of the social problems of material survival. In the era when technological advances and cybernation have brought into question the exploitation of man by man, toil, and material want in any form whatever, the cry "Black is beautiful" or "Make love, not war" marks the transformation of the traditional demand for survival into a historically new demand for life. What underpins every social conflict in the United States today is the demand for the realization of all human potentialities in a fully rounded, balanced, totalistic way of life. In short, the potentialities for revolution in America are now anchored in the potentialities of man himself.

What we are witnessing is the breakdown of a century and a half of embourgeoisement and a pulverization of all bourgeois institutions at a point in history when the boldest concepts of utopia are realizable. And there is nothing that the present bourgeois order can substitute for the destruction of its traditional institutions but bureaucratic manipulation and state capitalism. This process is unfolding most dramatically in the United States. Within a period of little more than two decades, we have seen the collapse of the "American Dream," or what amounts to the same thing, the steady destruction in the United States of the myth that material abundance, based on commodity relations between men, can conceal the inherent poverty of bourgeois life. Whether this process will culminate in revolution or in annihilation will depend in great part on the ability of revolutionists to extend social consciousness and defend the spontaneity of the revolutionary development from authoritarian ideologies, both of the "left" and of the right.

24

The Conspiracy of Law

Howard Zinn

There is, of course, some irony in speaking of the law itself as a conspiracy, when the law so often hounds others as conspirators. But beyond that, there is sense in using a term that suggests a collective will, lending a systematic character to events. What is different about the conspiracy of law from that of men is that men are not initiators but executors; there is no overall planning by men, but men carry out acts which lead to certain consistent results.

The human intent in the long-term social development is missing, but there is human purpose on the individual level; the scheme of the social structure is internalized as a variety of individual motivations which, as they are acted out, realize certain consequences with remarkable regularity. We are familiar with such motives. Marx, Weber, Michels, Harry Stack Sullivan taught us something about them: the desire for profit in business, for power in politics, for efficiency in bureaucracies, for approval by "significant others." Working in and around all these other motives is the social need for legitimacy, which reduces many of the complex requirements of modern society to a simple rule which, if followed, will maintain all results as before: Obey the law.

I use the term "conspiracy" therefore to retain the idea of systematic results. The word "systematic" avoids the extreme claim of inevitability, which has brought forth a fury of rejoinders (especially against Marx); it suggests, rather, strong tendencies and overall consistency. I use it also to retain the human element in our modern complicated system, even if this is diffused and differentiated, to insist on individual human responsibility. Otherwise, looked on as unmalleable monsters, such systems reduce us to impotency. We carry out the "will" of the structure by what we do. And it will take our action to thwart that will.

Radical critics of society (as well as the chief administrators of that society) have sometimes adopted "conspiracy theories" in which various groups of men have been accused of plotting against the rest of us. Radicals are led to this by their accurate perception of the repetitiveness of certain phenomena in modern society — war, racial hatred, political persecution, poverty, alienation — and by a false conclusion that this must be the work of a plot. The effect of this conclusion is to lose potential allies, who are properly dubious that there is evidence for a plot; it also misleads friends, because it turns them toward superficial actions aimed at particular plotters rather than at larger structural defects. (If anyone is innocent of exaggerating evil it surely must be the black South Africans, but I once heard a black man from Johannesburg say, "I don't want to exaggerate our situation, because it will mislead *me*.")

Since I am not defining "conspiracy" in the customary way, by whether or not it breaks laws, I must find an end for this conspiracy which is beyond the realm of law, and so I will find it in the violation of ethical goals. As a rough guide, I will use men and women's equal rights to life, liberty, and the pursuit of happiness, and speak of law conspiring against these rights.

This is still a crude test, but it is better than "the rule of law," which has no ethical content that I can see. What would seem to be an inherent ethic of stability turns out to be quite dependable, as we find the rule of law in practice creating certain kinds of stability at the expense of other kinds: national at the expense of international, civil at the expense of personal; or as we find that a "peace" enforced by the rule of law is purchased at the price of disorder.

In our general overestimation of the benefits of that modernization (industrialization, urbanization, science, humanism, education, parliamentary government) which followed the feudal era in the West, we have magnified the advantages of "the rule of law" supplanting "the rule of men." Our histories show varying degrees of reverence for the Magna Carta, which stipulated what are men's rights against the king; for the American Constitution, which made specific (and supposedly limited) the powers of government as against the people; and for the Napoleonic Code, which introduced uniformity into the French legal system. Writing to the new king of Westphalia in 1807, Napoleon enclosed "the constitution of your kingdom" to replace "arbitrary Prussian rule" with "a wise and liberal administration," and urged him: "be a constitutional king." The comment of historians Robert Palmer and Joel Colton on Napoleon (*A History of the Modern World*) bears out my point: "Man on horseback though he was, he believed firmly in the rule of law."

The modern era, presumably replacing the arbitrary rule of men with the objective, impartial rule of law, has not brought any fundamental change in the facts of unequal wealth and unequal power. What was done before — exploiting men and women, sending the young to war, putting troublesome people into dungeons — is still done, except that this no longer appears as the arbitrary action of the feudal lord or the king; it is now invested with the authority of neutral, impersonal law. Indeed, because of this impersonality, it becomes possible to do far more injustice to people, with a stronger sanction of legitimacy. The rule of law can be more onerous than the divine right of the king, because it was known that the king was really a man, and even in the Middle Ages it was accepted that the king could not violate natural law. (See Otto Gierke, *Political Theories of the Middle Age*, Notes 127-134.) A code of law is more easily defied than a flesh and blood monarchy; in the modern era, the positive law takes on the character of natural law.

Under the rule of men, the enemy was identifiable, and so peasant rebellions hunted out the lords, slaves killed plantation owners, and radicals assassinated monarchs. In the era of the corporation and the representative assembly, the enemy is elusive and unidentifiable; even to radicals the attempted assassination of the industrialist Frick by the anarchist Berkman seemed an aberration. In *The Grapes of Wrath,* the dispossessed farmer aims his gun confusedly at the tractor driver who is knocking down his house, learns that behind him is the banker in Oklahoma City and behind him a banker in New York, and cries out, "Then who can I shoot?"

The "rule of law" in modern society is no less authoritarian than the rule of men in premodern society; it enforces the maldistribution of wealth and power as of old, but it does this in such complicated and indirect ways as to leave the observer bewildered; he who traces back from cause to cause dies of old age inside the maze. What was direct rule is now indirect rule. What was personal rule is now impersonal. What was visible is now mysterious. What was obvious exploitation when the peasant gave half his produce to the lord is now the product of a complex market society enforced by a liberty of statutes. A mine operator in Appalachia (in a recent film made by Vista volunteers) is asked by a young man why the coal companies pay so little taxes and keep so much of the loot from the coal fields, while local people starve. He replies, "I pay exactly what the law asks me to pay."

The direct rule of monarchs was replaced by the indirect rule of representative assemblies, functioning no longer by whim and fiat but by constitutions and statutes, codified and written down. Rousseau saw clearly the limitations of representation, saying, "Power can be transmitted, but not will." And: "The English people think that they are free, but in this belief they are profoundly wrong. . . .Once the election has been completed, they revert to a condition of slavery: they are nothing." The idea of representation, he says, "comes to us from the feudal system, that iniquitous and absurd form of Government in which the human species was degraded and the name of man held in dishonour."

The conspiracy of law occurs in the age of literacy and makes the most of power of the printed word. Thus, the potential for hypocrisy, which is man's gift to the universe through symbolic communication, is enormously expanded. In slavery, the feudal order, the colonial system, deception and patronization are the minor modes of control; force is the major one. In the modern world of liberal capitalism (and also, we should note, of state socialism), force is held in reserve while, as Frantz Fanon puts it (*The Wretched of the Earth*), "a multitude of moral teachers, counselors, and bewilderers separate the exploited from those in power." In this multitude, the books of law are among the most formidable of bewilderers.

History, which comes of age in modern times and reaches the status of a profession, is used selectively, politically. In our histories, we make much of the great transition to "modern" times, thus obscuring the continuity of injustice from the premodern to the modern era, from the rule of men to the rule of law. And when it suits us, we become completely a historical — for instance, when we talk as if liberal democracy really did have an immaculate conception out of some noble compact among men, rather than out of the bloody struggles of ambitious and profiteering revolutionaries. David Hume tries to straighten us out: "Almost all the governments which exist at present, or of which there remains any record in story, have been found originally, either on usurpation or conquest, or both, without any pretense of a fair consent or voluntary subjection of the people" *(Of the Original Contract)*. Hume also neatly disposes of Socrates' talk of our "obligation" to obey the laws of the state in which we reside as based on some mythical original "contract" by saying, "Thus, he (Plato) builds a Tory consequence of passive obedience on a Whig foundation of the original contract."

The decade of the 1960s, as we know, has been marked by widespread disorders. This, even in the absence of other evidence, might make us suspect the nation's claim to be the leader of "the free world" and make us wonder if its staggering production (fifty per cent of the world's output) were being used in a rational way. We need not listen to the radical critics, only to government reports and other sources devoid of subversive intent, to reinforce our suspicions: the Kerner Commission tells us race prejudice is pervasive and virulent; the *Statistical Abstract* tells us that forty million

Americans have trouble just getting adequate food and shelter; *The New York Times* tells us that the oil companies, through government quotas, extract five billion dollars a year in excess profits from the American consumer; the national television networks tells us enough of the war to suggest that Sonmy is not an aberration but one stark instance of that colossal atrocity which is American military action in Vietnam.

We have been through periods of national self-criticism before. But this one is different. Previous protests were limited, addressed to what were seen as unhealthy growths in an otherwise admirable society, and quickly remedied. Thus, abolitionist calmed down when slavery was made illegal, despite the persistence of semi-slavery and racism. Populists, and radicals of the 1930s, were cooled by Wilsonian and Rooseveltian reform legislation, and by the easing of hard times. The anti-imperialist movements dies out when the glaring wrong of the Spanish-American War faded. the current disaffection of the ghettos comes not in a depression but in a period of "prosperity"; urban riots take place not in reaction to a wave of lynchings but shortly after a battery of "civil rights laws" has been passed by Congress; the protest against the Vietnam War has turned against national military policies in general; lack of faith in the political system grew while liberals (Kennedy and Johnson) were in the White House; disillusionment with the judical system becomes most manifest during the era of the "Warren Court" and its expansion of procedural rights.

In short, the target of discontent is not an abnormal event: a depression, lynchings, a particularly brutal war, the Sacco-Vanzetti case. The target is the normal operation of American society. The problem of poverty is no longer one of hard times but of good times. The problem of race is not in the South but in the whole country. The problem of war is not a specific adventure but the entire foreign policy. The problem of politics is not conservative Republicans but liberal Democrats. It is no longer the norms, but the aberrations of American culture, which have come under scrutiny, criticism, attack. That is why the current movement of protest is so important, why it will not fade away; why it will either grow or be crushed in a frenzy of fear by those in power.

When it is the *normal* functioning of society which produces poverty, racism, imperial conquest, injustice, oligarchy — and when this society functions normally through an elaborate framework of law — this suggests that what is wrong is not aberrational, not a departure from law and convention, but is rather bound up with that system of law, indeed, operates through it.

History argues against the notion of aberrational wrong; it shows the persistence over centuries of the social ills that bother us today. The maldistribution of wealth in America goes back to the colonial era; Bacon's

Rebellion, indentured servitude, and the labor struggles of the nineteenth century all testify to a class structure which spans our entire natural history. Mistreatment, to the point of murder, of blacks and Indians stretches from seventeenth-century Virginia and the Pequot Wars, through slavery and the extermination of the Plains Indians, down to the murder of black men in the Algiers Motel in Detroit. From the Sedition Act of 1798 to the Rap Brown statute of 1968, we have passed laws to jail protesters in times of tensions. And the war in Vietnam is only the most recent of a long series of acts of aggressive expansion by this country, from a tiny strip of land along the Atlantic to the point where our hydrogen missiles and our soldiers encircle the globe.

All this happened not in violation of law, but through it and in its unblinking presence. It is not a straight-line progression of identifiable evil. If it were, we would have caught on long ago. The persistence of the system's traits is hidden by ups and downs, backs and forths, and bewildering succession of bad times and "good" times, conservative leaders and "liberal" leaders, war and "peace." We are left somewhat breathless, and in the end persuaded of the basic kindness of the system (we who have time to think, talk, write about it have indeed been treated rather kindly). Only now have we suddenly awakened, startled by a new thought — that it is not just the "bad" times and the "bad" leaders, and "bad" wars, that what is wrong is built into the whole bloody system, at its best as well as at its worst.

We have always been naive about what seemed like games of chance; we had eras of depression and eras of prosperity, times of war and times of peace, times of witch hunts and times of justice, times of lynchings and times of civil rights laws. "And so it goes," in Kurt Vonnegut's phrase. It is like roulette; sometimes you win and sometimes you lose; you win, you lose, you lose, you win. Indeed, no one can predict in any one instance whether the little ball will fall into the red or the black, and no one is really responsible. Yet, in the end, in roulette, you almost always lose. What keeps you from suspecting a conspiracy is that "almost" (*sometimes* somebody wins) and the fact that no one spin of the wheel has been contrived — it is just the historic totality that has a predictable direction.

Thus with the social structure. There are enough times of reform, enough times of peace, enough reactions against McCarthyism, to make up that "almost." And each event itself seems to come from a crazy concatenation of individual decisions, group conflicts, personality quirks, trials and errors, with no overall purpose or plan. It is just the *results* that, on inspection, show a pattern.

If the pattern is indeed as I describe it, there are important implications for our attitude toward law, and our willingness or unwillingness to disobey the law. Much of the caution against civil disobedience in the United

States is based on the essential goodness of our society, whatever might be the admitted wrong of a particular law or partial condition. For instance, in the symposium *Law and Philosophy,* John Rawls says he assumes at the start, "at least in a society such as ours, a moral obligation to obey the law," with the premise that "the legal order is one of a constitutional democracy." In the same symposium, Monroe Beardsley urges caution against disobedience because of "every individual's general stake in the whole legal structure..." In a paper delivered last year at the American Political Science Association meetings, Joseph Dunner writes:

> I submit that while there is frequently not only a moral right but even a moral obligation to practice civil disobedience under conditions of political despotism, the advocacy and practice of civil disobedience in a democracy, far from "expressing the highest respect for law" might easily be one of the means used by totalitarians for the deliberate destruction of the democratic process and the establish-ment of their despotic rule.

This is the general presumption of most American writers on the subject of civil disobedience: that the United States, as a "constitutional democracy," is a special case. In this country, presumably, the law works mostly for good; therefore, respect for the law is of such a value as to create a strong case against diminishing that respect by acts of civil disobedience.

The evidence on how good a society is seems crucial to any argument on civil disobedience. It was on this basic ground of *fact* that Hume challenged Socrates, for Socrates' decision to submit to Athenian law was based on the supposition that when Athenians remained in the community it was a sign that they enjoyed its benefits; otherwise they could have left at any time. Hume argues: "Can we seriously say that a poor peasant or artisan has a free choice to leave his country, when he knows no foreign language or manners, and lives, from day to day, by the small wages which he acquires?"

For us too, our perception of the facts is crucial. It is not time that we reconsidered the easy judgment, passed on in an atmosphere of self-congratulation from one American generation to the next, that we indeed have "democracy," that there is such a polarity between our system and other systems as to require a different attitude to law and disobedience? I am arguing here that the evidence on the functional realities of our system, as opposed to democratic theory and political rhetoric, does not justify such an overriding respect for the laws. Rather, most of these laws have supported, through vagaries and deviations, a persistent pattern of injustice through our history. How do the laws, and the accompanying culture of "the rule of law," maintain that pattern of injustice? I would list a number of ways:

1. The idea of a *system* of law, to which we are asked to give general and undiscriminating support, disguises the differences among various categories of law. We are made aware of our constitutional rights, in the Bill of Rights and other provisions, from the earliest grades in school, with such fanfare and attention as to persuade us that these are the most important parts of our law; when we think of "respect for law" we are likely to think of these benign provisions of law which speak of rights and liberties. But we are told very little, so little as to escape our consciousness quickly, about the vast body of legislation which arranges the wealth of the nation: the tax laws, the appropriations bills (on the local level as well as the national level), and the enormous structure of law which is designed to maintain the property system as is — and therefore the distribution of wealth as is. One has only to look at the curricula of law schools, and see students staggering through courses titled *Property, Contracts, Corporation Law, Torts,* to understand how much of our legal system is devoted to the maintenance of the economic system as it now functions, with its incredible waste, with its vast inequities.

Consider the public relations job that has been done on the birth of the Bill of Rights in 1791, and how little attention has been paid to Alexander Hamilton's economic program, promulgated around the same time. The Bill of Rights was hardly more than a showpiece for a very long time, but Hamilton's program of tariffs, the assumption of debts, and the national bank were the start of a long history of federal legislation creating a welfare system for the rich. (See Charles Beard's essay of 1932, "The Myth of Rugged Individualism," for an account of the many ways in which the government in the nineteenth and twentieth centuries passed laws to aid big business.) From Hamilton's "Report on Manufactures" to the current oil depletion allowance, this bias of national legislation toward the interests of the wealthy has been maintained.

It is not just the volume of legislation which is important, but the force of it. The existence of a law, or a constitutional provision, on the books tells us little about its effect. Is the law immediately operative (like a tariff) or does it require long litigation and expense and initiative (like the First Amendment) before it is of use to anyone? Is it given prompt attention (like the assumption of debts) or is it ignored (like the provision that "Congress shall make no law...abridging the freedom of speech, or of the press.")?

We have a striking illustration from those early days of the Republic. The First Amendment was so little observed that hardly seven years after it went into effect Congress passed a law, the Sedition Act of 1798, which indeed did abridge the freedom of speech, and with such vigor as to send ten persons to jail for their utterances. One could hardly claim that the First Amendment was being enforced. On the other hand, the Excise Tax on whiskey (needed to pay off rich bondholders on the Assumption scheme) was so efficiently enforced that when small farmers in western Pennsylvania rebelled against the tax in 1794, Secretary of the Treasury Hamilton led the troops himself in putting them down. The government enforces those laws it wants to enforce; that fact is part of the American legal tradition.

Ironically (in view of the customary assumption that the legal system guards us against anarchy), it is the laws, either by what they provide as they are passed or by what they permit when they are not passed, which contribute to the anarchy of the economic order. They either permit or subsidize the unfettered spoilation of natural resources; they permit, indeed pay for, the production of dangerous things — poisons, guns, bombs. The allocation of the nation's colossal wealth to the production of either weapons or junk takes place not contrary to law but through a vast network of contractual arrangements.

2. The idea of a system of law disguises another distinction in categories of laws: between laws which protect us against bodily harm and laws which protect property from theft. When we are cautioned against chipping away at the structure of law, what is usually uppermost in our minds is that the law protects us from the constant danger of assault, rape, and murder. But most law-enforcing is designed to protect property, not human beings. Most crimes, by far, are crimes against property, not against persons. (In 1966, there were 120,000 offenses against persons and 1,670,000 offenses against property.)

We are constantly reminded of the priorities of law enforcement — property over human beings — by the repetition of certain events: the policeman shooting someone who has committed a petty theft (a man who steals a million dollars in a price-fixing swindle is never personally harmed, but a kid who runs off with five dollars is in danger of summary execution); police cars killing or injuring people in mad chases after robbers (a recent report to the American Medical Association said five hundred people die each year as a result of police auto chases).

The quality of justice depends on who is the person assaulted, and what is the nature of the property crime. On the same day in February 1970, the Boston *Globe* reported the results of two trials. In the case of policemen who admitted killing two black men in the Algiers Motel in Detroit, and were charged with conspiring to deprive persons of their civil rights, the verdict was acquittal. In Texas, a man who stole seventy-five dollars from a dry cleaning store was given a sentence of a thousand years.

Most of our legal system is designed to maintain the existing distribution of wealth in the society, a distribution which is based not on need but on power and resourcefulness. Most criminal penalties are used not to protect the life and limb of the ordinary citizen but rather to punish those who take the profit culture so seriously that they act it out beyond the rules of the game. Property crimes are a special form of private enterprise.

3. Seeing the legal system as a monolith disguises the fact that laws aimed at radicals, while pretending to protect the society at large, really try to preserve the existing political and economic arrangements. The Espionage Act of 1917 (even its title deceives us into thinking its aim is protecting the community) sought to prevent people from communicating certain ideas to soldiers or would-be soldiers which might discourage their carrying on a war. The Act begs the question of whether carrying on the war is a blessing to the society at large or a danger to it.

The Smith Act provision against teaching the violent overthrow of the government assumes the government is not evil enough to deserve being overthrown. The Selective Service Act assumes the draft protects us all when indeed it may take our sons to die for someone else's privileges. This is a small class of laws, but its psychological impact on the right of protest, ("Watch your step, or else...") can hardly be overestimated. It stands ready for use any time dissidence threatens to become too widespread. The recent Chicago "conspiracy" trial is an example.

4. The three distinctions I have made so far are intended to illustrate how the general exhortation to preserve the legal system as if it were a benign whole glides over the fact that different kinds of laws serve different purposes. More justifiable laws (for free speech, against rape or murder) stand in the front ranks as a noble facade concealing a huge body of law which maintains the present property and power arrangements of the society. Buried in the mass is a much small body of law which stands guard against those who would rebel in an organized way against these arrangements.

Underlying these distinctions is a more fundamental one: between rules of conduct, which are necessary for human beings in any social order to live with one another in harmony and justice, and those rules which come out of some specific social order, the product of a particular historical culture. H.L.A. Hart speaks of "primary rules of obligtion" *(The Concept of Law)*, which include restrictions on the free use of violence and "various positive duties to perform services or make contributions to the common life." These rules are not enforced by the coercive techniques of modern society but rather by "that general attitude of the group toward its own standard modes of behavior."

Bakunin distinguished between "natural laws," created by the facts of human nature, and "juridical laws," like the law of inheritance. What separates Hart from Bakunin is his acceptance of the need for "secondary rules" in more complex societies. I would claim that Hart accepts too easily the need for these secondary rules, but the distinction he makes is important because it enables us to examine more closely than he did himself the possibility of a society, even a modern one, that would be guided by primary rules. The distinction takes us out of our present social arrangements and back to an examination of what laws are necessary and just on the basis of human nature. We can look backward to primitive societies (as Hart does) but also forward, in a utopian (eu-topian) imagining about the future. The ideology of any culture tries to obliterate the distinction between what is humanly necessary and what merely perpetuates that culture.

5. We make a fetish of "obedience to law" (put more delicately by philosophers as the concept of "obligation") without making it clear to all citizens of whom this obedience is demanded that government officials have an enormous range of choice in deciding who may and who may not violate the law. One person's failure to honor the obligation is ignored, another's is summarily punished.

The most flagrant illustration of this is in racial matters. When I speak of selective enforcement of laws on racial equality, I am not speaking of the South but of the national government. Before the Civil War, the legal prohibition against the importation of slaves was ignored by the national executive, but the Fugitive Slave Law was enforced by armed soldiers (as in the rendition of Anthony Burns in Boston). From 1871 on, with a battery of statutes giving the national government the power to prosecute those denying constitutional rights to the black man, every President, liberal and conservative, from Hayes through Theodore Roosevelt, Woodrow Wilson, Franklin Roosevelt, John F. Kennedy, and Lyndon Johnson, refused to use that power on behalf of the black man. As one example, under Attorney-General Robert Kennedy, a series of violations of the constitutional rights of blacks in Albany, Georgia, in 1961-62 led to only one federal prosecution — against black and white members of the civil rights movement in Albany who had picketed a local merchant.

Unequal law enforcement in racial matters is most obvious, but it is also true in economic questions, where corporations violating the law may be ignored or gently rebuked; note the light sentences given in the General Electric price-fixing case, where millions were taken from the consumer. We find it also where rank and status are involved, as in the military. In 1966, an American Army captain in Saigon, found guilty of fraudulently doing off with imported silk, military planes and Treasury checks, was allowed to retire with a pension; in 1968, various enlisted men who sat in a circle and sang "We Shall Overcome" to protest conditions in an Army stockade in San Francisco were sentenced to years in prison at hard labor, on charges of "mutiny." Selective enforcement of the law is not a departure from law. It is *legal*.

6. Also concealed from the public, as it is bidden sternly to honor the law, is the record of law enforcement agencies in breaking the law themselves. This includes wiretapping by the FBI (admitted by FBI agents in court proceedings at various times) and countless cases of assault and battery, up to murder, by local police.

7. A restricted definition of "corruption" in our culture leads to cries of outrage against politicians and businessmen who break the law for their private aggrandizement. What is thus hidden from the public is the larger corruption of the law itself, as it operates to distribute wealth and power. Thus, our history books draw our attention to the Teapot Dome scandals and other legal shenanigans of the Harding Administration, while ignoring the far more serious (not only because of its scale but because of its permanence) reallocation of wealth that took place legally, through the tax laws proposed by Secretary of the Treasury Andrew Mellon and passed by Congress in the Coolidge Administration.

Similarly, the headlines parade Adam Clayton Powell's payroll padding, and bury the legal appropriation of the citizen's money by contracts to General Dynamics and Lockheed, by huge subsidies to poor farmers like James Eastland and Herman Talmadge. Thus, one Supreme Court nominee is pushed aside because of acts of dubious legality, while another breezes through the Judiciary Committee because he is legally proper, though morally more opprobrious than the first. We forget that the problem is the structure of the roulette wheel, not the occasional appearance of a dishonest croupier. The responsibility for what we see around us belongs to the legal system itself, not the deviations from it.

8. The rule of law, whatever its effects, is restricted by our national boundaries. International law, being far weaker, permits even greater selectivity in adherence to it. Contracts, and compensation for expropriated property, are likely to be given strict attention, while prohibitions against the use of force to settle international disputes will be ignored, as in Vietnam. While at home it can be claimed that we get a modicum of order along with injustice, in the international arena we observe neither order nor justice.

9. Attached to the law in our culture is the notion of solidity as against transience, of the stable against the erratic. Hegel, in the preface to his *Philosophy of Right,* asks that we recognize the rationality in the state, as that in nature, rather than leaving us all "to the mercy of chance and caprice, to be Godforsaken." But this attractive quality of "rationality" conceals the motive of thwarting change, the demand of "law and order" against reform and revolution. Thus, Hegel denounces his colleague J.F. Fries for a speech on the state in which Professor Fries said, "In the people ruled by a genuine communal spirit, life for the discharge of all public

business would come from below, from the people itself." Fries was punished by the German government for participating in the Wartburg Festival of 1817, and Hegel's translator, T.M. Knox, comments, "This was a liberal demonstration in favor of German unity and Stein's reforms. Hegel supported both of these but he held that enthusiastic demonstrations were no substitute for thinking and could only lead to immorality and anarchy."

The claim of permanence and rationality has some truth, but its other side is the natural tendency of law (at its best) to represent past conditions, past needs. As Professor Richard Wasserstrom has put it (in his talk "Lawyers and Revolution," given to the National Lawyers Guild in July 1968), "the law is conservative in the same way in which language is conservative. It seeks to assimilate everything that happens to do that which has happened." In an age where change has become exponential, this natural disability of law is especially marked. Granted, there is a value in acting on rules and principles derived from long-term experience as opposed to acting only on the ephemers of the moment. But that experience must not become an absolute; rather, it should be weighed constantly against the fresh perceptions of existential reality.

For such a mediation between past and present, Nietzsche is a better guide than Hegel, about whom he seems to be speaking when he talks (*The Use and Abuse of History*) of "the historically educated fanatic of the world process" who "has nothing to do but to live on as he has lived, love what he has loved, hate what he has hated, and read the newspapers he has always read. The only sin is for him to live otherwise than he has lived."

10. The law neither has to be violated nor does it need to *do* anything drastic in order to maintain existing inequities in wealth and power. It needs only to renew itself in the same basic patterns, to enlarge the scale but retain the same theme, to permit reforms, but within limits. At the time of legal codification (as in the United States Constitution, for instance), the basic pattern of modern life was set: the irrationality of a productive system driven by business profit; the concentration of political power in deputies, of judicial power in magistrates; the control of communication by schools, churches, and men of wealth. From that point on the system of law needed only elaboration, and it was resilient enough to absorb gradual reform. It performed as Madison predicted it would, to cool, through its political system of representation, any possible passion for tumultuous change, and to control any "rage" on the part of the propertyless. With the basic patterns set, it could afford a certain magnanimity in its pronouncements of equality before the law. Anatole France's comment is still apt: "The law in its majesty draws no distinction, but forbids rich and poor alike from begging in the streets or sleeping in the public parks."

11. So far, I have been talking of the passage of laws by legislatures and the enforcement of laws by the executive. By the time the law appears in the courtroom, to be applied by judges, juries, lawyers, and marshals, it has already been subject to enought of the social strictures mentioned above so as to make injustice probable even before the judge has taken his seat on the bench. But inside the judicial process, all of the built-in ordinary *legal* mechanisms act to reinforce what society has ordained.

The sociology of the judge needs to be considered. The awesome black robes conceal men who come to their posts through the most sordid corridors of local politics, or by political appointment. If cronyism appears on the Supreme Court (Truman and Vinson, Kennedy and Whizzer White, Lyndon Johnson and Abe Fortas), then how much more often must it be true on the local level, where most judicial decisions are made?

The judge is monarch of the courtroom: he decides the composition of the jury; he decides what evidence is admitted or excluded; what witnesses may be heard or not heard; what the jury may listen or not listen to; what bounds lawyers must observe; even what lawyer the defendant may have; what limits the jury must stay within in making its decision. He can dismiss a case, or so charge the jury as to make conviction certain. His background is middle- or upper-class parents, law schools, private clubs. His mind is in the past. His environment is limited: a splendid city apartment, a home in the country, the courtroom itself. The world of anguish, of social protest, is a threatening dark form on his window shade. In the play *The Chalk Garden* the old judge, off duty, muses about the man on the bench: "The line on the judge's face is written by law, not life."

Most law is decided on the local level, and while there are occasional exceptions, far more typical is the evidence of narrowness, class and race prejudice, and a hatred of social rebels. Judge Elijah Adlow, senior judge of the Boston municipal court, told a leader of a tenants' movement (who had helped a destitute family move — illegally — into a vacant apartment and was charged with assault after he had been beaten by police), that he would have to go to jail "unless you change your philosophy." But behind the glamorous injustice of the occasional Adlow or Julius Hoffman there is a parade of obscure judges making obscure decisions for obscure defendants, putting them away and out of sight.

The sociology of lawyers — the socialization of law school, the practice of obsequiousness before judges, and deals with prosecutors — is too long a story to tell in detail. The sociology of juries includes a process of unnatural selection which turns up, again and again, white middle-class citizens of orthodox views, common prejudices, and obedient disposition, most middle-aged or old.

The economics of justice in America — the systematic prejudice against the poor at every stage — the arrest, the setting of bail, the trial, the choice

of counsel, the sentence, the opportunity to appeal, the chance of parole —
is too well known to need documentation. (A newspaper item of last week:
Dozens of inmates in one New York jail had spent from six months to two
years behind bars, waiting for their trials, because they could not afford
bail — all this while they are presumed to be innocent, and while whatever
innocence they had is long gone.)

As one moves up from municipal courts to state supreme courts and federal courts, the basic sociological and economic facts of justice change very
little, but this is concealed by a certain regal mustiness of the atmosphere
which puts a coat of respectability on a fundamentally inhuman process.
What Herbert Read described in British justice differs only in detail (see his
essay "Chains of Freedom," in *Anarchy and Order*) from the American
judical system:

> The independence of the judiciary is symbolized in various ways. By
> means of wigs and gowns, the participants are dehumanized to an
> astonishing degree. If by chance, in the course of pleading a hot and
> flustered barrister lifts his wig to mop his brow, an entirely different
> individual is revealed. It is as if a tortoise had suddenly dispensed
> with its shell. The whole business is carapaceous; a shell of custom
> and formality against which life, plastic and throbbing, beats in an
> effort to reach the light.

12. The main decisions have been made outside the courtroom, by the
society and the culture that brought this combination of persons to this
place at this time. But this is made explicit by the deliberate attempt of
courts to limit the scope of argument and decision, thus ensuring that court
decisions will have minimum effect on the direction of society. On the
appeals level, including the Supreme Court, this means deciding cases on
technical or narrow grounds wherever possible, postponing fundamental
questions as long as possible. It has been most difficult, for instance, in
cases of draft resistance, to get the Supreme Court to rule on a question far
more important to society than the disposition of one resister: Is the war in
Vietnam illegal?

This attitude is expressed by one of the judges in Lon Fuller's mythical
case of "The Speluncean Explorers," when he refuses to deal with the
moral complexities of a community decision to sacrifice one person so that
others might live: "The sole question before us for decision is whether these
defendants did, within the meaning of NCSA Sec. 12A, willfully take the
life of Roger Whetmore."

Not so mythical are the actual cases of political protesters hauled into
court on ordinary criminal charges and prevented by the judge from airing
the political grounds of their actions. (Theodore Mommsen put it well:
"Impartiality in political trials is about on the level with Immaculate Con-

ception: one may wish for it, but one cannot produce it." Quoted in Otto Kirchheimer, *Political Justice*.) It should make us all pause to know that within the space of a few months similar pronouncements were made in a court in Moscow and a court in Milwaukee. The Moscow judge refused to let a group arrested for distributing leaflets in Red Square against the Russian invasion of Czechoslovakia discuss anything political; the only issue, he said, was: Did they or did they not break the law in question?

The Milwaukee judge similarly refused to let the priests who had burned draft records explain their motivation. The only question, he said, was: "Did the defendants commit arson, burglary, and theft?" When one witness began to discuss the ideal of civil disobedience, the judge interrupted him with what must be a classic judicial statement: "You can't discuss that. That's getting to the heart of the matter."

That is also getting to the end of my argument, which is always, of course, the beginning of another. A general "obligation to obey the law" is a poor guide in a time when revolutionary changes are needed and we are racing against ominous lines on the social cardiograph. We need to separate whatever there is in law that serves human ends from everything else that rides along with it, on the backs of so many people. We need to get away from pleasant abstractions and look at the functional reality of the legal structure which guides our society: its sociology, its economics, its human consequences.

Philosophical speculation tells us that civil disobedience may be necessary under certain conditions of injustice. Historical evidence, the facts of the lives of people around us, tells us that those conditions exist and they they are maintained by the present structure of law. To know this is only the beginning. I have tried here, by inculcating a proper disrespect for "the rule of law," only to put us at the starting point, in a mood to run. The same modern civilization which has given us unjust laws has given us great ideals. We need to learn how to violate these laws in such a way as to realize those ideals.

Each of us, depending on where we are in the social structure, must draw his own existential conclusion on what to do. In Tolstoy's "The Death of Ivan Ilyich," the proper, perfect, successful magistrate Ilyich agonizes on his deathbed about his sudden awareness that his life has been wasted, useless, wrong:

> "Maybe I did not live as I ought to have done," it suddenly occurred to him. "But how could that be, when I did everything properly?" he replied. "If I could only understand what it is all for! But that too is impossible. An explanation would be possible if it could be said that I have not lived as I ought to. But it is impossible to say that" — and he remembered all the legality, correctitude and propriety of his life.

Sources

George Woodcock, "Anarchism Revisited," *Commentary* 46 (August 1968).

Sam Dolgoff, "The Relevance of Anarchism to Modern Society," *Libertarian Analysis,* (1971).

C. Wright Mills, "Letter to the New Left," *New Left Review* (1961).

Staughton Lynd, "The Movement: A New Beginning," *Liberation,* 14 (May 1969).

Murray Bookchin, "The Anarchist Revolution," *Schism,* 1 (Winter 1970).

Emile Capouya, "The Red Flag and the Black," *New American Review,* 6 (1969).

George Cairncross, "Anarchists—And Proud of It," *Freedom,* 33 (January 1, 1972).

M.C., "Why Terrorism is not an Anarchist Means," *Freedom,* 32 (January 30, 1971).

H.W. Morton, "Black Anarchy in New York," *Anarchy,* 67 (September 1966).

John O'Connor, "A New Consciousness and Its Polemics," *Anarchy* 1 (2nd Series), 1971.

Jack Robinson, "Some Secular Myths," *Freedom,* 32 (September 11, 1971).

Neville Fowler, "A Religious View of Anarchism," *Freedom,* 32 (May 29, 1971).

Justin, "Man—The Creator and the Destroyer," *Freedom,* 31 (August 22, 1970).

George Cairncross, "Education and the Democratic Myth," *Freedom,* 32 (October 2, 1971).

Anthony Fleming, "The Machinery of Comformity," *Anarchy,* 94 (December 1968).

P. Turner, "Towards Worker Control," *Freedom* pamphlet #7, 1971.

Carroll, Lakey, Moyer and Taylor, "Revolution: A Quaker Prescription for a Sick Society," WIN (November 15, 1972).

Murray Bookchin, "Post-Scarcity Anarchism," from *Post-Scarcity Anarchism* (Berkeley, California: Ramparts Press, 1971).

Howard Zinn, "The Conspiracy of Law," in Robert Paul Wolff, ed., *The Rule of Law* (New York: Simon and Schuster, 1971).

INDEX